Essays in
European Economic Thought

The William Volker Fund Series in the Humane Studies

Essays in
European Economic Thought

Translated and Edited by

LOUISE SOMMER

D. VAN NOSTRAND COMPANY, INC.

PRINCETON, NEW JERSEY

TORONTO   LONDON

NEW YORK

D. VAN NOSTRAND COMPANY, INC.
120 Alexander St., Princeton, New Jersey (*Principal office*)
24 West 40 Street, New York 18, New York

D. VAN NOSTRAND COMPANY, LTD.
358, Kensington High Street, London, W.14, England

D. VAN NOSTRAND COMPANY (Canada), LTD.
25 Hollinger Road, Toronto 16, Canada

Published simultaneously in Canada by
D. VAN NOSTRAND COMPANY (Canada), LTD.

Library of Congress Catalogue Card No.: 60-15813

PRINTED IN THE UNITED STATES OF AMERICA

Preface

The present volume in the William Volker Fund Series in the Humane Studies brings together for the first time in English translation some of the most brilliant essays in economics written in Europe in the past decade.

In the hope of furthering among the English-reading public a familiarity with the ideas of some of the modern masters of economics, the sponsors of this project have culled from the vast assortment of books and periodical articles that have appeared in this field in German, French, and Italian in the last three-quarters of a century the seven papers that comprise this collection. Each one of the authors represented here ranks among the most distinguished economists of his age, and each of these selections may truly be considered as one of the gems of postclassical economic thought. Some have been excerpted from larger works of which they formed a section or a preface, while others were originally conceived and written as independent articles, but all are complete in themselves. They are as various in the range of their subjects as they are in the style of their presentation. Taken together, they constitute a unique collection of important contributions to economic thought that have lasting merit and deserve to be made known in wider circles than they could reach in the languages in which they were originally written.

It remains only to add that the translations provided by Dr. Louise Sommer faithfully reflect the clarity, precision, and elegance characteristic of each of the various authors' writing, and her scholarly notes should prove helpful in elucidating a number of points that the reader might otherwise have found obscure.

ARTHUR GODDARD

July, 1960

v

Table of Contents

A Note on the Authors

LUIGI EINAUDI (born 1874), statesman and economist, served from 1948 to 1955 as President of the Italian Republic.

CARL MENGER (1840–1921) was the founder of the Austrian School of Economics.

LUDWIG VON MISES (born 1881) is the author of *Human Action,* 1949, *The Anti-Capitalist Mentality,* 1956, and *Epistemological Problems of Economics,* 1960, as well as many other books in German and English. Born and educated in Austria, he taught for many years at the University of Vienna. Later he was professor at the Graduate School of International Studies in Geneva. He is now visiting professor at the Graduate School of Business Administration at New York University.

PAUL PAINLEVÉ (1863–1933), mathematician and statesman, was a member of the French Chambre des Députés from 1910 to 1928 and served as its president in 1924. In the first World War he joined the cabinet, first as Minister of Public Instruction, later as Minister of War, and finally, from September to November, 1917, as Prime Minister. He again became Prime Minister in April, 1925.

LUDWIG POHLE (1869–1926) taught economics at the University of Frankfurt and at the University of Leipzig. From 1910 to 1921 he edited the *Zeitschrift für Sozialwissenschaft.*

JACQUES RUEFF (born 1896), author of many important books on economics, is a member of the Institut de France (Académie des Sciences Morales et Politiques). He served in various eminent positions in his country's economic and financial administration. At present he is judge at the Court of Justice of the European Coal and Steel Community.

FRIEDRICH FREIHERR VON WIESER (1851–1926) was one of the three economists who are generally referred to as the older Austrian School—the other two being Carl Menger and Eugen von Böhm-Bawerk.

1

Toward a Systematic Classification of the Economic Sciences*

CARL MENGER

Ever since the appearance of my "Inquiry into the Methods of the Social Sciences" discussion concerning the epistemology and methodology of economics has been incessant. In the literature that has since proliferated on this subject, including even some recently published university lectures, the position I have taken has become the object of sometimes contradictory judgments. In particular, the views I have set forth regarding the types of problems to be solved by inquiry in the field of economics, as well as my treatment of the important related question of a systematic classification of the economic sciences, have met with no less vehement opposition than friendly acceptance. All this, and even the many misunderstandings which usually accompany discussions of questions of such a general nature, would yet not have persuaded me to re-enter the controversy. However, in view of the present state of economic studies in Germany, I am convinced that only full clarity concerning the whole complex of problems requiring

* "Grundzüge einer Klassifikation der Wirtschaftswissenschaften," *Jahrbücher für Nationalökonomie und Statistik,* ed. J. Conrad, New Series (Jena: Gustav Fisher, 1889), XIX, 465-496. The original German-language text was republished in "Kleinere Schriften zur Methode und Geschichte der Volkswirtschaftslehre," *The Collected Works of Carl Menger* (London School of Economics and Political Science, London University, 1934-1936), III, 187-218.

1

investigation in the field of economics can save us from adopting one-sided attitudes, with all their pernicious consequences both practical and theoretical.

The Historical School describes the origin and development of social phenomena, and—with the exception of a few especially biased authors—it makes a serious effort to discover their laws, in the sense of external regularities in their coexistence and succession. However, this school refrains from analyzing complex economic phenomena: it does not trace them back to their psychological causes or to ultimate component elements that would still be accessible to perceptual verification. Such a procedure cannot provide us with a *theoretical understanding* of economic events.

To be sure, many abuses have brought theoretical analysis into disrepute. This is especially true of efforts to arrive at knowledge and understanding of economic facts by way of an aprioristic construction. But no less harmful has been the failure to realize that economic phenomena are temporal events and therefore show developments that ought to attract the attention of theoretical inquiry. To the great detriment of our science, the adherents of this school regard the mere *description* of concrete economic events and of external regularities in their relations as the only legitimate goal of economic study. They thereby overlook the fact that historical investigation is no substitute for theoretical analysis, nor is the latter either excluded or rendered superfluous by the fact— equally neglected by the Historical School—that economic phenomena exhibit a development in the course of time. Historicism has simply turned its back on theoretical analysis. But is it not the task of our science to find the particular form that is adequate to the specific character of economic events? In trying to avoid the mistakes of aprioristic social philosophy, and to a certain extent also those of the social physicists and social biologists, the Historical School has fallen into the still greater error of renouncing theoretical analysis, and with it theoretical understanding, of social phenomena. Thus the scientific character of economics has become altogether questionable. The solution of the methodological problems involved is an urgent necessity of our science.

Although the attacks directed against me in this controversy challenge me to a reply, I do not intend to deal here with economic theory or with the diverse tasks which it has to fulfill. In view of the present state of our understanding of methodological issues, questions concerning the nature of economic theory—including its different branches and its distinctive problems, as conditioned by the specific character of its object—must doubtless be considered as providing the most controversial, and therefore the most attractive, theme for investigations into the methodology of that science. However, any study of the above-mentioned problem seems to me to be quite futile as long as *the preliminary question of the position of economic theory within the entire domain of the economic sciences in general* remains unresolved. The Historical School has failed to pay enough attention to the distinctive character of the problems confronting the sciences of history and statistics on the one hand, and economic theory and applied economics on the other; nor has it taken into sufficient consideration the essential differences among these main branches of inquiry within the field of political economy itself. The exponents of historicism have not maintained a sharp enough distinction between the "method of historical inquiry" and the so-called "historical method in economic theory and applied economics." They have especially misinterpreted the specific place of questions of applied economics within the complex of problems to be solved by theoretical analysis. In their eyes the only worthwhile goal of scientific research is a compilation—arranged on the basis of external principles of classification—of historical, statistical, theoretical, morphological, and practical studies referring to economics. Under such circumstances how is it possible to deal specifically with the whole set of problems to be solved by economic *theory* without having previously clarified either its position within the domain of the other economic sciences or the outlines of a system of classifying the economic sciences in general?

1. *On the Classification of the Economic Sciences*

The results of the investigation of reality by the different sciences have in practice been divided into separate domains in accordance with two essentially distinct principles of classification: on the one hand, according to the nature of the objects of inquiry, i.e., the different *fields* of reality which constitute the subject matter of scientific cognition; and on the other hand, according to the different lines of scientific inquiry, i.e., the different *methods of approaching* reality.

The distinction between the sciences of nature and the sciences of man, the division of the former into sciences of organic nature and of inorganic nature, the further subdivisions within the different fields of the organic and of the inorganic world (petrography, botany, zoology, and so forth), and the constitution of separate sciences of law, political theory, sociology, economics, etc., all rest upon the first principle of classification.

However, the progress of the sciences and a deepening interest in specialized problems of research has led to further classifications based upon the second principle. Within each specific field of reality different lines of approach have gradually developed into distinct disciplines and sciences corresponding to the need for an independent presentation of their results.

The search for an understanding of reality may be pursued, within each field, in two basic directions. It may be oriented towards knowledge of *concrete* phenomena and their concrete relations in space and time, or towards knowledge of their *general* nature and their general interrelations (i.e., relations of coexistence and succession among generally determined phenomena).

The first approach leads either to the *statistical* [1] or to the historical sciences: to the former if the concrete phenomena of particular fields of reality are viewed from the static standpoint, and to the latter if we take the point of view of evolution. The second direction ramifies into the *morphological* and the *theoretical* sciences, respectively: the former if what we are aiming at is knowledge of the generic form of the phenomena in a given field (their common structure), and the latter if the object of our knowledge is their relations and internal connections (i.e., their laws).

Our scientific interest, however, is not confined only to the exploration and the understanding of reality. Besides the above-mentioned lines of inquiry, there is within each field a tendency toward the establishment of principles and procedures aiming at a purposeful *shaping* of phenomena, i.e., effective interference with the course of events. The systematically organized results of these efforts are characterized as the *practical* or applied sciences.

The different lines of approach which we have mentioned—the statistical, the historical, the morphological, the theoretical, and the practical—have to be distinguished, by virtue of their formal differences from one another, not only within each distinct field of reality, but also within each subdivision in its turn; and the same holds true with regard to the further ramifications within these major types of science.[2]

The classification of the natural sciences according to the different kinds of natural substance, on the one hand, and the different lines of approach to them, on the other, has in part been long since completed and is in part still going on. Nobody in the field of the natural sciences would confuse the description of *concrete* natural substances in their static state, or of the course of *concrete* natural events of historical significance, with a *morphology* of natural phenomena. Even in treating of phenomena belonging to the same field, one does not fail to make a distinction between, for instance, the history of the animal world and systematic zoology, or between the history of man and a morphology of the races of mankind. In the same way a line of division is drawn between the morphological and the theoretical natural sciences. For instance, systematic petrography, botany, zoology, and anatomy are separated from physics, chemistry, and physiology. Finally, the same holds true of the theoretical and the applied sciences. The natural scientist does not confuse pure chemistry with applied chemistry, or mechanics and physics with so-called mechanical technology, or anatomy and physiology with surgery and thereapeutics.

To be sure, in particular cases practical considerations, such as regard for the appropriate arrangement of the scientific data or the rather rudimentary state of development of a particular branch of inquiry, might nevertheless induce one to combine the results of different approaches in the natural sciences purely for purposes of presentation. But no investigator of nature would conceive of "progressing" to the development of a single, comprehensive nat-

ural science embracing all statistical-historical, morphological, theoretical, and practical knowledge concerning nature, or even concerning one of its specific fields, assembled in a loosely organized
conglomeration—a veritable mass of ἄμορφος ὕλη! * The distinction
between the historical-statistical, the morphological, the theoretical, and the applied sciences—and within these major types between still further articulated subdivisions—is accepted without
question by every clear-thinking natural scientist. In the field of
the political sciences too, no doubt exists as to the difference between, for example, statistics, the history of political institutions,
political theory, and applied political science. The same holds true
in the field of jurisprudence with regard to the distinction between
the history of law, legal doctrine, and legislative policies.

In the domain of the economic sciences, however, the above-
mentioned development is in many respects still in an imperfect,
and even embryonic, state. The classification of the economic
sciences into the historical-statistical, the morphological, the theoretical, and the applied is far from being generally recognized.
The confounding of historical-statistical descriptions, morphological studies, "laws of economic phenomena," and principles and
procedures for effective action in the economic sphere is still the
rule in the literature on political economy, while a separation of
the economic sciences according to their formal differences would
still appear to be the exception. Moreover, it should be emphasized that this practice of indiscriminately lumping together the
results of different types of scientific approach is not dictated
exclusively by considerations of a didactic nature,[3] nor is it confined only to writings devoted to popular instruction; it is widely
prevalent also in works with pretensions to a strictly scientific
character.

The explanation of this fact is to be found primarily in the
hitherto rudimentary development of the economic sciences.
Many other disciplines likewise present the appearance, in the
early phases of their development, of a conglomerate mass, assembled on external principles, of historical-statistical, morphological, theoretical, and practical information about a definite

* [Translator's note: Greek for "amorphous matter."]

field of phenomena. In other realms of inquiry also, disciplines corresponding to different lines of inquiry have branched off only gradually and tentatively and have thus developed into independent sciences. As soon as economists have a clear understanding of the importance that a systematic approach has for the *demonstration,* and especially for the *understanding,* of the internal interrelations of the results of scientific inquiry, and as soon as they become aware of the impossibility of coherently presenting the results of different lines of approach within one and the same system, the natural course of development of scientific knowledge in the domain of economics will necessarily lead to a systematic ramification of the economic sciences similar to that which has already taken place in all other fields.

2. *On the Necessity of Separating Economic History, Economic Theory, Morphology, and Applied Economics* [4]

It is in many respects the methodological insufficiency of the Historical School that hampers the above development in German political economy, and that has even reversed the progress made thus far. The economists of this school envision a *universal science of economics* that should embrace any and every kind of knowledge about things economic in a neatly uniform order. They vehemently reject the idea of marking off one discipline from another, although such a division would in no way destroy the intrinsic coherence of each. They even stigmatize this separation as a regressive step, as "an artificial dismemberment of an intrinsically coherent subject matter"; or if there is agreement in principle regarding the classification of the economic sciences, it is interpreted in such a way as in reality to annul it altogether.

Now such a universal science of economics reveals itself not only as an absurdity from the point of view of scientific systematics, but as an impossibility if the above postulate of scientific procedure is taken at all seriously. I have no intention of discussing the altogether fantastic notion of dealing even with economic history and statistics within a "system" of political economy which also includes morphological, theoretical, and practical informa-

tion about economics. I simply cannot conceive of a system of political economy, or even of a treatment of it to some extent and
in some sense organized, which would simultaneously embrace
the whole of the economic history and all of the economic statistics of all ages and all nations. The *independent* treatment of
economic history and economic policy is an absolute necessity.
This, and only this, is what we are concerned with; neither the
citation of historical-statistical facts for the purpose of exempli-
fying the theoretical and practical truths of political economy
nor the use of history and statistics as ancillary sciences in laying
its foundations is at issue here.

Nor is what has been said above in any way opposed to those
summaries of economic history and economic ideas which usually
precede the exposition of our science. They are but introductions
to the study of political economy—synopses of the respective
sciences serving the above-mentioned didactic purpose—which in
no way obviate the need for, or replace an independent treatment
of, economic history, economic statistics, and economic literature.
The assertion that economic history and statistics as such can be
dealt with in a system of "political economy" embracing at once
morphological, theoretical, and practical questions rests on a misunderstanding.[5]

3. On the Idea of Combining Economic Theory and Applied Economics Within a Unified System

However, serious doubts must be voiced regarding the idea
of organizing economic theory and the principles of economic
policy into a systematically unified science. Each of these has its
own particular system corresponding to the specific formal principles upon which it is constituted. To unite them would involve
one or the other of two alternatives: either one would have to fit
the principles of economic policy into the system of economic
theory and demonstrate the laws of certain economic phenomena
in an incidental way by establishing an external connection between the principles and procedures of the economic policies re-

lating to them, on the one hand, and theoretical knowledge on the other; or one would have to accompany the systematic exposition of the principles of economic policy with incidental theoretical demonstrations. Both of these alternatives not only are logically possible, but, as experience has abundantly taught us, are actually feasible. Whoever recalls the historical development of scientific knowledge and appreciates the importance, for both methodology and systematics, of a division of the sciences based on formal principles, will recognize in such procedures nothing but a symptom of the still undeveloped state of the economic sciences.[6]

It is the failure to appreciate this fact for which I reproach my opponents. Their error consists in regarding the union of economic theory and applied economics, rather than their separation, as progress and even as a methodological postulate. Actually our efforts should be directed towards furthering the separate treatment of the theoretical and the practical, since this is of the greatest importance for the development of our science. But wherever, because of the backwardness of the latter, such a separation is not yet advisable, scientists should endeavor to prepare the way for it. There are, however, economists of the Historical School who tend to regard the above-mentioned development as a kind of regress, and who conversely consider any retrogression in this respect as scientific progress.

The argument of F. J. Neumann in favor of the opposed view [7] is quite untenable. It is not true that the division of political economy into economic theory and applied economics must necessarily lead to "awkward repetitions." This opinion rests upon two prepossessions, both widespread among German economists: that each individual science must present *all* the results of inquiry referring to a definite field of phenomena, and that there are no sciences which *presuppose* the knowledge of other sciences. Physiology is based on a knowledge of anatomy, while surgery and therapy presuppose a knowledge of both these sciences; chemical technology rests on a knowledge of chemistry; mechanics, on a knowledge of mathematics; etc. The opinion that the classification of the sciences according to formal principles leads to repetitions is so far from being correct that it is in fact diametrically opposed to the truth. The function of economics is not to provide us with an incomplete and arbitrary collection of theoretical and useful information organized on external principles. On the contrary, it has the task of organizing all the results of scientific inquiry relating to economics into an intrinsically coherent and well-articulated system. Once our economists realize this, the most expeditious means of attaining such a goal will be seen to consist in separating the theoretical and the applied sciences.

Still less convincing as an argument *against* such a separation is Neumann's contention that it would often necessitate defining different concepts specifically for each of the two divisions, theoretical and applied, of the economic sciences. Even if this were the case, the separate definition of the "concepts" in question would be a problem of economics the evasion of which could hardly be considered as a scientific solution. Neumann does not seem to be aware that he has here touched upon a sore point of the economic sciences. It is true that some of the most important terms are understood in a totally different sense by economic theory and by applied economics. One need only think, for example, of the way in which such concepts as capital, ground rent, interest, and so on, are used in economic theory, on the one hand, and, on the other, in public finance, particularly in treating of the taxation of profits. But can this conceptual confusion be used as an argument *against* the separation of economic theory from applied economics?

Finally, Neumann's proposal to replace the separation between economic theory and economic policy by a division of "political economy" into a *general* branch and a *specialized* branch rests upon a methodological misunderstanding, as I have already demonstrated elsewhere.[8] Economic theory no less than applied economics has its general and its specialized branches. But applied economics can no more be regarded as a specialized branch of economic theory, or the latter as the general branch of applied economics, than chemical technology can be considered as a specialized branch of chemistry, or surgery as a specialized branch of anatomy.[9] It is true that even if no distinction is made in the treatment of economic theory and applied economics, however imperfect such a system might be, a general and a specialized branch would still have to be distinguished, just as they are in every methodically organized scientific work. This fact, however, has nothing to do with the question that concerns us here. The bifurcation of each branch of economics into a general and a specialized section, and the separation of the economic sciences into the theoretical and the applied, are two distinct methodological problems that should not be confused with each other. The former refers to the intrinsic systematics of particular economic sciences; the latter, to the classification of the economic sciences in general.

4. Can There Be Independently Valid Morphological Sciences of Economic Phenomena?

It is doubtful whether the development of economics will lead to an independent systematic morphology of economic phenomena, nor can we be at all certain what place the results of morphological inquiry will have within the system of the economic sciences in general.

Not every theoretical discipline has an independent morphology as its counterpart. Even within the realm of the natural sciences, those which are purely theoretical, i.e., essentially the result of analytic-synthetic methods, such as chemistry and physics, do not have any particular morphologies corresponding to them. Wundt has rightly pointed out, with respect to the problem of a real separation between the individual branches of the different natural sciences, that, for example, the classification of chemical compounds is usually not separated from the theory of chemical phenomena.[10] However, he explains this "strange circumstance" on the one hand by "the relatively undeveloped state of chemistry, in which the functions of description and explanation are not yet sharply distinguished," and, on the other, by "the deep-rooted traditions of natural history, according to which only things found in nature, and not those artificially produced, are treated as objects of the separate systematic sciences." Here Wundt, excellent epistemologist though he is, seems to me to have misunderstood the real reason for a practice that is of great importance to economic inquiry as well.

Morphological knowledge, as far as it is the result of a real analytical reduction of complex phenomena to their elementary factors and of an isolating synthesis of the latter, has no independent significance. It subserves the needs of theoretical work, and its treatment comes to be bound up, for purposes of convenience, with that of the laws of synthesis of the respective phenomena, i.e., with the corresponding theoretical sciences. Indeed, in the absence of such morphological knowledge, these laws cannot even be formulated. The systematic presentation of the combined results of both approaches is thus seen to be dictated not by considerations of convenience alone, but also by their intrinsic congruity. The situation is quite different, however, where our immediate concern is not with *understanding* complex natural phenomena by means of analysis and isolating synthesis, but with *describing* them, as in mineralogy, botany, zoology, etc. Here, of course, the description of forms, the morphology of the respective fields of phenomena, assumes an independent significance, and the synthesis of the results of inquiry in separate systematic sciences corresponds only to the independent interest that we take in such knowledge.

Science is presented with a similar problem in the field of economics. Here too the question may arise—not whether the morphological approach is justified in general, for no doubt exists on that score—but whether, side by side with economic theory, a morphology of economic phenomena is of independent interest and whether the latter should accordingly be assigned an independent position, alongside economic theory, within the system of the economic sciences.

To this question the methodological principles that we have here set forth provide an answer that proves to be in full accord with the actual development of economics up to the present day. The elementary factors that theoretical analysis discloses in complex economic phenomena have no independent significance within the system of economic science; their morphology does not correspond to any independent scientific need.

It is therefore altogether appropriate that they should be treated as an integral part of economic theory as far as the latter deals with the laws of synthesis of elementary economic phenomena. What usually introduces systematic treatises on economic theory under the rubric of "Principles of Economics," but is incorporated into the body of the presentation by the more rigorously systematic economists, is chiefly nothing but a morphological description of the essential elementary factors of complex economic phenomena. There is as little scientific need for an independent morphology of these elementary economic factors as there is in the case of elementary natural phenomena and the combinations of them that are obtained by means of an isolating synthesis.

On the other hand, it seems to me that at least where our primary and immediate concern is not with *understanding* complex economic phenomena by way of analytic-synthetic inquiry, but with *describing* them in all their complexity and multiformity (in which noneconomic factors also play a role), their systematic morphology does take on an independent scientific interest. In addition to the effort to achieve a theoretical understanding of economic phenomena—and even long before the need for it appears in inquiry—there is an endeavor to study them in their complexity, as they are presented by experience, and in their multiformity, which is the product of the simultaneous operation of a diversity of spatial and temporal influences. It is here that morphology enters the system of economic science. Serving as a supplement to the historical sciences, where they offer but a collective image of concrete economic events within definite spatial limits, it has the task of presenting a systematic survey of the complex phenomena of economics in general.

To be sure, the first steps taken in this direction have so far been pitifully inadequate. No doubt, too, the results of such lines of investigation not only could be, but, in the present state of economics, are in fact already, an integral part of that science, particularly in its more highly specialized branches. Yet it does not seem to me to be altogether out of the question that methodological studies in the field of economics might some day emerge from their present subordinate position as a part of economic theory or as themes for monographical dissertations and finally develop into a fully independent systematic science.

5. *A Survey of the System of Economic Sciences*

A complete system of the actual economic sciences will therefore comprise the following:

1. The historical sciences of economics: *economic statistics* and *economic history*. The former has to investigate concrete economic phenomena from the point of view of statics and within definite spatial limits, while the latter has to study them from an evolutionary standpoint and to combine them into a unitary, organic structure.
2. *The morphology of economic phenomena,* whose function consists in the classification of economic facts in accordance with their genera, species, and subspecies, as well as the demonstration of their generic form, i.e., the description of the common structures of different groups of homogeneous phenomena.
3. *Economic theory,* which has the task of investigating and establishing the laws of economic phenomena, i.e., the regularities in their coexistence and succession, as well as their intrinsic causation. I have already called attention to the appropriateness of combining the morphography of basic economic phenomena with economic theory (see above p. 12).
4. *Practical or applied economics,* which teaches us the principles and procedures by which generally determined economic aims may be most effectively realized in different circumstances and in the light of existing scientific knowledge.

6. The Classification of the Economic Sciences as Conceived by the Historical School

The economists of the Historical School view the classification of the economic sciences from an essentially different methodological standpoint.

Here the confusion between historiography and sociology, i.e., between economic history and political economy (regarded as a branch of sociology), first makes itself apparent. I have already commented upon the difference between the tasks of these sciences and have pointed out the impossibility of dealing with history and statistics—the history of all ages and all nations—in a single system of sociology, and with economic history and economic statistics in a single system of political economy. If a certain number of social philosophers still cling to this error, the reason is that they consider it as the function of historical inquiry not to investigate and describe the evolution of *concrete* nations and their cultures, but rather to discover the *laws* of their development. However, distinguished historians have long since rejected this view as an error and as a misunderstanding of the essential task of historiography. Roscher's definition of political economy as "the philosophy of economic history" is a belated echo of this antiquated conception of history.

Even greater is the conceptual confusion concerning the relationship between economic theory and applied economics.[11]

Every variety of positivism, even a type less extreme than that embraced by the economists of the Historical School, finds it difficult to form a correct conception of the applied sciences.[12]

One will search in vain in Comte's classification of the sciences for a clear and consistent treatment of this problem, nor does the methodology of the Historical School offer any really serious solution of it. Within the system of the social sciences, what relation does the science of administration have to sociology? And what position do the principles of economic policy hold, especially in relation to economic theory, within the system of the economic sciences? To such questions, which can hardly be avoided by the methodology of our science, no satisfactory answer has been given either by Comte's positivism or by the historicism of German political economy. The latter has even denied the independent significance of applied economics.

It is true that the sciences which treat of the principles and procedures for the realization of generally determined human goals have no *absolute* significance, in the sense in which the word is understood in the attacks that the Historical School has launched against this idea. However, this is not a serious objection to the validity of such disciplines. It is patently erroneous to assume that identical procedures in different circumstances, especially in different ages and in different nations, lead to identical results and have in this sense an absolute meaning. However, this mistaken conception of the nature and the tasks of the applied sciences has no bearing on their validity. The function of these disciplines is to demonstrate how given, generally determined goals of human action can be attained under different typical conditions *by methods specifically appropriate to different kinds of circumstances.*

I do not propose to deal here with the question whether the physiocratic or the classical school of economics has really labored under the aforementioned error as completely as our historicists would have us believe. I leave to others the task of elucidating this point and of rectifying, in respect to the doctrines of *applied* economics, the distortions in the treatment of our science for which the Historical School is responsible, in the same way that this correction has already been made in respect to the history of the development of all the principal doctrines of economic theory. In any case, the above conception of applied economics is an error, but one which is in no way crucial to the question of the independent validity of that discipline in the sense in which we have defined it.

However, it is said, "the applied sciences, whatever they may do in the way of investigating and demonstrating the *different* procedures suited for the attainment of different typical objectives in different typical circumstances, are nevertheless deficient in that they fail to take into consideration the distinctive peculiarity of each of the *concrete* cases actually encountered in practice; and consequently, at least in this respect, there is a mistaken absolutism in the solutions that they offer."

This objection too rests upon a prepossession, viz., the mistaken idea that applied economics is to be conceived, if at all, only in the sense of a "set of prescriptions" for the concrete cases encountered in actual practice.

The applied sciences do not offer us "recipes" for taking action in every single *concrete* case. There are no sciences of this kind—sciences which would exhaust the whole of life's fullness and multiformity and which would prescribe for us from the very outset the procedure to be followed in each individual *concrete* situation. No applied science, no matter how complete, could possibly do this. Applied sciences in this sense exist only in the fantasy of our historicists. What the applied sciences can and do provide are not recipes for concrete cases. Therapy, technology, and the principles of economic policy are not mere sets of prescriptions. They show us how *generally* determined human goals of a specific kind can be most effectively realized in the light of diverse circumstances. Evidently what is referred to here is the attainment, by means of a *variety* of procedures, of different kinds of objectives under similar conditions and of the same kinds of objectives in different types of circumstances. This is far from providing us with prescriptions for every occasion. The ends aimed at by men are unique in each concrete case, and so are the circumstances in which they have to be attained. No applied science, no matter how highly specialized, could possibly exhaust the individual particularity of every single situation encountered in actual experience.

Here, *in this respect,* the practical man is required to have recourse to his essential insight into phenomena and their interrelationships and to rely upon his own inventiveness. Just as the applied sciences in general are based upon the theoretical, so the scientifically trained technician tries, on the basis of his theoretical insight, to modify, to refine, and to adapt to the unique requirements of each concrete case the procedures indicated by the applied sciences as suited for goals and conditions that are determined only in a general way. It is *only in combination with his theoretical insight* that his knowledge of the applied sciences enables him to specify, in each concrete case, the procedure appropriate to it—or, if one will, the "prescription" for it. Indeed, there are many situations in practical life, with its ever-changing conditions and exigencies, in which the applied sciences, at their current level, are completely useless, leaving the practical man at the mercy of his own theoretical insight and his native faculty for synthesis and invention. There are instances when even the surgeon, the therapist, and the technologist have only their theoretical insight into the essential nature of things and their interrelations to fall back upon. Although the applied sciences, no matter how fully elaborated, can never, as we have said, be merely a set of prescriptions, yet, in combination with the theoretical sciences, they serve, in innumerable cases that constitute the rule of practical life, as the guiding star of the scientifically trained technician.[13]

What, then, it may be asked, is the use of the applied sciences after all? Can they not be dispensed with entirely, as too roundabout? Is it not more appropriate for practical purposes to familiarize oneself exclusively with theory, or at least with history, and thus determine directly, on the basis of these sciences, the procedure corresponding to each concrete case?

Whoever argues in this way—and our economists of the Historical School actually seem to have fixed upon a position very much like this—misunderstands the exigencies of practical life. Historical knowledge, however comprehensive, and theoretical insight, however profound, into the essential nature of things and their interrelations, are far from sufficient in themselves to enable one to decide in a concrete case with the required certainty, rapidity, and completeness upon the most appropriate procedure for getting things done. Theoretical insight has to be associated with the faculty of synthesis and inventiveness, and these are endowments that are to be found only among a limited number of exceptional and especially talented minds. The applied sciences provide us with the sum total of the results achieved in man's effort to find appropriate procedures for the attainment of his practical goals. This knowledge represents the accomplishment not only of scientific research, but also of the greatest inventive geniuses—the really "practical" men in the strict sense of the word—and includes as well a stock of particular experiences accumulated in practice. Whether because of the imperfect state of development of this kind of knowledge, the ever-changing patterns and requirements of life's practical situations, or special peculiarities of circumstance, the applied sciences may fail to offer an immediate and well-founded prescription for action in a concrete case; yet even then they provide a systematic survey of all the procedures that have been found to be effective in attaining similar goals, and they thereby, to some extent at least, lighten the task of selecting, on the basis of theoretical insight, the means appropriate to the end in view in a given case.

Thus, besides the theoretical sciences, the applied sciences have an eminently independent significance. To call into question, for instance, the utility of surgery, of therapy, of technology, or of the principles of economic policy would argue a complete disregard for the requirements of practical life. These disciplines challenge the sagacity, the experience, the ingenuity, and the diligence of their practitioners to the utmost degree. To place them on a par with "cookbooks for handy reference," as Kleinwächter does,[14] is an aberration comparable to that of certain "practical" men who consider theorizing as idle toying with ideas.[15]

However, it is said, the applied sciences are not sciences in the strict sense of the word, but only scientific studies.

This objection, I believe, does indeed amount to playing with the word "science." It is true that some epistemologists refuse to call these disciplines sciences on the ground that the name "science" in its strictest sense is to be applied only to those disciplines which provide us with an *understanding* of things and which are susceptible of *systematic* demonstration. On this basis, as we know, even *history* has been denied the character of a science. This is a serious error. As far as the applied sciences are concerned, such a judgment is mistaken because disciplines that lend themselves to systematic treatment not only *describe* the procedures for the attainment of generally determined human ends, but also provide us with an *understanding* of them. The applied sciences not only enable us to act in a mechanical way, but at the same time make us aware of the reasons for our action. They are fully entitled to be regarded as sciences in the strict sense of the term in so far as they provide a systematic account of human goals in any one field of endeavor and demonstrate the appropriate methods of attaining them. Terminological controversies over whether these disciplines are properly to be called sciences in some particular sense of the word or whether they are to be labeled "mere scientific studies" will not affect in any way their independent significance and value in the sphere of scientific knowledge, which is all that concerns us here.

7. *Further Observations on the Classification of the Economic Sciences as Conceived by the Historical School*

It is incorrect to assert that the applied sciences in general and applied economics in particular establish general principles "without taking circumstances into account." It is also incorrect to say that they are "just sets of prescriptions" and that they can be replaced by theoretical disciplines or even by mere historical studies. On the contrary, these sciences are of the greatest independent significance for both theoretical research and practical life. Their development in both breadth and depth requires no less talent and zeal than does that of the historical, morphological, and theoretical disciplines. Why, then, in the light of all this, are these practical sciences rejected by our economists of the Historical School? The reply is: It is the task of science to be concerned solely with fact and not with value. Science has to teach us what *has been,* what *is,* and how what is *has come to be;* but not, what *ought to be.*

Accordingly, it is asserted, disciplines like surgery, therapy, technology, or the principles of economic policy are not sciences, and the effort to elaborate and perfect them is misdirected, for they do not teach us what *was,* what *is,* or how what is *has come to be,* but rather, on the basis of this knowledge, they concern themselves, in a certain sense, with what *ought to be.*[16]

Let us, by all means, give to positivism its due share of credit for having liberated us from aprioristic speculation in the sciences that have the real world for their object. However, its helpless incapacity to deal with the applied sciences, and especially with the applied social sciences, seems to me not so much a proof of the invalidity of the latter as a symptom of the *insufficiency* of the positivistic conception of the social sciences. If we understand by the term "applied sciences" disciplines having the task of teaching us the most effective way in which certain human goals *could* be realized under given conditions and in the light of our judgment at the time, then I am inclined to believe that the applied sciences will continue in full vigor and enjoy a flourishing development long after the insufficiency of positivism, even in the field of *theoretical* inquiry, will have become generally recognized.

The objections cited here against the independent validity of applied economics are thus seen to be complete misconceptions. They are certainly far from justifying the opinion that in the field of social inquiry in general, and of economics in particular, the applied sciences should be replaced by a mere description of what was and what is, i.e., by "economic history and especially a record of the outcome of the attempts that have hitherto been made to improve economic conditions."

History and statistics, together with the common experience of life, are important foundations of the theoretical sciences. The latter, however, for their part constitute the foundation of the applied disciplines. These too rely upon experience and, what is more, upon an experience that is comprehensive, well-founded, and systematically organized. They are far from rejecting experience or from minimizing its significance. Economic history, economic theory, and the morphology of economic phenomena are important, and even indispensable, auxiliary sciences for applied economics. However, the latter has an independent function, which is essentially different from that of the above-mentioned sciences. As long as the practising surgeon and the therapist do not confine themselves to the study of human history, anatomy, and physiology, or the practising technologist to that of chemistry, mechanics, and physics, there will continue to exist, side by side with history and sociology, applied social sciences of the greatest significance for both theory and practice, even though positivism cannot fit them into its system.

The present confusion concerning the *methods of the applied sciences* in this field will come to an end as soon as it is realized that the cognitive goals of the latter are essentially *different* from those of the other economic sciences. In basing themselves upon historical and theoretical disciplines, the applied sciences draw upon experience to the greatest extent. But in their endeavor to establish the principles and procedures for attaining the goals of human action, they do not confine themselves to the mere description of what the inventive spirit of man has already accomplished. They are not concerned exclusively with past experience. They are equally the product of inventive genius and the faculty of intellectual synthesis. Progress in the applied sciences is the result not only of the scientist's zeal in collecting data, but also of his ingenuity and resourcefulness. The assumption that social scientists should, as a matter of principle, restrict themselves solely to the historical description of the results of man's activity involves the renunciation on the part of science of any concern for meeting new needs and even for influencing in any way the conduct of affairs in all those cases for which no precedent so far exists. Not scientific knowledge, but administrative authority would then determine every innovation in the field of applied economics.

It should be clear from what has been said so far that the applied, as well as the historical and the theoretical, social sciences have an independent significance and validity—that their cognitive goals and their methodologies are different—and also, as I have shown above, that their separate treatment is essential for the intrinsic systematics of each of these sciences.[17] Hence no doubt should exist any longer concerning the relationship between the *morphologies* of social phenomena and the applied social sciences. I have elsewhere pointed out that the morphological approach is valid also in the domain of political economy. And beyond that, I must say that it is indeed gratifying to note, in the methodological discussions of the economists of the Historical School, the increasing emphasis that has recently been placed upon morphological considerations. I welcome this as a sign of the growing conviction among them that our science has the task not only of investigating and describing *concrete* economic phenomena and their development—of being, in other words, something more than mere historiography—but also of dealing with their *generic* aspects. In any case, those who hold to the opinion that a morphology of economic phenomena could be substituted for applied economics in general, or for the sciences of business management in particular, simply fall into a new error. Indeed, a morphology of economic phenomena could by no means take the place even of economic theory, although the connection between theoretical knowledge and certain branches of morphological investigation, particularly those that are concerned with evolutionary changes, is quite as close here as it is in the natural sciences. Those who regard a morphology of economic phenomena and of their historical development as the only legitimate branch of inquiry in the field of economics (besides, perhaps, economic history and economic statistics) fail to understand the independent function and significance not only of applied economics, but of economic theory as well. The one-sidedness manifested by such a confusion of the morphological and the theoretical in the field of economic inquiry surpasses even that involved in the lumping together of economic theory and applied economics.

8. *Rebuttal of Some Recent Attacks on My Methodological Position*

While I was preparing this paper, my attention was called to Brentano's *Über die Ursachen der heutigen sozialen Not,*[18] and Kleinwächter's *Wesen, Aufgabe, und System der Nationalökonomie.*[19] Both these authors take the opportunity to present their methodological views, which in part are in direct opposition to my own. Since their conception of the classification of the economic sciences reflects the prevailing view on this subject, it seems appropriate to give it some attention here.

Brentano takes the position of the "vicar of Wakefield," that the honest man who marries and raises a large family does more good than the man who stays single and babbles about the population. But instead of drawing from this the obvious conclusion that the honest man who organizes cartels or shares in their profits is more useful than the one who only lectures on them, Brentano derives the practical application that "endless chatter about *what* should be done and *how* it should be done without ever getting anything done"—in other words, concern with the goals and the methods of inquiry—amounts to the "contraction of intellectual debts." [20]

Now I too am of the opinion that a methodology, no matter how fully elaborated, is not sufficient in itself for the development of the sciences.

There is, to be sure, between the elaboration of a systematic method and the satisfactory completion and perfection of a science an immeasurable distance that can be bridged only by the genius of the scientist. An active talent for inquiry has often, even in the absence of a fully developed method, created a science or transformed it in an epoch-making way—something that no methodology by itself has ever succeeded in doing. Techniques of procedure, although of incomparable importance for the performance of the subsidiary tasks of science, are of minor significance for those great problems that only the genius can solve.[21]

However, as long as such a genius has not yet appeared in the field of economics, erroneous methodological doctrines still hamper the development of important branches of our science. Under these conditions I think the value of methodological inquiry can hardly be overemphasized by any of us. "It is," says Kant, "already a great and necessary proof of good sense or judgment to know what questions one should ask from a rational point of view." Economic inquiry has the aim of teaching us not only this, but also what to do in order to get reasonable replies to reasonable questions. Why, then, just in this field, should such investigations imply the "contraction of intellectual debts"?

In this respect the natural sciences are in an enviable position, because they have long since had an essential awareness of their cognitive goals and procedures. Nevertheless, they do not by any means reject methodological questions, least of all where serious doubts arise concerning the aims and methods of inquiry. Suppose there were to appear a group of natural scientists who refused to recognize as valid any but a descriptive approach to nature, limiting themselves, for example, to the morphology of natural phenomena or even only to the theory of evolution, and who would accordingly reject not only the mathematical sciences as an idle game played with abstract concepts, but even the applied natural sciences as a mere aberration from the true path of inquiry. In that case, provided that their more sober-minded colleagues did not simply prefer to pass over such prejudices in silence, methodological questions would immediately come to the fore also in the field of the natural sciences.

In the domain of the social sciences, however, we are not in the same fortunate position. It is not at all clear what social phenomena are specifically or in what way their distinctive nature must determine the goals and methods of inquiry. There is more than enough room here for misunderstanding and prejudice. Even attitudes as one-sided as those we have described above are within the realm of possibility. Indeed, it is by no means inconceivable that such prejudices might gain currency within certain scholarly circles and that men obsessed by them might have the power to decide on the most momentous issues affecting our economic life. Under such circumstances it can hardly be gainsaid that methodological questions, far from being entirely without significance, are of paramount and urgent importance and demand of all of us our best efforts toward their clarification.

The need for a thoroughgoing reorganization of the social sciences is an undeniable fact. However, I shall not enter here into a discussion of whether such an undertaking is still to be regarded in our time as naive and unconsidered, or whether criticism of other investigators' work is even possible in the absence of clarity concerning methodological issues. But there is no doubt that the finest flower of the German mind sprang from the ground of inquiries concerning *"what* should be done and *how* it should be done." Indeed, it is precisely this that constitutes, to a considerable extent, the distinctive feature manifested by the development of German thought. Scholarly zeal, very respectable, to be sure, but rather confused as to the aims and methods of scientific inquiry, is what I think is responsible for the biased tendency of the German Historical School of economists. It is not as unlikely as Brentano seems to believe that a deeper study of methodological questions may make German economists once again aware of the types of problems to be solved by our science and may thus put an end to the one-sidedness that has had such a pernicious effect upon the development of the economic sciences in Germany. However, I am of the opinion that we can attain to a broad view of the types of problems to be solved by economics only by way of comprehensive methodological investigations subserving no extraneous ends of any kind. Incidental methodological dissertations, on the other hand, subjoined to specialized studies of other questions, often serve the sole purpose of placing the particular merits of these works in the right light. Being little more than adornments added to special investigations of quite a different kind, they necessarily bear within themselves the seeds of partiality.

The foundation of a methodology of the social sciences is the most important epistemological task of our time. Our most distinguished epistemologists have directed their scholarly endeavors for the most part towards the great goal of contracting that "intellectual debt." Indeed, I myself would like to be such a contractor of intellectual debts. Would that I could solve the methodological problems in the field of the social sciences! Even the more modest service of having advanced their solution by an essential step deserves—considering the present level of methodological understanding—to be esteemed at least as highly as any purely descriptive monograph, even one as meritorious as Brentano's own study of the trade unions of England.

Brentano speaks in a similarly derogatory way of the endeavors of the "new abstract school" to bring about the reform that economic theory so urgently needs if it is to become a truly scientific foundation for applied economics, and thereby also for economic policy. Although attacking these "new abstract thinkers," he does not find them guilty of errors in the field of economic theory. He is even fair-minded and candid enough to recognize the progress that it owes this particular group of scientists.[22] And yet this progress, strangely enough, has come not from the Historical School, which has been in existence now for about half a century, but precisely from the "abstract school," which is charged with being remote from life. In spite of this, Brentano does not miss any opportunity to demonstrate his disdain for "abstract theory," which he seems to regard as an idle game played with ideas. Why? Because abstract theory has not succeeded in abolishing poverty! [23] The investigations of the "abstract scholars" seem to him of no value whatsoever, and the adherents of the "abstract school" appear even "incomprehensible" as long as their theoretical inquiries have not succeeded in "conjuring away either poverty or the dangers to the social order resulting from it." [24]

I shall deal with this idea in greater detail in another place, where I propose to discuss the different lines of theoretical inquiry with particular reference to mathematical economics. There I shall further examine the circumstances connected with the reproach that "abstract" economics is only a conceptual game or, as some would have us believe, a system of abstract theorems contradicting experience and derived by way of deduction from certain a priori axioms. These and other similar prejudices that have recently been championed with much zeal, especially in German economics, I shall make the object of an exhaustive inquiry. But here I must observe, in opposition to Brentano's thesis, that the judgment he passes on the theoretical work of the "abstract scholars" seems untenable to me no matter what branch of economic theory is involved. Brentano seems to forget that economic theory, even when it is interpreted, as it may be, as a science having the real world for its object, has to investigate the nature of economic phenomena and their interrelations and thereby to provide us with an *understanding* of them. On the other hand, it is the task of the applied (or so-called "practical") sciences, and specifically of applied economics, to teach us the principles and procedures for effective intervention in the economic system in the light of different circumstances. Brentano overlooks the fact that theoretical economics or some specialized branch of it can not very well be reproached for solving the problems peculiar to it and not those that are properly within the sphere of the *applied* sciences.[25]

How biased Brentano's point of view is may be seen from the fact that he declares "abstract" economic theory to be of no value, but not on the ground that it is *utterly* incapable of solving problems of economic welfare. He scorns all the "controversies about concepts in which the abstract school is absorbed" only because "abstract" economic theory is unable to solve a special problem of public welfare, viz., the abolition of "social danger." He reminds one of those well-known medical specialists who hold that the natural sciences are all very well, yet scorn them because theories cannot cure a diseased eye or heal a sore leg, and who therefore cannot understand how anyone can devote time and effort and even his entire life to such theoretical inquiries.

Moreover, Brentano does not realize that by demanding this kind of achievement from *science* he puts his own morphological studies in a bad light. After all, Brentano did not originate the idea of trade unionism, of arbitration offices, etc., nor has he, as far as I know, directly called them into being. He is not the Schulze-Delitzsch of these institutions, but only a distinguished expositor and historian of them. Even if they were to abolish poverty, as Brentano predicted and still in part assumes, even if his forecast of their operation and development had proved to be perfectly correct, he still could claim for himself only the merit of being their monographer, i.e., a theorist in economics. Not he, but the institutions he describes, would have abolished poverty, and they would have done so even without his descriptions. Yet it would hardly be reasonable to reproach him for this, since he has accomplished, to the best of his ability, what the scientific description of different kinds of economic phenomena has the task of accomplishing. For this reason, it seems to me, it would only be fair if he too demanded of theorists that they do no more than the theoretical sciences or particular branches of them can do by their very nature, namely, what their specific tasks require them to do.

Brentano's attack upon "abstract" economic theory is mistaken. But I myself am inclined to think that the latter is open to justifiable criticism on quite another score, namely, its failure, in its present state of development, to solve the very problems with which an "abstract" theory of economics has to be specifically concerned.

Economic theory, in my opinion, will do justice to its task only when it provides us not alone with knowledge of the external regularities in the coexistence and succession of economic phenomena, i.e., with empirical laws, but also with an *understanding* of them in their intrinsic relations. Only in this way can the theoretical foundation be laid for the solution of *all* the problems of economic policy. The inability to abolish poverty is not the only respect in which the science of economic welfare has proved its practical insufficiency in consequence of the present defective theoretical understanding of the nature of economic phenomena and their essential interrelations. The helplessness of administrative authorities in the face of economic crises and the uncertain and fumbling attempts made by even the most distinguished statesmen in dealing with problems of monetary, commercial, industrial, and agricultural policy are only too evident symptoms of the unsatisfactory state of applied economics, which, in its turn, reflects the backwardness of economic theory. The inadequacies of economic policy are but the corollary of an economic theory that leaves to the arbitrary judgment of politicians the answer to such questions as whether duties on grains raise their price in predominantly grain-importing countries, whether higher grain prices raise the price of bread, or whether duties on coffee, petroleum, and tobacco or other indirect taxes raise the price of the corresponding articles of consumption.

No one is more deeply conscious than we theorists, whose heads, according to Brentano, are filled with "abstractions," of the imperfection, even the fundamental weaknesses, of the prevailing economic theory and of its insufficiency as a basis for applied economics. Where we differ from Brentano, however, is in the conviction that science as well as economic policy can be perfected only by a deeper understanding of the nature of economic phenomena and their essential interrelations. It is our belief that in economics, as in all other fields of practical activity, only the progressive improvement of all branches of theory can bring about progress in the applied sciences and thereby also the perfection of practice itself. It is therefore one of the most important tasks of those of us who work in this field to cultivate the study of economic theory in all its branches.

However, this task will in no way be advanced by erroneous and biased conceptions concerning the cognitive goals of economic theory or by depreciatory remarks in regard to the endeavors to reform it or particular branches of it. In his criticism of our theoretical investigations Brentano adopts an unfair attitude from the very outset by demanding of them that they forthwith abolish poverty—in other words, that they do the impossible. Nor is he, it seems to me, quite just in his judgment of what these investigations have already accomplished within the sphere of their competence or what, assuming that they are correct, they are called upon to accomplish.

I should like to add here only one remark regarding Brentano's attitude toward the applied sciences.

I believe that in struggling against the idea that life "may be controlled" by *theory*,[26] Brentano has fallen prey to an altogether baseless apprehension resulting solely from his defective conception of the system of the economic sciences. To be sure, false theories can lead, and often enough have led, the applied sciences based upon them into errors on their part. Erroneous theories in the field of anatomy and physiology, for instance, have had a pernicious influence on surgery and therapy, and thereby indirectly also upon medical practice. In the same way, false economic theories have been responsible for errors in the principles of economic policy. Erroneous ideas concerning the nature of the wealth of nations and the function of money in the national economy have, for example, contributed essentially to aggravate the errors of mercantile economic policy; and the erroneous theory of value developed by the classical school has unquestionably had an essential influence on practical affairs in the demand of the socialists that the entire product, or its equivalent value in money, should belong to the workers. False theoretical doctrines can doubtless give rise to false principles for the conduct of practical affairs and to ineffective procedures or inappropriate policies based upon them, but a *theory* that could "control" life is a contradiction in terms. Economic theory too can offer us only a true or a false statement of the laws of economic phenomena; it can represent life falsely, but it can no more control life than chemistry or physics can.[27] Hence the question whether the economic sciences have the task of "controlling" life, if it arises at all, can in any case refer only to applied economics.

But if by "the control of life" one means to refer to the fact that applied economics has the task of teaching us the principles and procedures for an effective policy of intervention on the part of the state, or of associations analogous and subordinated to it, then the above question must be answered unconditionally in the affirmative, for this is precisely the function that applied economics is, by its very nature and, indeed, by definition, called upon to perform. It "controls" the economic system in just about the same way as nature is "controlled" by technology, or the human body by surgery and therapy. In any case, this reproach is one that the specialists in the field of applied economics will find it easy to treat rather lightly.

If the reproach contained in the passage quoted above has any justification at all, it surely cannot mean that applied economics is to be blamed for performing its specific function of aiming at the improvement of life in general, but for going about this task *in the wrong way*.

Here, indeed, the question arises whether applied economics should in principle confine itself to recording the results of past experience and whether—at least from the standpoint of a strict scientific method—it should be absolutely prevented from *also* proposing such ways and means of attaining human goals as are not borrowed from past experience, but are the result of intellectual synthesis and inventive thought.

In this regard, I believe that a science that would confine itself to the description of existing institutions and administrative measures and to waiting for their results with the intention of also "describing" them at a later date must, in principle, abandon any claim to a leading position in questions of economic policy and dwindle to that of a mere history of the activity of administrative authorities and institutions of collective self-help. No one can possibly deny the importance of experience to the applied sciences, nor would anyone even wish to call it into question in the slightest degree. In requiring that disciplines for the conduct of practical affairs be founded upon the theoretical sciences, we are demanding for the former the most comprehensive empirical foundation, one which can be subjected to the most penetrating criticism and which includes everything that enables us to acquire "an insight into life." To restrict these disciplines exclusively to the task of describing past institutions and tendencies and their effects would argue a complete disregard of the innumerable innovations in the economic system that are to be attributed to the work of specialists in applied economics.

Brentano apparently fails to recognize the great practical importance of the creative and inventive spirit or its influence upon the applied sciences. If those working in the field of the applied sciences, as well as men engaged in practical affairs, had always shared Brentano's opinion that science should confine itself to "observing nature" and to noting the principles of its development, and if they had made this the exclusive rule of their conduct, then we should have run the risk of still having to live in caves and of clothing ourselves in hides "discovered in nature," and—in the absence of any higher ethical principles—of preserving the institutions of slavery and serfdom to this very day. Brentano seems to have taken too literally Roscher's dictum that the sole task of our science should be "the simple description, first, of the economic nature and needs of the different peoples of the world; then, of the laws and institutions designed for their satisfaction; and finally, of the greater or lesser effects they have had," and that whatever exceeds this "simple description" is to be regarded quite literally as a "collection of prescriptions." [28]

What may well be the strongest point in favor of the conception of applied economics and its task that we have set forth here is that it opens the way for the presentation of new proposals for the organization of economic life. As long as these are sound and are realized in practice, people can always be found to "describe" the different ways of organizing the management of practical affairs and to "observe nature" once again in order to learn their underlying principles. In any case, however, nothing seems to me more certain than that in the field of economics "a real service can be rendered to science, fatherland, and humanity" not only by "descriptions," but also by intellectual synthesis and the inventive spirit, especially when these are combined with an ever-growing fund of experience.

NOTES

1. For my conception of the *statistical* sciences, see my *Untersuchungen über die Methode der Sozialwissenschaften* (1883), pp. 253 ff.

2. See my *Untersuchungen über die Methode der Sozialwissenschaften* (1883), pp. 3 ff. and pp. 249 ff. For other discussions of this point, see L. Cossa, *Guida allo studio dell' econ. pol.* (1878), pp. 14 ff.; M. Block, *Journal des écon.* (1883), pp. 67 ff.; E. Sax, *Das Wesen und die Aufgaben der Nationalökonomie* (Vienna, 1884), pp. 21 ff.; E. v. Philippovich, *Über die Angabe und Methode der polit. Ökonomie* (Freiburg, 1886), pp. 3 ff.; L. Walras, *Eléments d'éc. pol.* (1889), pp. 34 ff.

3. A presentation combining theoretical with practical knowledge is justified wherever certain parts of a theory are of specific importance for a particular applied science. In demonstrating a particular practical application of the natural sciences, one may draw upon all the theoretical knowledge relevant to one's purpose, setting it forth either by way of introduction or by means of incidental references in the body of the presentation itself. The economist who deals with a particular practical application of economic theory, or of any branch of it, may do likewise. The author of a work on monetary, commercial, and agricultural policy or on indirect taxation may use whatever theoretical knowledge is specifically required to support his thesis, either in his introduction or in incidental references in the body of his work. He may do the same with the results of the sciences of history, statistics, technology, husbandry, forestry, mining, etc. But it is clearly understood that this in no way obviates the need for an *independent* presentation of the above-mentioned sciences.

4. See my essay "Zur Kritik der pol. Ök." in Grünhut's *Zeitschr. für das privat- und offentl. Recht* (1887), pp. 754 ff.

5. See my *Untersuchungen über die Methode der Sozialwissenschaften* (1883), pp. 352 ff. and *Die Irrtümer des Historismus in der deutschen Nationalökonomie* (1884), pp. 12 ff. The experts in the field of historical research are in substantial agreement on this point. Bernheim, in his *Lehrbuch der historischen Methode* (1889), pp. 68 ff., vehemently criticizes the conceptual confusion of those social philosophers who regard the science of history, not as an independent discipline, but as a

branch of sociology, with allegedly the same aims, tasks, and methods as the latter. Bernheim says, "This is almost as erroneous as it would be to regard history as a branch of politics, merely because both are concerned with the state. Sociology, it is true, is concerned with the same object as history, i.e., with human society, but in a totally different way. . . . The whole outlook and approach of sociology is fundamentally different from that of history, since the latter endeavors to learn what man, as a member of society, has everywhere become, how this development has taken place, what has been accomplished by every social group, every people, every prominent personality, in all their individuality. . . . Sociology is an auxiliary science of history. But it is in no way the aim of the latter to establish general types and factors, or even laws, of development. . . . The sociologists belonging to the biased group that fails to recognize this fact declare the only theme of historical science to be what they themselves seek to abstract from history for their own purposes."

6. The separation of economic theory from the applied sciences as far as *presentation* is concerned is no more an "unnatural dissection of a homogeneous subject matter" than is the separate treatment of chemistry and chemical technology or of mechanics and mechanical technology. The assumption that such a separation of the sciences necessarily involves a disintegration of *knowledge* must in any event be considered as one of the most naive of existing prejudices. A scientifically trained physician is familiar not only with therapy, but also with anatomy and physiology, although these sciences have long since been treated as independent.

7. G. Schönberg, *Handbuch d. pol. Ök.*, I (1885), 134 ff.

8. See my *Untersuchungen über die Methode der Sozialwissenschaften*, pp. 246 ff.

9. This error is especially obvious in Kleinwächter's characterization of the relationship between economic theory and the principles of applied economics as that of "different *parts* or *chapters*" of one and the same science. (See *Jahrbücher*, New Series, XVIII [1889], 603.) Brentano also makes a distinction between general *or* theoretical economics and specialized *or* applied economics. (*Die klassische Nationalökonomie*, pp. 28 ff.)

10. *Logik* (1883), II, 230.

11. On the confusion of *economic theory* with the *general* branch and of *applied economics* with the *specialized* branch of political economy, see above pp. 10-11.

12. "Every practice presupposes an ideal; the thing to be done is never a fact; empiricism leaves every practice to the hazard of the passions." (C. Secrétan, *Études sociales*, 1889, p. 205).

13. We must distinguish in the domain of economics, just as we do in other fields of human activity, between the so-called *practical sciences* and *practice* itself. The former have the task of teaching us the procedures by which certain economic aims, determined only in a general way, can be most effectively realized in different circumstances. In actual

practice, on the other hand, on the basis of the above-mentioned sciences and of one's own (theoretical) insight into the essential nature of things and their interrelations, one has to determine and to follow the procedure uniquely appropriate to the concrete case with which one has to deal. The confusion in the field of economics between the practical sciences and practical activity is one of the chief reasons why there are so many methodological misunderstandings. What chiefly contributes to this error is the fact that the practical sciences are often designated as the *applied* sciences, since they are based upon the theoretical sciences and presuppose a knowledge of them. It is clear, however, that the applied sciences in the above sense should not be confused with practice. Surgery, a practical science, is, in its relation to anatomy and physiology, an applied science. Yet no one would confuse the activity of a practising surgeon with the *science* of surgery.

14. *Ibid.*, p. 603. Kleinwächter seems to be ignorant of the reasons why the words *"or the so-called practical arts"* are an appropriate addition to the expression "the applied sciences." The reason lies in the double meaning of this term, which designates, on the one hand, especially in the older philosophy, ἡ περὶ γἀνθρώπινα φιλοσωφία, i.e., *all* the sciences of man, and, on the other hand, the *applied* sciences in the modern sense (as opposed to the *theoretical* sciences). The added words are intended to eliminate a possible doubt as to the *meaning* in which the expression "applied science" is employed. In any case, it takes a rather extravagant fancy to draw from them the conclusion that Kleinwächter does that the applied sciences are something like "cookbooks for handy reference that the Minister of the Interior or of Commerce consults each time he proceeds to draft a bill or an ordinance, in the same way as a cook refers to her cookbook when she has to prepare a roast in an unusual way." In my opinion, an official usually knows that there are no prescriptions in the art of public administration, but only general principles and procedures to be *reasonably* applied in the specific cases in which he is called upon to act. Besides, he does not wait until the moment when he begins to draw up a law before familiarizing himself with the principles of legislation. A minister who behaved in that way would be like a military commander who would "look up" the general principles of strategy only immediately before or during the battle. Such a bizarre conception of the manner in which public affairs are conducted can hardly avail to disprove the independent validity of the applied sciences.

15. Those who are opposed to treating applied economics as an independent science might find it worthwhile to consider how the founder of the strictly scientific treatment of mechanical technology characterizes the very essence of that science: "Technology," says Karl Karmarsch, "is often denied a separate status as a science—although only by those who do not understand its nature and aims. One would think that its entire content consists of a combination of fragments of chemistry and mechanics. . . . Technology is based on natural history, physics, chemistry, and mechanics. . . . But the mere combination of all these *auxiliary sciences* in one person does not necessarily constitute a technologist."

And he rightly emphasizes that from an accumulation of purely descriptive literature technology developed only after its materal had been interpreted, investigated, and treated in a scientific way. (*Geschichte der Technologie* [1872], pp. 1 ff.)

16. In view of what has been said above, it is hardly necessary to observe that the applied sciences do not force upon us any *absolute* "*ought*," but that they only teach us the way in which certain generally determined ends can be attained in the light of our judgment at a particular time and *provided that we want to attain them at all*. The applied sciences do not contain, as Kleinwächter thinks (*Jahrbücher für Nationalökonomie und Statistik,* New Series [1889], XVIII, 603 ff.), a command to pursue any aims in particular. They merely show us how we have to act (or, if one will, how we *ought to act*), on the basis of our judgment at a particular time, if we *want* to attain a given end; whereas it is the historical, the morphological, and the theoretical sciences that provide us with knowledge of the past and the present and of the nature of phenomena and their interrelations. This distinction between the tasks of the applied sciences, on the one hand, and those of history, statistics, morphology, and the theoretical sciences, on the other, is expressed, in a way that can hardly be misunderstood by any unprejudiced person, in the statement that the former do not deal with what *is,* but with what *ought to be.*

17. See above pp. 7-8.

18. *Über die Ursachen der heutigen sozialen Not. Ein Beitrag zur Morphologie der Volkswirtschaft.* Lecture delivered on the occasion of assuming the professorship at the University of Leipzig, April 27, 1889 (Leipzig, 1889).

19. In *Jahrbücher für Nationalökonomie und Statistik,* New Series (Jena, 1889), XVIII, 601 ff.

20. *Loc. cit.,* p. 1.

21. See my *Untersuchungen über die Methode der Sozialwissenschaften* (1883), pp. xi ff.

22. *Die klassische Nationalökonomie* (1888), p. 7; *Die Ursachen der sozialen Not* (1889), p. 3.

23. From an essentially different standpoint F. J. Neumann, in the recently published first part of his *Grundlagen der Volkswirtschaftslehre* (Tübingen, 1889), opposes the tendencies of the Austrian school of economists. Neumann has been concerned with economic theory not only in his "younger years" or in a merely cursory way. Unlike many of his German colleagues, who became aware of the untenability of "classical theory" and perhaps also of their own incapacity for reforming it, Neumann has not thrown theory overboard completely or confined himself exclusively to the investigation of "parallelism in economic history" and a rootless eclecticism. Neither has he ever failed to recognize the importance of economic theory to applied economics and to economic policy. We can unqualifiedly agree with Neumann's statement that it was precisely practical problems that impelled him to embark upon theoretical investigations and showed him how to set in order the

theoretical foundations to which one has to revert in the discussion of the above questions (*ibid.,* p. v.).

In economic theory itself an essential progress in Neumann's thought is also to be noted. He arrives at the conclusion (pp. 251 ff.) that the standpoint represented by the opponents of the theory of value that he had himself hitherto favored—a theory of particular importance for our science because of its bearing upon the theory of prices and the doctrines connected with it—is to be given "preference over the interpretations of Hufeland, Lotz, Hermann, etc.," the very men whose essential views he had formerly espoused. By openly acknowledging this revolution in his fundamental doctrines, he has rendered an inestimable service to economic theory.

However, the reader of Neumann's work will find this concession scarcely conceivable. His book is introduced by a criticism, extending over some two hundred and fifty pages, partly petty, partly even misinterpreting the very authors to whom he owes his present better insight. Many of his objections against particular details of some of the theories that he now recognizes as essentially valid are to be attributed simply to the fact that in the introductory section of his work, devoted to general doctrines, he takes only a partial view of the necessary consequences that the standpoint he now accepts has for the specialized doctrines of economic theory. This lack of clarity is what is mainly responsible for the chief deficiency of his work: his trivial prolixity and a tendency toward the consistent evasion of the crucial points in the problems he discusses.

24. *Die Ursachen der sozialen Not,* p. 5. Brentano directs this criticism in particular against those authors who have attacked the basic error in the theory of modern socialism. As if those who seek to refute the socialists' erroneous idea that labor is the sole source of value or other similar errors in fact "believed," as Brentano maintains, that by doing so they could immediately conjure away all the dangers to the social order! Such dangers can be created by erroneous theories only in an *indirect* way; hence, it stands to reason that their refutation can likewise contribute only in an *indirect* way toward removing those dangers. However, this is not a valid objection to the refutation of erroneous theories. Brentano, after all, seems to have forgotten that he has himself only recently devoted a lecture, which he also had printed and published (*Die klassische Nationalökonomie* [Leipzig, 1888]), to the criticism of economic theories that he regarded as erroneous, without, as far as I know, succeeding in abolishing poverty, not even—and this is what seems to me, under the circumstances, to be a far more serious failing on his part—the poverty still existing here and there in the field of economic theory.

25. Brentano so far fails to recognize the limits of the different economic sciences and the nature of economic theory that he even suspects the efforts to reform the latter to be a method of justifying and sanctioning the existing economic order, in evident disregard of the fact that inquiry into the nature of economic phenomena and their interrelations does

not contain any value judgment implying their "perfection." (*Die Ursachen der sozialen Not,* p. 28.)

26. *Loc. cit.,* pp. 29 ff.

27. An essentially different question has been raised by Wundt (*Logik* [1883], II, 591 ff.). His problem is whether "abstract" economic theories (which, in his sense, are true only under specific assumptions) may be *directly* transformed into prescriptions for practical action. I believe that —quite apart from erroneous doctrines—even correct "abstract" theories cannot properly constitute the sole and immediate basis of the principles of practical action. One must take into consideration differences of circumstance as well as empirical probabilities. Even principles of practical action are not universally applicable prescriptions, but rather rules for the conduct of affairs that have to be applied with due regard for the distinctive peculiarity of each concrete case. Abstract theory can serve as the foundation of an applied science, just as the latter can form the basis of actual practice, only by virtue of a determinative procedure—if one may be permitted to use such an expression.

However, this is not, I think, a peculiar feature of the economic sciences, but a general characteristic of the relationship of "abstract" theories to the applied sciences based upon them. Technologists, surgeons, and therapists, for example, apply the laws of physics, chemistry, mechanics, and even physiology, not directly, but only by means of the above-mentioned determinative procedure. The difference here is only one of degree, not of kind. In any case, the fact referred to by Wundt, that in abstract theorizing about economic questions our conception of "what *ought to be*" helps to determine our view of "what *is,*" as far as this does not involve a complete confusion between theoretical and applied science, is not, I believe, a feature peculiar to "abstract" economic theory alone. No doubt science has often enough been led astray by certain practical motives that have operated to give it a tendentious direction. However, it is not only "abstract" economic theories that are open to this reproach, but also, as recent experience has demonstrated, the "concrete" ones as well—including even economic history and statistics. To impute to those who work in the field of "abstract" economic theory a special propensity toward biased distortions of this kind or even merely toward error would be, it seems to me, more than unfair.

28. *Grundlagen der Nationalökonomie* (1854), §26 and §29.

2

The Theory of Urban
Ground Rent*

FRIEDRICH FREIHERR VON WIESER

Preface

The theory of urban ground rent, which I here submit to
the public in a separate reprint, appears at the same time as an
introduction to a detailed study made by Dr. W. Mildschuh entitled "Residential Rents and Land Values in Prague," recently
issued as Part I of Volume IX of the Wiener Staatswissenschaftliche Studien. Although I occasionally refer in a few places in the
text to figures arrived at by Dr. Mildschuh, my presentation is
nevertheless complete in itself, and I therefore feel justified in
publishing it independently in the hope that in this form it may
be of interest to readers seeking an explanation of the theory. A
few words are needed to clarify the relationship between my
work and Dr. Mildschuh's.

This paper was inspired by a discussion of the theory of urban
ground rent which I conducted about six years ago in my seminar
in economics at the German University of Prague. With a view

* Introduction to Dr. W. Mildschuh, *Mietzinse und Bodenwerte in Prag*, Wiener
Staatswissenschaftliche Studien (Vienna and Leipzig: Carl Deuticke, 1909), Vol. IX,
Fasc. I. Also issued as a separate reprint. Republished in *Gesammelte Abhand-
lungen*, ed. Friedrich A. v. Hayek (Tübingen: J. C. B. Mohr—Paul Siebeck, 1929),
pp 126-163.

to verifying the theory there developed, Dr. Mildschuh, one of the participants in the seminar, declared himself willing to make a study of the data available for Prague and its suburbs. The assessment of the Austrian tax on residential rents, being calculated on the basis of an official register in which all the rents paid in a municipality are scrupulously recorded year by year and dwelling by dwelling, furnishes the scientific investigator with a wealth of data such as no researcher, no matter how diligent, could succeed in assembling elsewhere. Dr. Mildschuh has earnestly and judiciously sifted through this entire mass of material on tax assessment, as well as all the available information offered by the official registers of landed property, mortgage records, and other sources. He has, in fact, expanded the scope of his original project in all the directions in which theoretical interest extends. Every student of the theory of urban ground rent will benefit from the completeness and clarity with which he has placed before the reader the actual conditions bringing about an increase in rent in a town which, in the period under examination, was going through the transition to a large modern city.

Originally I intended to supplement Dr. Mildschuh's work with a comprehensive theoretical dissertation. Unfortunately, lack of time prevented me from doing so, and I have had to limit myself to an introductory essay confined to the exposition of only what is absolutely essential for the understanding of the statistics he presents. I have had to set aside any consideration of their wider implications and in particular to abstain from discussing the extensive literature concerning this subject. Nor have I been able to enter into the related problem—so important for Austria —of the shift in the incidence of our taxes on residential rents. I refer in this connection to the official minutes of the inquiry conducted by the Austrian Ministry of Finance in the fall of 1902 into the question of revising the tax rates on inhabited dwellings. On that occasion I presented a detailed statement of my position on the subject. In regard to this problem Dr. Mildschuh likewise provides comprehensive data, and I think one is warranted in assuming that his documentation will not fail to impress the reader even in the absence of any theoretical commentary. I could not very well have provided such a commentary at this time without entering deeply into polemical discussions, but I reserve the right to publish it independently.

The theory of urban ground rent that I propose to expound here I already presented on the occasion of the aforementioned inquiry, although only in a condensed form. Even at that time I was able to refer for corroboration to certain results obtained by Dr. Mildschuh in his treatment of the data from Prague. I trust I am not wrong in assuming that his work, now submitted to the public in its completed form, will provide the theory set forth here with a broad empirical verification.

The Theory of Urban Ground Rent

Every theory of urban ground rent has to begin with an exposition of the Ricardo-Thünen theory of agricultural ground rent. Today we have become so unfamiliar with the ideas which gave rise to that theory that it seems advisable first to discuss Ricardo's personality as a scientific investigator. This can be done in a few words. Ricardo is generally considered as hyperabstract. Indeed, he is often described as the most resolute opponent of empirical inquiry. In fact, however, his chief limitation seems to have been his incapacity to detach himself sufficiently from reality. He lacks the ability to analyze complex phenomena into their elements; he is wanting in depth of penetration; and even his exceptionally keen perspicacity is at bottom but the shrewdness of a businessman schooled in the practical affairs of life. His very insistence on simplification, on which he is so emphatic, is just the practical man's way of disregarding everything but the actual results and of ignoring all the factors in the background that may have played a role in the shaping of events. He thus makes it impossible for himself to arrive at a true explanation. That is the reason why he had to resort to artificial explanations that appear to us today as unempirical abstractions. The fact is that his formulas are ultimately drawn from the large stock of popularly accepted beliefs, of which he was a remarkably observant student. It is understandable that science in its early stages, as long as it had to be content with only half the truth, should have admired these surprisingly concise formulations as complete solutions. Only recently has it been realized that they block access to the other half of the truth and that one has to accomplish the difficult feat of freeing oneself from their seductive charm and of trying new paths if one wishes to discover the whole truth.

Today this work has been achieved in great part, and as a result many of Ricardo's theories have finally been found to be untenable. Others are on the point of being discredited and are still held only in outward form until the right theory, of which we are already on the track, is fully established. It is his theory of ground rent that has best withstood the corrosive influence of critical examination. This is easily understandable. The explanation of agricultural ground rent does not require very deep scientific penetration. There are only certain prominent peaks of value that have to be illuminated, if one may be permitted the metaphor, while the whole complex network of other value phenomena, with all their interconnections, may be left in darkness. Even if one is unable to explain the formation of prices or the essential nature of costs, it is relatively easy to demonstrate that pieces of land that are exceptionally well favored or soil that is especially fertile, since they keep costs low, yield the owner a surplus above the price of his produce. Here was a problem that challenged Ricardo's best scientific abilities. Yet even here he failed to achieve a definitive formulation: his theory is lacking in certain refinements, and for all its apparent precision it conceals intrinsic contradictions that have to be winnowed out. However, as it doubtless provides a faithful representation of most of the phenomena involved, Ricardo's theory of ground rent is, in view of the nature of the problem, assured of lasting value. Whatever it still lacks in theoretical completeness is added of itself once it is fitted into the framework of a completed theory of value and price formation.

The problem of urban rent seems to be closely related to that of agricultural rent. In both cases what we have to deal with is a differential rent that can be regarded as the peculiar benefit deriving from the permanent advantages that certain especially favored pieces of land offer the proprietor. In both cases, too, these advantages are due to favorable location. And in both cases it is the scarcity in the amount of such land that exerts an influence upon the formation of rent. If conditions in both cases correspond in so many respects—and still others could be mentioned—then there must follow a certain correspondence in the result. Nevertheless, there is no feasible way of effecting a transition from Ricardo's theory to a theory of urban rent. The advantage to the agricultural producer offered by relatively favorable land or by soil that is exceptionally fertile consists in the fact that they keep his costs of production comparatively low. This, at least, is the only advantage investigated by Ricardo, and quite rightly, since the other advantage that is offered, namely, that better land also yields better crops, is of no special theoretical interest. For urban land, however, the contrary is true: here it is of no theoretical interest that in certain cases the conditions of the subsoil help to keep the costs of construction comparatively low; the theory of urban rent is concerned exclusively with those advantages that are provided, directly or indirectly, by location. But location, as such, has nothing to do with the costs of construction. It will not do to assert that central locations are more favorable because they serve to keep these costs comparatively low and that the graduation in rents that one finds as one passes from the center of town to outlying areas is to be accounted for by the difference in these costs. Hence, the theory of agricultural ground rent has to start, as Pantaleoni rightly observes, from the fact that for fruits of the soil produced at unequal costs equal prices are obtained; whereas the theory of urban rent must be based on the fact that with equal costs unequal prices are obtained.

This contrast goes even deeper. We have already observed that the basic idea of Ricardo's theory of ground rent can be understood without entering into the subtleties of the theory of price formation. Indeed, one has no need to refer to the latter theory at all: agricultural ground rent, in its primary form, does not presuppose a market. Even in the self-sufficient domestic economy of the rural household the surplus obtained will be imputed, as its rent, to the more fertile land, which produces the same quantity at lower cost. Urban rent, on the other hand, is entirely a phenomenon of the market. To explain it one needs a fully perfected theory of the formation of prices, and, what is more, one has to adjust this general theory very precisely to the special peculiarities of the market in urban rents and to develop it farther in this direction.

This is what we shall attempt to do in what follows. But first it is necessary once again to revert to the matter of savings in costs. So far we have spoken only of the costs of construction, but apart from these perhaps other costs might come into question too. A tenant, if he lives in a relatively unfavorable location, has, under the circumstances, to make daily use of means of transportation that, in the long run, put him to considerable expense. There is hardly anybody who would not be willing to pay correspondingly more for a dwelling place so situated as to save him "costs" of this kind. Should it not be possible to derive from these facts a law of urban rent that, in essence, would coincide with Ricardo's law? Ricardo speaks, to be sure, of savings in costs on the side of supply, which do not appear in the price, whereas we are concerned with savings in costs on the side of demand, which would raise the price; but both really amount to the same thing. One must start from the fact that the total outlay for rent plus the "costs" of transportation occasioned by the location of one's place of residence will amount to a certain sum for each level of income. Thus, as in the case studied by Ricardo, prices (the total outlay) would be equal, while "costs" would be unequal. Hence the owner of a dwelling so situated as to save transportation costs would receive a higher rental for it; in other words, he would earn a differential rent in the strictly economic sense of Ricardo's theory.

There can be no doubt that such calculations are actually made quite often and that they are one source of urban rent. But only a small part of the rents actually received come from this source. It would be quite erroneous to assume that everybody who lives in the outlying areas has to go into the center of town every day. Most of the families who live on the outskirts describe the more or less narrow orbit of their daily lives within the area of the outer reaches themselves. Nor can costs of transportation alone explain either the range or the number of the actual differences that exist between the rents paid in different localities. The gradations in the fares charged for different distances on the mass transportation lines, even in a very large city, are generally small and few in number, and then only for long distances. But what a difference there is between residential rents within each of these transportation zones and, even more, between one zone and another! The greatest disparities are to be found in the central sectors over very short distances—so short, indeed, that no means of transportation is needed at all. It is clear, therefore, that a tenant's appraisement of the advantages of any particular location is, in the main, determined by considerations of a quite different kind.

The theory of urban ground rent has to discover what these are and what role they play in determining rental values on the market. For this purpose it is advisable to begin by assuming the case of a town with a relatively stable or slowly increasing population. A large modern city springs up so rapidly that many of the connections between the different factors involved are too confused to be easily analyzed. Therefore, the discussion of the special case of the market in residential rents in a large modern city, with particular reference to the related question of speculation in land, will be reserved for our conclusion, since it can be more readily understood once one has grasped the law governing more stable phenomena.

The case we propose to take up first is, in fact, approximately that of the towns of Austria up to 1848 and even into the eighteen-sixties, the years of economic upswing. Let us consider the case of a town that has already outgrown its medieval walls and is now spreading out quite freely, but, for the time being, only very slowly, into the surrounding countryside. The predominant type of dwelling is the rented house; the privately owned home is becoming less common. (As long as the latter is still the prevailing type, a market in residential rents has not yet fully developed.) We shall assume a situation like that which prevails generally in Germany and Austria, where, contrary to the English custom, several families share the same floor of an apartment house. Although the theory of urban ground rent is essentially the same in either case as long as the market in residential rents is sufficiently extensive, its treatment is greatly facilitated if it is confined to one definite type, and we shall therefore make use of this helpful procedure.

In a town with a slowly growing population, residential rents will, in the long run, have to cover at least the cost of production if the supply of buildings is to keep pace with the demand. These costs are divisible into two types. The first consists of the original investment and comprises construction costs proper, including the average profit of the builder as well as the capital expended for the acquisition of the building lot itself, which, however, in this calculation of minimum costs, is to be reckoned only at the value of arable land. The second comprises current expenditures annually required for the house, namely, taxes, costs of administration and maintenance, and amortization of the invested capital. The rentals received should exceed these annual costs by an amount such that the customary interest on the still unamortized capital invested in the building can be paid from the remaining surplus. Ground rent is already included in the lowest residential rental paid. This is evidently true at least of agricultural ground rent, which is capitalized in the value of arable land; but it is also true of urban rent, for if one wishes to acquire property for urban construction, one must bid more than its value as arable land.

Urban ground rent, however, comprises only a very small part of the lowest residential rental paid and will not be really high even in proportion to the value of the property as arable land; for under our provisional assumption of a slowly growing population, the market will favor a tendency toward the acquisition of new land for urban construction. Under the conditions we have assumed, we do not yet have to reckon with speculation in land, since urban demand is directly met by rural supply. The builder will be willing to pay the value of the property as arable land plus a certain premium, since this expenditure, when added to his others, is still not very great. Only a small premium will be required to induce some one of the many rural proprietors to sell his land. There is still plenty of agricultural land surrounding the town, much in excess of the demand (which we assume as rather limited) for new urban construction. Property on the outskirts of the town, in high demand for agricultural purposes, is available in abundance if viewed from the standpoint of urban demand.

As long as this remains the case, not more than the lowest residential rental, calculated on the basis described above, will, as a rule, have to be paid for the poorest urban locations. The situation is quite different, however, in the better sections of town. Since they are limited in number, only some of those seeking accommodations will find them there, and competition will therefore have to decide who these tenants are to be. The theory of price formation teaches us what the result of such competition is: only those tenants will be admitted who combine the most urgent need with the greatest ability to pay. But to attain their end they have to make their superior ability to pay effectual by so decisively outbidding their weaker rivals as to eliminate them entirely. To the first relatively small premium which the builder has to be willing to pay in order to outbid those who wish to use the land for agricultural purposes must now be added ever-increasing increments in view of the competition within the town itself; and the more desirable and limited is the space available, and the more affluent the class of those who have to be outbid, the higher this premium becomes. It is from this kind of bidding that urban ground rent is built up: it is that part of the residential rental which is offered as a premium, over and above the basic cost, for comparatively favorable locations.

This is a simple idea—as simple, indeed, as the idea that agricultural rent originates from savings in costs, and equally important. To appreciate its importance fully one has to make clear to what extent the urban market in residential rents demands this kind of competitive bidding, just as in the theory of agricultural rent everything depends on the extent to which savings in costs actually occur. The theory of urban rent has no other task than to determine the cost basis of the lowest residential rental paid and then to demonstrate the system of competitive bidding that is erected over and above this foundation.

In the market in residential rents this competitive bidding is carried on in some cases differently from the way it is in the market in business rents. We shall have to examine separately the manner in which prices are formed in each of these markets. We propose to begin with the market in residential rents, as it is the one that is the more important for the mass of the population.

The market in residential rents is divided into a greater or smaller number of sites graded according to their relative desirability. In towns built on the older pattern there is generally a nucleus that forms the hub of all municipal life. It is here that we find the town hall, the main church, the residences of the prince's court, the government buildings, and the cathedral. Here too we find concentrated all the other buildings that are representative of the town. Here all the objects of historical or touristic interest are collected; here all the pageantry of the town is displayed; here pulse the main arteries of its political, ecclesiastical, commercial, and social life. All those who play a role in civic affairs, all the people who want to see and to be seen, endeavor to dwell in this area. It is not always the geometrical center; it may even be situated on the periphery—for example, on the ocean or extending along one of the banks of a river. (One has only to think of Venice or Hamburg.) But wherever it may be, it is always from here that one measures distances in determining the relative desirability of different sites, even though distance alone is not decisive, for many other factors may also be of importance and may lead to all kinds of irregular configurations in the pattern of residential rents. Nevertheless, we shall provisionally assume a thoroughly regular town plan, arranged in concentric rings around a central section, although we are fully aware of the fact that in doing so we are idealizing the irregular phenomena actually encountered in reality. Idealization is a most useful expedient of which all the exact sciences take advantage. So, for instance, geometry starts with perfectly regular figures, although it is well understood that these are pure abstractions.

In our case the assumption of a concentric town plan faithfully represents the two most important facts characterizing the towns of the prerevolutionary period preceding March, 1848. The elucidation of the theoretical significance of this arrangement must be our first task, and apart from that everything else must be relegated to the background. The first fact is that most, if not all, of the poorer quarters were situated near the town border; and the other is that the better quarters, being densely concentrated in the interior part of the town, were in shorter supply according as they were more favorably located. What gives the urban market in residential rents its peculiar character is precisely the fact that the scarcity of the supply increases in proportion to the favorableness of the location. In this market the demand does not consist of parties who enter into competition all at once and just for once, but rather of groups competing successively and frequently in the whole graded series of rings surrounding the heart of the town. After the weakest bidders have been pushed into the outermost ring by their stronger competitors, the next higher stratum of tenants will be composed of the second weakest, who will be prevented from advancing further in than the second ring from the last by their inability to pay the rent (now raised higher by the renewed competition of the remaining bidders) demanded in the third ring; and so, by virtue of this continually renewed competitive bidding at every level, residential rents form themselves into a graded series comprising as many different steps as there are major residential sections, together with their respective subdivisions, until the highest rents include a premium that may well equal or even exceed the basic cost. If I may revert to an example that I used at the Austrian inquiry into the tax rates on inhabited dwellings, the highest residential rentals paid on the Stephansplatz in Vienna form one end of an unbroken chain that extends as far as the lowest rentals paid in the outermost suburbs, the whole of which, in the last analysis, is based on competitive bidding.

The major residential areas or quarters are quite different from one another in the character of their buildings. What a contrast there is between the streets and houses of the elegant districts and those in the poorer sections of town! In fact, if one were to judge from the outward impression that one receives even more from the older type of town plan than from that of the modern city, one would think that every district was sharply defined and demarcated from every other, i.e., not only fixed immovably to a definite location, but, above all, constituted as a residential area restricted exclusively to a certain class, in very much the same way as, in the strictest sense, the old Jewish quarter, the ghetto, indeed was.

If this were really the case, then, as soon as demand became more urgent, that pitiless law of residential rents which has recently been called "the brass law of rents" could in fact become operative; that is, the urgent demand for a supply that cannot be increased could be exploited in every dwelling, including the good and the best ones, so that tenants of every income level, even the middle and the highest, would be obliged to strain their resources to the utmost in order to secure a place to live. However, the market in residential rents should not be conceived in this way, still less the partial markets into which it is divided, for the connections among all of them are quite fluid.

Nevertheless, the picture that we have given of these connections as forming a concentric pattern is not altogether clear; at least it needs a more precise interpretation, perhaps even a correction, in order to avoid misunderstanding. For the town plan that we have taken as our model gives undue prominence to distance from the center as the one factor determining the relative desirability of different locations. Distance from the center is a given quantity whose economic consequences can, at best, be mitigated by an improvement in the means of transportation, but which, in all other respects, is fixed. The subdivisions in the market in residential rents, on the other hand, are by no means fixed in relation to one another, for in reality distance plays only a secondary role in tenants' appraisal of the relative desirability of different locations.

The primary factor is of social origin and one whose theoretical significance has thus far been neglected. Indeed, the whole theory of price formation has, in general, been treated up to now with far too little consideration to social influences. Choosing a place to live is like deciding whether one is going to travel first, second or third class on the railway: both decisions reflect one's sense of one's own social status, which is in turn affected by the pressure of conventional opinion. In these days of democracy, when all classes wear very much the same kind of clothing, the location of one's home serves more than anything else to indicate the social status that one claims for oneself, especially as one generally lives in the same place for some length of time and the reputation of the neighborhood is a matter of public knowledge. "Tell me the neighborhood you live in, and I'll tell you what you are." This is more or less the feeling that actuates tenants in choosing a place to live. Whether a location is good or bad is determined by the social class of the people who have settled there—even though, as we shall see later, people of different social classes may be found stacked, as it were, above one another on different floors of the same house. If, for instance, the sections in which the middle classes have settled are less highly regarded than the most elegant neighborhoods, the decisive reason is not that the former are further from the center of town, for this is not always the case, but that they are not occupied by people of distinction. One must add, however, that, as a rule, the less fashionable neighborhoods will be found at a greater distance from the center of town precisely because the central locations have been taken by the social elite.

Hence we may draw the important theoretical conclusion that the spatial extension of any neighborhood will, in the long run, always accommodate itself to the size of the social class or the number of people of a given income level who live in it. In the concentrically arranged urban community which we have imagined, one must always assume that there are as many major residential zones as there are major levels in the town's social hierarchy. These large zones are divided into smaller ones corresponding to the finer gradations within each income level and are again still further subdivided according to their distance from the center of town. If the ranks of a particular social class increase, the neighborhood that it occupies will in the long run also expand by the construction, sooner or later, of streets and of houses built in its characteristic style of architecture, at the expense of the people of lower income level inhabiting contiguous areas. When Wallenstein erected his palace in the "Kleinseite" of Prague,* he provided the space he needed by buying some sixty houses from poor people in the area and razing them. Thus, the example of the powerful Duke of Friedland served to widen the zone whose residents could pass as elegant.

To summarize: the subdivisions of the total urban market in residential rents are as freely extensible in relation to one another as the latter is in relation to arable land. These partial markets, in both the area of their extension and the architectural style of the buildings within them, express the specific stratification of urban society, as determined not only by income distribution, but also by conventional views regarding the type of accommodation required by each social class. The upper classes feel obliged to maintain a certain standard of living suitable to their position, while those in more modest circumstances find it necessary to live in more densely populated areas and even to sublet their apartments or take in lodgers.

The well-known distinction made in the German textbooks on economics between goods of which the supply can be increased at will and goods of which the supply can be increased only at higher costs of production needs to be supplemented, if we are to understand the urban market in residential rents, by a third category, for we can consider dwelling places as goods of which the supply can be increased by the payment of a premium. The condition required by the "brass law of residential rents," namely, that of rigidly restricted partial markets, is absent here. The different social classes are not confined to specific zones of fixed extension and therefore do not find it necessary to strain their resources to the utmost in an exhausting competitive struggle within each zone. Competition in this case is confined to outbidding weaker rivals living in contiguous areas by just enough to force them to release the desired ground.

The rich enjoy less of an advantage in bidding for a place to live than they do in buying staple foods, for which they need to

---

* A zone in the city of Prague. [Translator's note.]

pay only what the poorest classes can afford. But, on the other hand, they are in a better position in the market in residential rents than they are in the market for diamonds, which they bid up to luxury prices by competition among themselves. The market in residential rents thus stands somewhere in between: the rich have to strain their resources, but only as far as is required to outbid weaker competitors of lower income level living in contiguous areas, who, for their part, have already had to overcome the competition of still weaker bidders. This statement is in full accord with the well-known empirical fact that the proportion of income allotted to the payment of rent decreases with increasing income, even though the need for a place to live could in this case be more richly satisfied.

Here we have found a first point of vantage from which we can look back at Ricardo's theory of prices. According to Ricardo, there can be a law of price formation only for goods that can be regularly reproduced, because their prices have to adjust themselves to given costs. However, the prices of goods having scarcity value, such as precious stocks of wine, do not conform to any law, but depend upon the whims of the consumers and the ups and downs of their financial circumstances. They are, if one may say so, capricious prices. So far Ricardo.

Now the rents paid for the most desirable urban locations form a graduated scale no less closely integrated than that which is exhibited in the formation of the prices of commodities produced in branches of production operating with the utmost regularity. Dwelling places are no doubt scarce in every town, but they are goods of which the supply can be increased by the payment of a premium, and they therefore faithfully reflect, in the rents paid for them, the economic stratification of the townsfolk. Urban residential rents are in no sense capricious prices. Just as their gross amount conforms to a stringent law, so likewise does their net yield over and above costs, which constitutes ground rent in the strict sense of the term. Urban ground rent also conforms to the economic stratification of the people of the town and shifts only gradually with it. The modern theory takes full cognizance of the fact that the "objectively" given costs of production have their basis in subjective valuation. The constancy in the cost of the goods and the labor most widely needed in production is attributable to the fact that they are objects of demand for mass consumption. The law of urban ground rent and the law explaining the formation of commodity prices ultimately coincide in that they both rest on the solid ground of mass social phenomena.

The market in business rents is likewise composed of several independent subdivisions. For the wholesale trade this market is to be found in a central location, the best being in the vicinity of the Exchange. Separately situated we find the highest governmental and municipal offices, the houses of parliament, and the like, generally, however, in buildings of their own and only under exceptional circumstances in rented quarters. They too seek to be centrally situated, but they are not all together in a district restricted exclusively to them. Finally, there is a rent market for retail business. The following observations refer to this type of market.

Like the market in residential rents, it is composed of partial markets among which the connections are quite fluid. However, the market in business rents is much more restricted than the market in residential rents. The only commercially important sites and streets are those in which traffic is relatively dense, in particular the hub of the town, into which all roads lead and from which they radiate in all directions, and then too, of course, the large arterial avenues themselves. It is not necessary to elaborate any further on a phenomenon so well known, but one fact not usually discussed needs to be emphasized, namely, that such a location represents one of the most effective means of advertising. Since the partial markets in rents for retail business follow the major traffic lanes and expand only along with them, their range is less extensible than that of the partial markets in residential rents, and therefore the competitive struggle for desirable business locations is correspondingly much keener.

Even more important from the theoretical point of view is a second difference. The increased profits obtained from businesses situated in advantageous locations increase the fund available for competitive bidding, and since this is true for all enterprises that can be carried on within a given area, competition on the side of demand increases in intensity. The amount of the premium that one has to pay in order to secure a favorable location for one's business is determined not only by the lower profits that weaker competitors, after having been squeezed out, will make outside the preferred area, but also from the higher profits that they had hoped to realize if they had succeeded in finding a location within it.

Nevertheless, the opinion so often heard that the urban businessman works only for his landlord is incorrect. The general law of marginal utility that governs the formation of commodity prices applies also to the market in business rents to the extent that the conditions that it presupposes are in fact given, since the problem is almost never that of "the only possible site," but, as a rule, involves a certain choice among different locations. At least the more successful entrepreneurs in a given part of the market can afford to pay a premium that is not within the reach of competitors still left in the area who are operating at a lower profit. Yet business rents always do rise higher than residential rents, and in the most desirable locations they stand considerably higher. The same holds true for the central market in wholesale business. The graduated scale of residential rents may be likened to a vault that arches upward from the border of the town to its center. Above this, in the area of the main arteries of commerce that radiate from the center, the highest business rents rise still further upward, like the ribs of the vault and the central steeple over the dome.

So far we have been concerned only with what may be called the rent of location. One must also raise the question whether the architectural plan of urban construction does not, like agricultural management, give rise to a rent of intensity. The question can be easily answered. Such a rent of intensity does indeed arise. But, just as the rent of intensity from agricultural land is always only the enhancement that higher fertility and greater proximity to the market add to an original rent, so the rent of intensity on urban land is only an enhancement of the original rent of location. In the favorable locations the builders have a chance to increase the rent by increasing the capital invested in construction; and the better the location, the greater the opportunity for an increase in rent. Here an increase in capital enables one to build in a narrower space, to a greater height, and with greater luxury, and by thus increasing horizontal, vertical, and qualitative intensity, to earn a higher rent in all these directions. But it is obvious that this rent will always remain a rent of location.

The town of our fathers and grandfathers exhibits, as we proceed from the border to the center, a gradual transition in architectural styles, starting with houses of still half-rustic construction, with a wide courtyard and garden and consisting of a ground floor only, or of a single story of very simple structure. The more we proceed inward, the fewer become the gardens, and the more narrow the courtyards, owing to the construction of outbuildings in response to the demand for them; the fewer become the additional subsidiary rooms as the predominant consideration of tenants in outbidding one another becomes the turning of all available space to immediate use for living quarters; the more floors are superimposed upon one another, since they help to increase the rent by multiplying the land's capacity to accommodate occupants; the more costly the materials used in construction, the more artistic the labor employed, and the more luxurious the fixtures and installations, since it is with these that one hopes to satisfy the pretentions of—and thereby to attract—the class of tenants both ready and able to pay the highest rent. So manifold are the ways of increasing intensity by way of construction, so simple is, in general, their theoretical interrelationship, that only a few additional remarks are required.

As far as horizontal intensity is concerned, it will be opposed in the richer neighborhoods by a counterpressure in the direction of qualitative intensity, that is, toward greater comfort and, in addition to other luxuries, the luxury of more room for each family. Needless to say, this has to be paid for at higher cost, since the provision of more space where ground is already so precious requires a great increase in capital investment. If, on behalf of the wealthier classes, building regulations are demanded for such areas prohibiting the full utilization of the available space for apartment houses and requiring houses with gardens, the influence that these classes have on the administrative authorities will tend to be used to their own advantage. They will want the government to take measures to restrain the vexatious competition occasioned by an excessively heavy demand for space, to prevent the increase in the price of land brought about by crowded construction, and to make possible, precisely in this part of the town, a spacious style of building at lower cost.

As for qualitative intensity, it must be noted that landlords seek to earn not only interest at the prevailing rate on the capital invested in construction, but, even more, the highest rentals obtainable from competitive bidding in any area. Hence they will decide in favor of a relatively expensive type of construction only if the entire capital investment offers the prospect of yielding a return, over and above interest at the prevailing rate, that is at least equal to the differential rent deriving from the advantages offered by a favorable location; otherwise they could utilize the same amount of capital more profitably by a more extensive investment spread out over a wider area. By attracting the richest tenants, among whom competitive bidding must, of necessity, reach the greatest heights, they can even expect a further increase in differential rent.

Of the greatest theoretical interest is the increase in intensity obtained by vertical construction. We have to begin by considering how tenants appraise the different floors of the same building. For a retail shop, location on the ground floor is preferred. Certain other business establishments may be situated to equal, or perhaps even greater, advantage on higher floors. The installation of elevators, however, has brought about important changes in these respects. In urban areas that are built up, ground-floor apartments are considered less desirable, the main floor being greatly preferred.* Some tenants even have a preference for still higher locations, where there is better light, purer air, and less noise

---

* By "ground floor" in continental European parlance is meant the street floor. What is called the "main floor" is in reality the first floor up the stairway or the elevator. [Translator's note.]

from the street. In general, however, most tenants above the main floor are more conscious of the disadvantages than of the advantages of living so high up, and from here upwards, therefore, apartments as well as business lofts are the less valued the higher they are situated; or, in other words, from here on up the increments in the premiums offered in competitive bidding become progressively smaller. Finally, everywhere—in inferior locations at a lower point, in the better locations at a higher point—a floor must be reached above which a higher bid can no longer be obtained.

If the interests of the owner of the building were the sole deciding factor, one story would continue to be superimposed upon another until a point was reached at which the rent obtainable from any further elevation would no longer defray the cost of its construction. In such a calculation he would have to take into account the fact that every additional story would cost him proportionately less, since the ratio of the cost of the foundation and the roof to the total costs of construction will be calculated with a correspondingly larger divisor. Besides, as we have already mentioned, people of different income levels may very frequently be found above one another on different floors of the same building. In most sections of town the upper floors are inhabited by families of relatively low income, who are less sensitive to the inconveniences of living higher up and for whom, therefore, a more economical type of accommodation suffices, so that the builder saves money on them and can still have a surplus in spite of the fact that he charges them less.

Subject to all the reservations we have mentioned, we can formulate a rule or, if one may be permitted the expression, a "law," which could be called the law of diminishing returns on residential quarters. It calls to mind the law of diminishing returns on agricultural land and must be taken into account in a complete theory of urban ground rent just as its analogue is in Ricardo's theory, except that, of course, it produces different effects, depending upon the peculiar structure of the market in urban rents. In this market, as we know, price is directly determined by costs only in quarters inhabited by the very poorest tenants; the price paid for better quarters rises above costs as a result of competitive bidding. The law of diminishing returns on residential quarters makes it clear that the lowest-paying quarters are found not only in the poorest areas lying on the outskirts of town, but well within the interior. The border of the town, if the latter is conceived in the sense of a market, extends not only outward, but upward. The rising line of premiums paid as a result of competitive bidding thus curves in a double direction: horizontally, from the outskirts to the interior of the town, according to the varying character of its residential zones; and vertically, from the top to the ground floor in each house.

These two concatenated series of prices always counterbalance each other. The rent for each apartment is weighed, on the one hand, against the rents paid in other streets and neighborhoods for the same floor (or also for higher or lower floors inhabited by the same social class) and, on the other hand, against the rents paid on higher or lower floors in the same house.

American skyscrapers show how high the border of a city can be pushed. Such gigantic buildings, to be sure, can be erected only here and there, and then only for business purposes. Nevertheless, our towns could rise much higher towards the interior if landlords were not hampered by our building regulations, which restrict the number of floors for the sake of the general welfare. Since the effect of these regulations is to broaden and flatten out the town's vertical profile, the result is that in the areas where rentals are the highest, the buildings with the greatest number of floors are generally the most remunerative, because the competition for their top floors still produces a premium over and above costs, i.e., a rent in the strictly economic sense. Only in the poorer districts might it happen that a rent can no longer be earned on the highest floor still permitted by the building regulations. And it could even happen—as is, for instance, the case in Prague—that houses in a given area are not built as high as the law permits them to be, simply because the rent that could thereby be earned would no longer cover the costs of construction. In any house in which the number of floors is kept down solely by force of law, the ground rent—that is, in a house of several stories, the sum of the premiums, over and above costs, yielded by competitive bidding on all the floors taken together—will, of course, be likewise reduced.

In spite of this reduction brought about by building regulations, the rent derived from an advantageous location will, in favored areas, be very considerably increased by virtue of the fact that it can be made to yield a rent of intensity. It will be recalled that we concluded our earlier discussion of what we have called the rent of location by comparing residential rentals to a vault arching upward from the border of the town to its center. This vault will soar considerably higher by virtue of the rent of intensity. Towards the interior there will be an upward gradation in the increments that competitive bidding can yield per unit of surface utilized and a consequent increase in the intensity of construction. As the space available for the construction of apartments becomes more congested, they will be arranged in superimposed levels. Finally, in the preferred locations, the more elegant style of construction will raise the basic costs above which premiums have to be offered in competitive bidding. As the rentals paid for such apartments arch upward, like a vault, over the most highly favored locations, the ground rent included in them will also rise, and no special proof is required to show that the curve of the latter will necessarily rise more steeply than that of gross rentals paid.

And now a word about the large modern city. As a consequence of the "lure of the city," its circumference has increased enormously in comparison to that of earlier days. The demand for new accommodations is, as a rule, continually growing and is often even urgent. As a further consequence, the market in urban rents is fundamentally transformed in many different ways.

Let us discuss first the immediate effects brought about by the enormous extension in the area occupied by the city, and let us assume provisionally, as we have up to now, a concentric arrangement in its layout. Even on the assumption that the cost of the poorest accommodations on the outer fringes of the city remains unchanged, gross rental values, as well as ground rents, are bound to increase considerably in the favored areas, and this applies as much to living quarters as it does to places of business. Residential rents rise because of the considerable increase in the number of concentric rings that results from the fact that the population is more widely spread out and more intensely stratified; and business rents rise because of the considerable increase in the number of business sections and, concomitantly, in the profits to be earned in the very best locations now that traffic has spread out and, at the same time, increased heavily in the most favored areas. Between center and border there are now located considerably more partial markets than before. The premium that one previously had to offer, over and above the rental paid at the town border, in order to secure a place further in the interior is now no longer sufficient because the whole scale of gradations in the amounts offered in competitive bidding from the border to the center has been considerably lengthened and its height considerably increased. Where one previously had to meet the competition of bidders at twenty different levels, one now has to reckon with perhaps forty, and the premium one finally has to pay in order to drive competitors from the field has to be larger because of their increased ability to pay.

In regard to this crucial point, I should like to call the reader's attention specifically to the facts that Dr. Mildschuh has brought out with reference to Prague.[1] The lowest cost of an apartment located on the outskirts of the city is today scarcely higher than it was in 1882 at what was then the border of Prague, since the increase in taxes and in the direct costs of construction has approximately been balanced by the decrease in the prevailing rate of interest. Yet in spite of this, residential rents in the interior increased considerably in this same period. No doubt one reason for this is that apartments today are more richly equipped, but the major part of the increase can be explained only by the intensification of competitive bidding. The figures adduced by Dr. Mildschuh show clearly that as a town extends its borders, the whole scale of rents from border to center gradually becomes more steeply inclined.

Although Prague has, for the most part, retained its concentric arrangement, one would by no means be justified in assuming that this is the general rule in large modern cities and in treating it theoretically as the prevailing type. With the growth of population the number of people in the upper-income brackets increased so greatly and so rapidly everywhere that they could no longer provide space for themselves in the central part of town simply by driving the poorer classes further out. Any attempt to do so would have been self-defeating, in view of the great difficulties involved in rebuilding and all the different kinds of resistance that traditional elements usually oppose to change. One had to resort to other expedients.

In Vienna, of course, a historical coincidence has made it possible to create an elegant quarter of very large extension immediately adjacent to the old central section of town. The latter was fortified, and the dismantling of the fortifications has made room for the fashionable "Ringstrasse" and a whole network of side streets. In Prague the situation was similar, for here too there was an old fortification, which has been partly razed. This, together with other local circumstances, has made it possible to erect, immediately adjoining the old hub of the town, elegant new residential areas, which in one sector have been extended further and further out from the center. These are the areas Dr. Mildschuh has especially examined. In the other towns of Austria, following, in general, the example of the capital city, the well-to-do families have still retained their traditional preference for the interior sections. However, the rapid expansion of Vienna has led to the development of richer neighborhoods farther out from the center, and the city now possesses a number of suburban areas of this kind. In Berlin and other German cities this arrangement is even more popular.

Does not such a development destroy the factual basis of the law that the graduated scale of residential rents is determined by competitive bidding for favored locations? If good apartment houses can also be built on the outskirts of the city, should one still have to pay a premium in order to get a good location? And what about cities that have stopped growing?

The formation of a city is the completion of a process that starts with the creation of separate islands consisting of good neighborhoods located on the outskirts. The distance of these residential sections from the center of the city increases as soon as it becomes the general practice of those in business or the professions to arrange their hours of work in such a way as to require them to leave home but once a day. Thus, the connection between one's place of work and the location of one's own home becomes less important, so that even if all of one's work always has to be carried on in the downtown areas, it is still possible to take up residence farther away, where a wide variety of advantages are offered that could not be provided in the central part of the city for even the richest people. All that then remains on the most expensive sites in the city are public buildings, the offices of big business, and monuments of historical or touristic interest. The residential sections, including even the most fashionable neighborhoods, are all situated as far outside the downtown area as the constantly improving means of transportation make it possible to be.

However, it should not be supposed that proximity to the center of the city and the convenience of the transit facilities to and from it are no longer considered as advantages. Other things being equal, these factors will still play a decisive role, but it will often happen that they will be outweighed by other advantages even more highly valued. A theory of urban rent that would make everything dependent exclusively upon proximity to the center would be applicable only to a rather limited extent to the large modern city. It would, of course, explain why rents are higher within the city and along the main arteries of traffic, but in regard to the residential sections it would take into account only one of the motives for competitive bidding—and one that, moreover, is becoming less and less significant. Besides, such a theory would have to meet the objection that it completely fails to account for the existence of good residential areas located well outside the city, right next to vacant land. Hence, it is important to observe, as we have already seen in the case of the old town, that proximity to the center is only a secondary consideration and that the primary factor is that of social stratification.

Consequently, we do not need to seek for any new theory in dealing with the large modern city. Today as in the past each social class will be in possession of just so much ground as befits its status in relation to all the others, and it will succeed in gaining possession of this ground for itself only by outbidding the less solvent classes. There will never be an abundant supply of vacant land at the disposal of the great majority of the inhabitants of a city, unless we suppose that its centripetal force will be compensated by a corresponding flight from the city and that the congested masses of houses existing today will be completely broken up and dispersed over a wider area like little villages.

Apart from proximity to the center there will always be some other characteristics—however indifferent some of them may seem—that determine the valuation, and the rich will always tend to occupy the necessarily limited areas offering the greatest advantages, whatever these may be. Today as in the past the primary factor is social prestige. The neighborhoods in which one can live "suitably," that is, in a manner befitting one's social position, will always be limited in number since one always wishes to live where other, "better" families have already settled. Even if the suburban areas sought out for the better quarters were not, for a variety of other reasons, already rather limited, they would in any case be restricted in order to protect them from the encroachment of the proletariat. The number of people energetic enough to liberate themselves from social prejudices and to choose their places of residence independently is very small—quite as small, indeed, as the number of independently acting individuals has always been within the memory of man—and only such a minority will take advantage of the possibility of settling down where rents have not yet been raised by the competitive bidding of their social peers.

It cannot be denied that the irregular layout of the modern large city possesses, under present circumstances, very obvious advantages over the concentric arrangement of earlier days. By reducing the social prestige of proximity to the center, the existing arrangement will no doubt help to lower residential rental values as well as ground rents. But it cannot altogether break down the system of graduated competitive bidding in the market in residential rents, even if we disregard the fact that, in the case of business rents, proximity to the center becomes the more important the greater the number of people for whom transportation through the center is the shortest route. It will be recalled that in describing conditions in the town of earlier days we represented residential rental values and ground rents as forming a kind of vault with a central dome and ascending ribs. In the modern large city this image is applicable only to the business districts. In regard to the residential sections, the pattern that we should have to draw today is highly irregular, with a number of larger or smaller domes, each spanning some local center, and yet all oriented, to some extent, towards the heart of the city and the chief centers of business.

We can bring this part of our discussion to a conclusion with the observation that the market in residential rents in a large city, although far more spread out and less easily surveyed, basically conforms to the same law of a graduated scale of competitive bids as the more limited, but at the same time more regular, market in the small town of earlier days. But we have not yet finished. The supply of and the demand for apartments will less easily adjust themselves to each other when the town is growing rapidly than when its population remains relatively stable. As a general rule, demand will take the lead, but sometimes supply will do so. The latter situation occurred in many Austrian towns and elsewhere on a large scale in the troubled times around 1873. Dr. Mildschuh devotes a thorough investigation to the effects that the crisis of that year had in Prague, thereby bringing to our attention facts that deserve a more precise theoretical interpretation. Many workers' families at that time were forced to leave town, the income of those remaining behind was sharply reduced, and in the outlying districts inhabited by the working class residential rents and land values declined considerably. It is very interesting to note that in the better sections of town rents and land values declined only moderately, and in the best neighborhoods least of all.

These facts would seem to constitute a powerful argument in favor of the opinion we have here opposed, namely, that the partial markets in residential rents are quite independent of one another. But if one examines the matter more closely, nothing more is proved than that the partial markets are, as their name indicates, merely parts of a large market in which prices are formed to a certain extent independently, without, however, completely losing their connection with one another. The different residential sections of the city are so sharply separated from one another that the available supply of accommodations in any given neighborhood does not easily find outside buyers of a different income level, nor does the demand for accommodations find it easy to penetrate into alien neighborhoods. This explains, among other things, why landlords in the better quarters are reluctant, even when vacancies occur, to accept the lower rent that poorer tenants, of whom there is always an abundance, are able to offer.

After the crisis of 1873, which in Prague affected the middle classes less than it did the industrial workers, the relationship between demand and supply did not change much in the better neighborhoods. There was no reason for the families residing in these sections to move out and establish themselves in the quarters formerly occupied by the workers, where inexpensive apartments were now available, nor could they have done so very easily without lowering their social status. Considerations of this kind play a role in determining the valuation placed on any given dwelling, and the great majority of tenants submit to this sort of social constraint even though it costs them dear. However, there is no doubt that if the emigration of workers from Prague had continued longer, residential rents would have declined even in the good neighborhoods as the pressure to outbid people of lower income level gradually diminished.

When the demand outstrips the supply, a whole chain of consequences of the greatest practical importance is produced, but these can only be touched upon in a theoretical investigation such as ours, which is oriented primarily towards the treatment of general principles. And so we wish merely to call attention briefly to the fact that the people who are at present moving into the city belong to a different social class from that of the residents who are already established there. As a result of increasing industrialization, the influx of proletarians into the large cities is today much heavier than it ever was. Thus, an ever-increasing class of needy and economically helpless workers, living on extremely low and insecure daily wages, makes its appearance in the market in residential rents. Districts of a pronouncedly proletarian character come into being, which are separated from the rest of this market far more sharply than is any other partial market, and a supply of a peculiar nature adapts itself to their condition. In the large cities rents are everywhere as high as they can be pushed as a result of the increase in the costs of construction and competitive bidding. In the proletarian sections, because of the impotence of demand in the face of the overwhelming power of those in control of the supply, housing conditions are very likely to be extremely wretched and rents exorbitant. This is a matter of the utmost importance for the municipal authorities, but it is of no special significance for the theory of urban ground rent, since these well-nigh isolated markets have as little effect on rents in other parts of the city as the usury market in emergency loans made to the improvident or to those in dire need has on the interest rates of gilt-edged securities and first mortgages.

Another set of problems of equal administrative importance—and hence naturally lending themselves also to literary treatment—but of no great theoretical significance, results from the fact that even outside the entirely proletarian districts there are markets in which the demand sometimes outstrips the supply. In such cases, speculators in building contracts, without business experience, moral integrity, capital, or credit, may enter the field; and it is they who are responsible for usurious practices in the building trades, the overburdening of mortgages with abnormally heavy interest rates, and unsound and costly modes of construction. The more widespread is the activity of such promotors, the more disastrous is its effect. It might even bring about a general rise in the minimum costs of construction and thereby, to that extent at least, finally affect the entire market.

A problem of considerable theoretical importance is presented by land speculation, another phenomenon prevalent in the real-estate market of a large city. This indeed needs to be discussed, but before doing so we must emphasize, in view of our immediately preceding remarks, that usury in all its many different forms will definitely be excluded from this inquiry.

There can be no doubt as to the origin of speculation in urban real estate. It began with the whirlwind growth of modern cities, which increased, in rapid sequence, gross residential rentals and the ground rents included in them, and, with these, real-estate values as calculated by the capitalization of ground rents. The speculator who purchases land at the right time can make big profits if only he guesses correctly the tendency of the market. Speculation has turned, by preference, towards vacant land on the outskirts of the city. Increases in real-estate values, reckoned per unit of surface area, are much greater in their gross amount in the good neighborhoods inside the city; but relatively, i.e., in proportion to the land values hitherto prevailing, they are greater outside the city, where, as Dr. Mildschuh, taking Prague as an example, demonstrates statistically, the capital invested yields a higher rate of profit. Besides, speculation inside the city is rendered difficult wherever buildings have already been erected because these buildings have to be purchased, with an investment of additional capital, as well as the land they occupy.

We have to distinguish sharply between speculation in land and usurious practices in the rental of land or of buildings. To be sure, the speculator too is lured by the expectation of inordinate profits, but he has to gain them by other means. The speculator endeavors to employ his superior knowledge of the market solely for the purpose of choosing the right moment to make his purchase and then biding his time until the right moment comes when the land can again be disposed of. Moreover, he operates in a free market, accessible in principle to everyone, even though not everyone speculates. The usurer, on the other hand, operates in a virtually isolated market which is shunned by any businessman jealous of his good reputation and which can therefore be more easily dominated. That is why profits from land speculation will not, on the average, be usuriously high. Adolf Weber has shown this to be true for a number of cities, and Dr. Mildschuh has done the same for Prague. He demonstrates that profits were exceptionally high only for such persons as possessed real estate that they had purchased at first hand or had acquired at approximately the value of arable land. Speculative purchasers entering the market at a later time must, as a result of their mutual competition, more or less anticipate in their purchase price the expected increase in value.

In characterizing the urban real-estate market as a free market, in which competition exerts its effect, we have to some extent already pointed to its most important distinguishing characteristic. There are many writers today who attribute a monopolistic power to land speculation. And does not this charge seem well founded? Can one resist the impression that the natural development of the large modern city is being stunted by an overwhelmingly powerful force, such as a private businessman could acquire only by monopoly? The town of our fathers and grandfathers presents the picture of a natural transition from the village beyond its borders, its towering and massive buildings quite naturally supplanting the simple rural houses of the countryside. The modern city, on the other hand, in many places builds its tenement houses right out to the very border. How else can the existence of these "rented barracks" in the outermost reaches of the city be explained if not by a "prohibition on building" dictated by a monopoly that crowds tenants together within narrow walls and refuses to release new land for building until demand is so hard pressed that it is prepared to pay ground rent for new tenements?

For the theory of urban rent, as we have developed it, tenements erected on the outskirts of the city present a problem of particular importance. We have declared that ground rent arises from the fact that in the better locations one has to pay a premium over and above the lowest rental paid in the poorest location. Is there an even worse location than that of the slums on the outskirts? For it now appears that here too there is not only an urban rent in general, but, corresponding to the extensive capital investment involved in such a large project, even a comparatively high rent of intensity. We have explained urban rent—in agreement with Ricardo in this respect—as differential rent. But where can one find a worse place by comparison with which the slums on the farthermost outskirts of the city would be considered as worth such a differential?

Conditions in Prague may help us to see in what direction the answer lies. According to Dr. Mildschuh's report, land speculation in Prague started in the boom years preceding the crisis of 1873. Consequently, in certain sections on the outskirts of modern Prague, as in other large cities, multiple dwellings are to be found advancing right into the surrounding countryside. And yet, as Dr. Mildschuh reports, there is not the slightest trace of a monopolistic organization in the Prague realty market. It must therefore be possible to explain the existence of big apartment houses on the outskirts, directly adjacent to a zone of vacant land, without any reference to monopoly.

But first we have to clarify the concept of monopoly. Monopoly is the domination of supply or demand by a single party, whether by a physical person or by some overt or covert association of a few or many persons. Limited competition should not be confused with monopoly. However limited competition may be, its power over the market is never as great as that of a true monopoly, since only the latter admits of a policy of unrestrained ruthlessness. The confounding of monopoly with scarcity has unfortunately become quite common since the founding of classical economics, although no less confusion is involved in speaking, on the other hand, of absolutely free competition, since there is nothing whatsoever in the economy the supply of which could be increased "at will."

In the same way, it is permissible to speak of a natural or actual monopoly only in connection with a completely isolated economic event. The possession of urban real estate does not in the least constitute a natural monopoly. In every large city there are thousands and thousands of separately owned pieces of land, and even in any particular neighborhood there is usually a considerable number. Besides, as we have seen, the differently situated sections of the city should in no way be thought of as partial markets that are rigidly separated from one another. Let us not forget that the supply of even the best locations can be increased by the payment of a premium, and all the more easily in a modern city, where less social prestige attaches to a central location. Still less can one speak of a natural monopoly at the border of the city, where the extended radius increases the circumference of the zones, since the supply is by nature less restricted here than in any other location. As long as speculation in land does not interfere, new urban property can, in general, be acquired at the expense of arable land, without requiring more than a small premium over and above the value of the latter.

Here, however, the emergence of land speculation has caused a change. Instead of the value of arable land, a higher value is fixed on tracts of land spreading over a rather wide area, corresponding to the anticipated extent of urban construction and the time it is expected to take. The anticipated urban ground rent will be capitalized, and from the capital value will be deducted the sum of the rentals not receivable during the intervening period of time up to the completion of the building program.

What degree of intensity of construction is here presumed? That is the decisive question. Evidently the speculator is faced with several possibilities. The longer he waits to start building, the more intensive will the demand have become, the greater will be the intensity of construction, and the higher the future gross rentals, the future ground rent, and the future value of the land will be; on the other hand, however, the greater also becomes the discount that has to be deducted from the future value of the land in calculating its present value. It is in the self-interest of the speculator to select from all the given possibilities those which, according to his appraisal, yield the highest present value.

What these will be will depend essentially upon the anticipated rapidity of the increase in population. On those points along the periphery where experience shows that the city is expanding but slowly, builders will immediately start extensive construction, in order not to lose the rents that can be garnered in the interim, as soon as there is any demand at all. The case is different, however, on those points along the periphery where the working-class quarters are expanding most rapidly. As long as the demand here is not yet sufficient to pay the prevailing rent for all the space available in houses customarily for rent in this area, the speculator will find it temporarily unprofitable to erect a big tenement house. But neither will he find it advantageous, under these circumstances, to build extensively, since he thereby forfeits the prospect of realizing, within a reasonable time, the high rental values that could otherwise be derived from construction on an intensive scale, unless he razes the buildings of simpler construction that he first erected and proceeds, in spite of temporary losses, to build tenement houses in their place.

If we take Prague as an example, the statistics presented by Dr. Mildschuh are very instructive in this respect. In front of the town gate of Strahow, in a slowly growing working-class neighborhood there has developed during recent years the village of Tejnka. Its houses are built in a semirural style. The construction of a tenement house here would not have paid, nor would there have been any advantage in postponing construction entirely. The suburb of Weinberge, on the other hand, which lies in the direction of rapidly advancing development, pushes forward with the construction of big apartment houses right into the fields, which at the same time are held free for the building of still more apartment houses. In both cases it is considerations of self-interest that determine the decision of the speculator in land, as he adjusts his conduct to the demand in the market. Everything is accomplished without monopoly or concerted arrangement, simply in the interest of each individual speculator, which, in turn, is guided by the conditions of the market.

No entrepreneur could proceed any differently in his calculations. The so-called "prohibition on construction" allegedly dictated by speculators enjoying monopolistic advantages proves to be nothing more than a decision of business policy that the urgency of the demand forces upon competitors on the side of supply. Perhaps an administrative agency, working on behalf of the entire community in the interest of social welfare, could find more economical ways and means of meeting this urgent demand than private industry does with its tenement houses. But the study of such questions, important as they are, lies beyond the goal of our theoretical investigation, which has to confine itself to the explanation of given market phenomena. And the conclusion that we have reached may be formulated thus: tenement houses situated on the outskirts, beyond a zone of vacant land, are the product of the free market of a large, rapidly growing city. Supply in the hands of private owners obeys in its way the will of urgent demand. This demand generates the centripetal force which, since the time the city was founded, has been crowding its inhabitants together and which still continues to do so even more than ever in the rapidly growing city of the present day. Just as coming events cast their shadows before them, so, in the light of present tendencies, we must expect that future residential areas will be even more crowded than they are today.

This relationship is much easier to understand if one clearly realizes that the so-called "border" of the large modern city is not in fact its border at all. Beyond the zone in which there are no buildings and opposite which tenement houses have not yet been constructed there is much other land on which an urban population has settled. Strictly speaking, the inhabitants of this area are also part of the city's population, since large numbers of able-bodied men, and perhaps even women and children, go into the city to work every day. Separated from what may be called the inner periphery of the city by a zone of vacant land there lies still farther out an "ultraperiphery." In criticizing my theory of a graduated scale of competitive bids, Mr. Auspitz, one of the experts called in the inquiry into the tax rates on inhabited dwellings, used this term half-ironically, but we can adopt it quite seriously. Such an "ultraperiphery" does indeed exist.

Naturally, however, it should not be thought of as forming part of a regularly developing concentric arrangement. The large modern city radiates differently in different directions, in one place nearer to the center, and in another farther out. Just as an ever-increasing number of the most fashionable people choose to settle on the outskirts, so also do certain members of the very humblest classes. They find it too expensive to live in tenement houses, and they go to work on foot or use the cheapest means of transportation. They live in a number of dispersed hamlets or in growing villages that gradually adopt urban characteristics, or even in real towns, nearer in or farther out, depending upon the facilities for transportation.

Just as the town of our fathers and grandfathers gradually overflowed into rural settlements, so, as we now see, does the large modern city, except that, in view of the enormously greater scale of the whole operation, the transitional zone is correspondingly very much larger and hence no longer lends itself as readily to a synoptic survey. Like a great fortress with its surrounding outworks, a large city is encompassed by all kinds of outlying suburbs.

The entire population is by no means crowded together in the very heart of the city. Only after having first traversed a rather wide zone of urban settlements outside the city proper does one come upon the tenement houses of the inner periphery. If these yield their owners a rent of intensity, this is entirely the result of their location, which possesses the advantage most highly appreciated by the mass of tenants, viz., immediate access to the center of the city and its numerous administrative buildings. In the most modest dwellings situated further out one pays the lowest rent; for apartments located on the inner periphery, one already has to pay a differential rent.

This development of the inner periphery is anticipated by the speculator. Taking into consideration the expected increase in future value to be produced by more intensive construction, he fixes a higher present value on land in this area. This very expectation of being able to proceed, within a relatively short time, to construction on a more intensive scale, acts, as long as it prevails, as a deterrent to more extensive construction. If, however, the development of the city comes to a standstill or slows down too much or spreads in other directions, the speculator has miscalculated and has at best to be satisfied with the lower rents to be derived from more extensive construction on land for which he has already paid a high price; at the worst, he has to forgo construction entirely. Under no circumstances does he have any power whatsoever to compel the construction of tenement houses, nor has he any claim to reimbursement for the money he has invested.

Obviously, the demand for accommodations in a particular place must, if it is to be satisfied, always cover the necessary costs, but these include only so much of the cost of acquiring the building lot as is equal to its value as mere arable land, for only to this extent is the amount paid by the speculator an already given quantity, fixed by the relatively alien market in agricultural land. Whatever he chooses to pay over and above this amount for land to be used for construction is a matter of his own speculation and risk; it does not figure as one of the necessary costs. If the speculation fails, this is the amount that, in the reckoning of accounts, has first to be written off as a loss. The speculator is never in a position to extort a higher rent just because he paid too much in the first place in purchasing his building lots; on the contrary, the rent that the demand is finally willing to pay is the measure of what it would have been more reasonable for him to have paid originally in acquiring them.

This line of reasoning is in accord with the interpretation advocated by Voigt. Dr. Mildschuh is an adherent of the opposite opinion, which he supports in a very interesting way.[2] He has found, by means of carefully compiled statistics, that in Prague, during the years 1870 to 1875, residential rents rose to an extent which cannot be explained by the increase in costs proper, and which evidently was related to the speculative increase in land values that began to occur at this time. As Dr. Mildschuh interprets this relationship, this speculative increase in land values raised the costs of building houses.

In reality, however, the connection between the rise in rents and the increase in land values has to be interpreted quite differently. The development of the "ultraperiphery" of which we have spoken was a concomitant of the speculation in land and was, indeed, brought about by the same cause, namely, the rapid growth of the city. The inner periphery had ceased to be the real border and became a preferred location, to which tenants could find admittance only by the payment of a premium in competitive bidding. Once residential rents increased on the inner periphery, all the other rents further in toward the center also increased, as a necessary consequence of the raising of the lower limit above which a premium had to be bid. Nor should one overlook the fact that during the boom the old bourgeois population living in the interior had grown rapidly in numbers and wealth and had become stratified into a diversity of social classes, the members of which had to outbid one another in the ensuing competition for dwelling space.

In concluding, let us once again revert to the distinction between agricultural rent and urban rent. The former springs from a productive process, the latter is a market phenomenon, and these two facts constituted our original starting point. Now that we know more precisely in what sense urban rent is a market phenomenon, we are in a position to determine its character definitively and to distinguish it from agricultural ground rent.

Regardless of whether a piece of land is fertile or not, extensively or intensively cultivated, or nearer to or farther from the market, its crop commands the same price in the market. From the price as such, therefore, we cannot tell how high a rent is left over for the owner of the land or even whether it yields a rent at all. In order to answer these questions, we first have to go behind the price and to take into account the elements that entered into its formation, namely, the processes of agricultural production and transportation. The calculation to be made for this purpose is theoretically very simple: it depends on the amount of the crop and its costs. In practice, however, even in the simplest cases, this calculation can be performed only very inexactly. In the process of production, which is repeated every year anew, the performance of the soil is so thoroughly bound up with that of capital and labor that we can make a clear and distinct separation among these three factors only in theory. This applies especially to the substance of the soil, which only in theory can be isolated and separated from the capital connected with it. We define it as the "indestructible" powers of the soil, but in practice who can separate these from the other powers of the soil?

Under the circumstances, the widespread notion that agricultural rent accrues undeservedly to the owner of the land stands in need of some qualification. Whatever one may say against the big landowner who reaps a profit from the toil of tenant farmers or of hired overseers and day laborers, the case is quite different with the farmer who tills his own land and himself participates in the process of agricultural production, wresting from the soil, by a difficult effort, sheaf by sheaf and fruit by fruit, what economic theory calls "rent," but what is, in practice, indistinguishable from the rest of the yield. The advantage of owning productive property which the free farmer enjoys and the proletarian lacks is not absolute. Everything depends essentially upon the distribution of the property, and generally this is such that the farmer is perfectly right in considering his agricultural "rent" as a well-deserved reward for his hard work. It is something he has to count on, and when he does not get it, his expectations are cruelly disappointed, since all his labor is oriented towards the hope of receiving a rent. For the big landowner, on the other hand, who manages his own estate, agricultural rent is combined with an entrepreneurial profit, at least in those places where modern law has freed landed property of restrictions on ownership and alienation and rewards more intensive cultivation by permitting the landowner to retain his title to the increased returns.

The case is different with urban rent. It is not concealed by an outer covering of uniform costs from which it has to be removed in order to be visible at all; it presents itself quite openly as a market phenomenon. The line of gross rental values ascending from the worst residential areas to the best makes clearly apparent the proportionate magnitude of urban ground rent. It is true that the prices charged for the use of urban land are likewise not quite clearly presented in the market, since gross residential rentals always include a considerable quota that has to be imputed to the capital invested in construction. This second factor, however, must be sharply distinguished, not only theoretically, but also practically, from the premium paid for location. Unlike the prices paid for agricultural land, those of vacant lots intended to be used for urban construction also contain capitalized ground rent quite independently, without any alien admixture whatsoever. These prices express, with the fluctuations brought about by the ups and downs of speculative expectation, nothing but land values, inasmuch as speculation derives them from the expected future rents. An entrepreneurial profit is earned only once during the lifetime of a house: at the time of its construction, or, to be altogether precise, also in smaller measure on later occasions when various additions to the building are made. It is only during the comparatively short period while the house is being built that entrepreneurial activity takes place. Its most important task consists in determining the ad-

missible degree of intensity of construction. Throughout the decades that follow, all that is needed is simple day-to-day administration, which the landlord can very well leave to an agent.

The rights of private ownership, which we so emphatically demand in the case of agricultural land for the sake of the increased
returns it makes possible, are not such an imperative necessity in
the case of the urban house. Urban rent is therefore not only more
clearly evident and more amenable to calculation than agricultural
rent, but also very much less affected by economic policy. And to
all this we must finally add the important fact that under present
conditions it is far more capable of a rapid increase. In the large
cities it rises steeply toward the major centers, and its ascent becomes ever steeper with the unceasing growth in population. The
resulting increases in rent accrue to the landlord undeservedly;
for, if one rightly understands them, they are unexpected, in the
sense that, once the construction is completed, it is no longer his
economic activity that is oriented toward the future, but at best
only his speculative expectations.

Consequently, urban rent is in fact that undeserved income
from rent which the followers of Ricardo speak of in connection
with ground rent. Without the necessity of any further effort on
his part, the urban landlord is assured of a continual rise in rent
in the better locations, which are always in scarce supply, simply
by virtue of the law of graduated competitive bidding and the increase in the number of bidders brought about by the natural
growth of the population.

There is still another important difference. All purchasers in
the same market pay the same price for the same fruits of the soil,
and hence all purchasers of the same produce bear an equal share
of the burden of agricultural ground rent included in its price.
The curve of urban rent, on the other hand, rises in such a way
as to burden tenants according to their ability to pay. The premium paid for preferred locations amounts to a kind of tax that
the tenants impose on themselves according to principles which, at
least in regard to residential rents, exactly correspond to the requirements of justice in taxation. By the inherent process of its

formation, urban rent readily lends itself to taxation by the community. However, in a theoretical dissertation such as ours, whose task is to explain how phenomena come into being, we cannot enter more deeply into this aspect of the question.

We must likewise leave for separate treatment the discussion of the great problems involved in a policy of municipal housing, contenting ourselves here with a brief summary of the conclusions that can be drawn in this respect from the theory of urban rent.

Only those who attribute all the hardships and inconveniences associated with urban housing, and especially the rise in rents, to a monopoly in urban land can indulge in the illusion that everything will be better when private monopoly is replaced by a more considerate and perhaps also more economical policy on the part of the public authorities. The explanation we have given of urban rent shows that it is demand, the pressure of competitive bidding on the part of the tenants, that is really responsible for the hardships involved. Most of the tenants are not satisfied to live in the same general locality; they attach great importance to living close together, since they wish to work together, to trade with one another, and to enjoy together the comforts and conveniences of urban life. Supply merely serves demand, executing the will of the latter over a given area, though naturally only in so far as doing so is within its power and serves its own interests. The enormous urgency of the demand that has crowded our cities so densely and raised them up so high cannot be mitigated simply by changing in one way or another the organization of supply.

No doubt a reasonable exercise of public authority could remove many of the evils now existing. Certainly far too little has so far been done in this direction. But the pressure of the demand sets a clearly evident limit on what can be accomplished by intervention on the part of the municipality. Building regulations may be able to set a limit on how high walls can be constructed, but they will not thereby succeed in setting any limit on how high ground rents can rise. In order to do so, one would have to find some means not only of discouraging people from living close together in crowded quarters, but also of equalizing the incomes of the different social classes as well as the relative advantages of different locations, since these are the factors that find expression in the graduated scale of rentals paid for accommodations in various parts of the city. Only if the factor of distance from the center could be entirely eliminated by advances in methods of transportation and if all class distinctions among the citizens could be abolished could urban residential rents be equalized and reduced to the insignificant premium that in any case has to be offered over and above the value of arable land.

NOTES

1. See specifically pp. 120 and 125.*
2. See especially pp. 74-75 and pp. 145-146 of his report.

* This and the following note refer to the text of the previously cited report to which this essay is an introduction. [Translator's note.]

3

A Critical Examination of Current Doctrines Concerning Wage Rates and Unionism*

LUDWIG POHLE

It is no exaggeration to say that among German political economists of the present day it is a widespread practice not only to present facts and examine their interrelations, but at the same time to evaluate and judge them from the standpoint of definite ethical and political ideals. This procedure is especially common in discussions dealing with the economic conditions of the workers. Just as the income of the wealthier classes was at first declared to be unjustifiably high, so now the wages of labor are said to be too low to provide the workers adequately with the necessities of life. Indeed, one is safe in saying that the common starting point of the wage theories developed by the socialists of the chair is the conviction—for it is only this, and not well-founded knowledge—that the worker, at least when he is isolated, i.e., not a member of a trade union, does not in today's economic order receive the income which by right is due to him. Many economists of the present day

* Die gegenwärtige Krisis in der deutschen Volkswirtschaftslehre, Betrachtungen über das Verhältnis zwischen Politik und nationalökonomischer Wissenschaft, originally published in 1912 and reprinted unchanged in 1921 (Leipzig, A. Deichert; Erlangen, Dr. Werner Scholl). The translation was made from pages 29-50 of the 1921 edition.

81

start from this arbitrarily accepted assumption in dealing with the question of wages. This becomes especially evident in the discussion of trade unionism. A few remarks are therefore in order concerning the manner in which this topic is treated in the writings of the orthodox socialists of the chair. It will then become clearly apparent that the whole phenomenon of unionism has been considered predominantly from the *political* point of view.

In discussing trade unionism, the socialists of the chair see their task as something more than a simple inquiry into the way in which the workers, by joint action, can influence wage rates, etc., and the means by which, in a particular case, they can eventually attain this influence. Although this is the problem that would have to occupy the foreground of the whole inquiry in a really scientific treatment of the economic aspects of trade unionism, it is generally disposed of very cursorily and rather superficially. The major emphasis is devoted to an attempt to show that the wages which the workers obtain with the help of their organizations are justified on the ground that they represent a really "just" distribution of income. The treatment of trade unionism in German economics today is more like apologetics than unbiased explanation. For the purpose of justifying trade unions and their activities, a whole set of theories has been developed that apparently have already come to be generally regarded as firmly established scientific knowledge, for they keep reappearing in nearly the same form in the writings of many different authors. At least some of the more important of these theories will be briefly set forth here, not so much with the intention of making an exhaustive criticism of the actual assumptions from which they start—although this too will be done in passing—as to demonstrate their pronounced political character; that is, to show that they do not owe their existence to the need of explaining certain otherwise incomprehensible phenomena, but that they are merely attempts to justify trade unionism and to represent it as socially desirable and useful.

We shall deal first with the doctrine that in the final analysis it is the workers who must bear the full brunt of the economic pressure exerted in the market. This theory has been especially championed by Sidney and Beatrice Webb in their well-known work on the theory and practice of trade unionism in Great Britain, a book which has been highly regarded also by German economists and which has had a great influence upon them.[1] In the chapter entitled "The Higgling of the Market" contained in the second volume, the Webbs provide an exceedingly biased representation, in which truth and falsehood are strangely intermingled, of the way in which the condition of the working class must finally be depressed by the combined effect produced by the consumers' endeavors to purchase everything they need as cheaply as possible and the competition existing among sellers. The consumer, who can distribute the favor of his custom according to his sovereign discretion among the stores in which he makes his purchases, will first depress retail sales prices by purchasing commodities where he can obtain them a few cents cheaper than anywhere else. The retailer passes this pressure on to the wholesaler, who in turn depresses the prices of the manufacturers by trying to exploit as much as possible the competition existing among them. Under the continuous pressure placed upon the price of his product, the manufacturer, in order to make a profit at all, finally tries to indemnify himself out of the wages paid to his workmen. Thus it is the workmen who ultimately have to bear the entire weight of this economic pressure.

". . . The impulse for cheapness, of which the consumer is the unconscious source, grows in strength as it is transmitted from one stage of bargaining to another, until, at last, with all its accumulated weight, it settles like an incubus on the isolated workman's means of subsistence." [2] The workman is therefore, according to this conception, the hindmost, whom, in the words of the old saying, the Devil takes.

The arbitrariness and insufficiency of this line of thought needs only to be briefly indicated. In the first place, it is a gross exaggeration to consider the seller as the one who in all circumstances is dependent upon the buyer. There are just as many cases in economic life where the buyer is dependent upon the seller. One must ask, first of all, how far this dependence goes. To what extent must the seller yield to the pressure of the buyer? If the seller must always, willy-nilly, be the one to give in, then it is really a miracle that such a large working class still exists. The fact that it can and does exist in spite of this pressure and even increases in number and raises its standard of living is quite easily explained as soon as we examine more closely who really comprise the class of consumers that exerts this enormous pressure and thereby enjoys the advantage of providing itself cheaply with the goods that it needs. We then see quite clearly that *the working class itself forms the main component of the mass of consumers.* But from this it follows that the same transaction that hurts the worker in his capacity as a producer must redound to his benefit in his capacity as a consumer, at least if we consider the economy as a whole and prescind, of course, from individual deviations and exceptions. It is indeed a completely untenable way of thinking in economic inquiry to regard the consumer as the independent first person in a series of economic relations that terminates with the equally independent and isolated worker or producer. If we traverse this series from beginning to end, we find ourselves again at the starting point. The first and the final links in the chain are identical and are connected by a personal bond; that is, it is a closed chain in which there is neither beginning nor end or in which it could just as well be said that any link can be considered indifferently as either the beginning or the end.[3]

The Webbs fail to give due recognition to these simple and quite obvious economic connections. It is evident that the real purpose of their theory that the working class ultimately has to bear the full weight of the economic pressure exerted by the consumers is only to prove that the workers need to be organized into trade unions. The latter are represented as bulwarks erected by the workers to restrain the pressure weighing them down or at least to mitigate its harshness, very much like the other bulwarks put up by sellers to avoid the pressure that buyers seek to exert upon prices. It is certainly quite correct to establish a parallelism between the organizations of the workers and those of other sellers, and one can even admit the legitimacy of the description of these associations as bulwarks. The Webbs, however, are not concerned with determining where such bulwarks might favorably be erected or what changes they might cause in economic life; but, by referring to these associations in connection with their doctrine that the workers are the ones who, in the final analysis, must bear the full brunt of this economic pressure, they seek from the very outset to give at least to those bulwarks of the workers the appearance of a higher necessity. Far from being ethically neutral, as every purely scientific theory should be, the Webbs' theory of trade unions already involves a considerable commitment to ethical presuppositions right from the very beginning. This theory presents trade unions in such a light as to make them appear as an institution designed to eliminate, at least to some extent, an evil that the workers are unjustly made to endure solely by virtue of the mechanism of the existing economic system.

But the Webbs apparently did not consider as altogether adequate for this purpose their theory that the workers are the ones who must finally bear the full burden of the economic pressure exerted by the consumers; and so, with the intention of bolstering their justification of trade unionism, they added a second theory and joined it to the first in an organic relation. This is the doctrine that the isolated worker finds himself in an unfavorable position vis-à-vis the employer in negotiating the conditions of a labor contract. Without a doubt this is the argument most commonly urged today in favor of trade unionism, especially in the German literature on economics, where it appears again and again. We therefore wish to submit it to critical examination, particularly in the form in which it has been stated in Germany. This theory constitutes a part of what might well be called the hard core of the doctrine of the socialists of the chair. It forms the basis of the whole picture of labor relations in modern economics as seen by many present-day political scientists.

Brentano and his school have shown a particular fondness for ringing all the changes on this theme that the isolated worker is in a prejudicial position in negotiating a labor contract, i.e., that he cannot by himself obtain the wages due to him. In order to see how arbitrary are the assumptions and ethical value judgments in which this theory abounds and just how far it aims at producing in those to whom it is addressed the ethical and political conviction of the necessity for trade unions in the present economic system, one has only to quote an extract from the theory, in the form in which Herkner, in his widely read *Arbeiterfrage,* has accepted it:

In receiving juridical equality in the negotiation of the labor contract, the worker is still far from receiving actual freedom on a par with that which the employer enjoys. If one grants that there is true freedom of contract only when each of the contracting parties is able to decline the other's offer without having to suffer disadvantages essentially more grievous than the other, then one cannot, as a rule, speak of a really free labor contract. The propertyless worker can practice his craft only by finding an employer who is prepared to place at his disposal the means of production necessary to his work. In the absence of employment the worker does not generally have enough resources of his own to keep body and soul together; he has to go on relief, with all its humiliating consequences. The employer, on the other hand, even if a labor contract cannot be negotiated, can either live off his fortune and the income it yields or do the work himself without depending upon assistants. No matter how great the economic inconvenience he may have to suffer if he cannot provide himself with outside labor, his situation is by no means comparable to that of a propertyless and unemployed worker. One is therefore quite justified in saying that the worker finds himself permanently in the position of a bankrupt who is forced to sell out at any cost and whose clearance sales at ruinous prices have become proverbial. . . . There is no doubt that the bare principle of liberty of contract, the attempt simply to subject the exploitation of labor to the laws of the market, the neglect of all those peculiar features which distinguish the worker as a lessor of his labor power from other lessors—all this has resulted in a monstrous misrepresentation of actual labor relations that has, on the whole, been to the detriment of the worker. For him the labor relation is a matter of life and death; for the employer, merely a matter of business. . . .[4]

In determining what basis this opinion has in point of fact, it suffices to observe that if there is really "true freedom of contract" (and herein lies the value judgment on which the entire theory depends) only when each of the contracting parties is in a position to decline the other's offer without having to suffer disadvantages essentially more grievous than the other, and if one accepts the rest of Herkner's argument in the passage cited above, then true freedom of contract is encountered very rarely in economic life. Under such circumstances the worker is by no means the only one who is handicapped in negotiating a contract. This is often the case with the consumer too. With the baker, for instance, who supplies me with my bread, I am not on a footing of true liberty, because if he refuses to furnish me with bread, if no contract to do so exists between us, I am the one who in that case suffers a greater disadvantage than he does. Without his bread I cannot hold out as long as he can without my custom. I lack the equipment as well as the skill to bake the bread for myself. For the baker, on the other hand, if I no longer buy his bread, this means perhaps only a loss of less than one percent of his customers. Just as in industry a relatively small number of employers often stand over against possibly a hundred times as many workers, so that the individual worker is of no importance for a large corporation; so, in the same way, especially in the big cities, there are several hundred consumers to each bakery. The individual customer, therefore, is of no importance for the sales of the baker, and thus the economic superiority of the baker over the individual customer is evident.

Now, as Herkner will no doubt be good enough to explain to me, if my baker charges too high a price, I am not on that account forthwith faced with the alternative of either forgoing bread entirely or baking bread myself under great difficulties and of inferior quality. If I refuse to pay the price demanded by my former supplier, I need only go to another baker; and the sole inconvenience I shall have to undergo is that of having to make a longer trip to purchase my bread. This objection is certainly correct. But *does it not apply in exactly the same way to the worker who is on the point of concluding a labor contract?* Is he not also free, if he is offered a wage that he thinks unjustifiably low, to look around for another job? To do so, of course, he will have to take the trouble to travel to another place or at least to another employer.

But what will happen if even the third or the fourth employer is unwilling to offer the worker a wage higher than what he considers as the minimum acceptable to him? Would this not be a perfect exemplification of the conditions actually assumed by Herkner's theory that the worker is the weaker party in the negotiation of a labor contract? Does not the worker in this case occupy a special position in economic life, one that leaves him only the choice between starving or accepting conditions of labor unilaterally imposed by the employer?

In fact, however, the relation of the worker to the employer is similar to that of the consumer to the baker.[5] The consumer might find himself very much in the same position as the one that we have assumed in the case of the worker. He too might find that the second, the third, or the fourth baker also charges for his product the same price as did his former supplier. And now he too apparently has the alternative of forgoing the consumption of bread entirely or of being obliged to undertake the onerous task of baking his own bread. Certainly, however, if experience can teach him anything, he will do neither the one nor the other, but, after having gathered information about what prices are being asked and paid elsewhere, he will find it more prudent to accept conditions as they are. He will then come to understand that the price that his former supplier asked him to pay had not been set arbitrarily nor was it the result of the fact that the economic position he occupies is less favorable than the baker's. The price merely reflects the market situation, i.e., the normal costs of production of the bakery business. And he will therefore repentantly repair to his old supplier in the full knowledge that the latter's interest coincides with his own.

Today, however, what makes it exceedingly difficult for the workers to arrive at a similar insight into their own situation with regard to their employers is the existence of all those theories, advanced for the most part by the so-called bourgeois economists, which hold that the workers occupy a relatively unfavorable position in the negotiation of a labor contract. After being assured that this is the result of a scientific investigation into their actual status in negotiations over wages, they must always assume that, unless they resort to special methods, they will be defrauded and cheated.

Yet this whole doctrine of the prejudicial position of the isolated worker is basically nothing more than a *petitio principii;* it is a value judgment masquerading in the guise of an economic theory. What apparently presents itself as the result of a scientific inquiry into the position of the workers in the negotiation of a labor contract is in fact only the consequence of the arbitrary prepossession, already assumed prior to the beginning of the inquiry, that the wages which the isolated worker receives are not those due to him. This whole theory, therefore, is a kind of pseudo theory; it explains nothing at all in economic reality. Its sole purpose is to convince us of the equity or inequity of certain wage rates. To attain this end more easily, it makes a great show of invoking economic concepts and thereby clouds the judgment of those who are not sufficiently capable of critical thinking. They are thus led to accept as a scientifically established fact the assumption that the isolated worker cannot, at least today, receive the wage which by right is due to him.

In this theory of the alleged prejudicial position of the workers in the negotiation of wage contracts there are only two features that are scientifically correct and relevant. First, we have, of course, to concede to Herkner that if the worker were not basically obliged to work, if he could just as well afford to live entirely on the income from his private means, the supply of labor would also be smaller and wage rates would be correspondingly different. And, as a strictly necessary logical consequence of Herkner's thesis, the demand must be raised that, in order to enjoy true liberty and equality in the negotiation of wages, the workers should all be born with fixed incomes sufficient to maintain them for life. For the resources of even the trade unions are not sufficient to provide assistance for the workers beyond a brief period of unemployment. After this is over, when the means of the trade unions are exhausted, the workers will be in the same position as before. To discover this trivial truth there was no need of such lengthy disquisitions on the worker's difficult position in negotiations over wages. One may well wonder what kind of economy would correspond to Herkner's ideal, in which no worker would any longer be obliged to work for his living, but would work only for the love of work or just to have something to do.

And, on the other hand, the theory that the isolated worker is in a prejudicial position in the negotiation of wage contracts is correct in that, under certain conditions that cannot be more closely examined here, concerted action on the part of the workers may be able to bring about better conditions of labor. But whether the higher wages that such concerted action is eventually able to obtain are to be considered as just and natural has to remain an open question for the scientific investigator. This is purely a question of political policy and ethics and therefore one which cannot be decided by the methods of science and which really has nothing at all to do with science. That the workers can, under certain circumstances, obtain better working conditions by concerted action than they could without resorting to such methods is an ethically indifferent fact that is in itself sufficient to constitute the starting point of a scientific discussion of the phenomenon of trade unionism. The specific task of such a scientific investigation would then consist in determining under what conditions and within what limits this is possible and to what extent it really occurs.

In the voluminous literature on trade unionism produced by the socialists of the chair it is not these problems that receive the major share of attention, but rather the ethical and political evaluation of trade unionism. Naturally, the points touched upon above are also dealt with. Accounts of the actual development of the trade unions are particularly abundant. But, for all that, the characteristic mark of this whole literature is the more or less distinctly expressed idea that trade unions are something desirable, that they help the workers to acquire a position of equality vis-à-vis the employer, and that it was the trade unions in particular that first secured for the workers a just wage or at least one that might be paid in good conscience. Many economists even go so far as to consider the increases in wages that have fallen to the share of the workers in the last decades simply as the achievement of the trade unions or at least give them the principal credit for it.[6]

The theory we have described above might today be designated, with very few exceptions, as the common intellectual property of the socialists of the chair. It is often presented in their publications with the pretension of being an assured result of science. I am far from pretending to attack this doctrine as such or even trade unionism. What I maintain is merely that these matters, which today occupy such a large place in what passes for scientific discussion and which form an essential part of what is taught to students in many German universities today, for the most part do not pertain to science at all.

This whole conception of trade unionism is shot through with value judgments. As evidence of how widespread it is in present-day science and with what naive self-confidence it is and can be presented as long as each author is in a position to appeal to the authority of many others who have taught the same doctrine before him, we need only cite the following passage from Sombart, who, of course, has always sought to surpass everyone else in the assurance with which he proclaims mere opinions to be well-established truths. It may be found in his booklet on the industrial labor movement (Göschen Collection, No. 209, pp. 46-47):

Nowadays every schoolboy knows that in the struggle for the best working conditions the worker is the weaker party, for he is constrained to sell his labor sooner than the capitalist is to utilize his capital, and this situation of itself gives rise to a keener competition among workers than among capitalists. It is no doubt true that in the final analysis, in order to be able to exist at all, they are both equally dependent upon each other; just as, for instance, the proprietor of a furniture warehouse and the peddling cabinetmaker could not exist without each other. And yet, in the final transaction, the cabinetmaker is handicapped. But the worker is nothing more than just such a peddler who cannot wait. This is the well-known situation that has led to the development of trade unions, whose task it is to enable the worker to wait: *Voilà tout.*

From this evaluation of the trade unions the author proceeds a few pages further on to point out the corresponding political consequences:

There could be no greater mistake than to pronounce a sentence of death upon trade unionism because of the remote possibility of a conflict between unionism and the public interest. On the contrary, it may be stated quite categorically that the labor-union movement has a beneficial effect not only upon the workers, but upon the general welfare of the people, and that the public authorities, both legislative and administrative, could not do better than to lend their aid to the further development of this movement.

In his recently published work *Sozialpolitik*,[7] O. V. Zwiedineck-Südenhorst describes the position of the worker in the negotiation of a labor contract in just the same way as Brentano, Herkner, and Sombart. He argues as follows:

In the absence of any common agreement among the workers, or at least of a feeling of solidarity on their part and of a single will in regard to working conditions, each worker, in consequence of his being constrained to find employment in order to earn a livelihood, must accept the conditions offered by the employer unless the force of the authorities intervenes in the stipulation of these conditions.

In a similar form this idea that the worker, in *individually* negotiating a labor contract, does not obtain what is due to him is repeated in L. von Wiese's *Einführung in die Sozialpolitik*.[8] As long as the modern state unconditionally adhered to the principle of the *individual* labor contract, the working class, according to von Wiese, "could never enjoy true liberty or make any progress."

Whoever seeks for still further evidence of the prevalence in German economics of the idea that the individual negotiation of a labor contract constitutes in itself an economic injustice has only to reread the articles dealing with the right of the workers to join labor unions and with related problems that appeared in the *Archiv für soziale Gesetzgebung und Statistik*, especially during the period when it was under the management of H. Braun. There the reader will again and again come upon the familiar doctrine, which we have already sufficiently described, that the worker does not get what is rightfully due to him when the labor contract is negotiated on an individual basis. This value judgment—which, however, is not presented as such, but as the logically necessary conclusion derived from the objective facts of the case—runs like a red thread through the majority of the essays dealing with labor relations.

Thus, it is this basic idea, for example—to mention but one instance of its kind—that serves as the principal foundation for the line of reasoning pursued in Dr. Löwenfeld's frequently quoted essay on breach of contract and the right of combination in connection with the reform of German industrial legislation.[9] This opinion, which simply reflects the prevailing doctrine in German economic theory, leads Löwenfeld to treat all labor contracts as if they were negotiated under the pressure of dire need and accordingly to plead for lenient judgment, as a matter of course, in case of a breach of contract on the part of the workers. The workers thereby take revenge, in a certain measure, for the wrong previously done them by the exploitation of their economic distress.

From a consideration of the special position that the worker allegedly occupies in the negotiation of the labor contract it is usual to derive at the same time a justification of trade unionism. It seems to be utterly impossible for the socialists of the chair to deal with trade unions as an object of purely scientific contemplation, as an institution beyond good and evil, and one that can consequently be treated dispassionately, without either love or hatred. Indeed, the end aimed at by their discussions is, as a rule, that of inducing a favorable attitude toward labor unions, of which they generally play the role of advocates. That what is involved here is, in the final analysis, a *political* judgment on trade unions is quite openly conceded by Herkner, for example. In his "Concluding Remarks" on professional workers' associations he himself observes that, in regard to trade unions as well as other social groups, the decisive question cannot be whether they are wholly good or bad, but whether their good effects predominate over the bad.[10] It thus becomes crystal clear that these scientists see their task not only as that of explaining phenomena, but as that of arriving at the same time at value judgments. This explains their need of operating with the categories of "good" and "evil," which usually have no place in science.

Whether or not the theories of trade unionism discussed above are derived from correct factual assumptions is not, therefore, of decisive significance in judging them. Even if they were perfectly correct in point of fact, such theories would have no place in science.[11] Science has no need of these doctrines for its purposes. It is, after all, the aim of every science to explain phenomena in the *simplest* way (for the principle of economy should not be ignored in formulating the tasks incumbent upon science), and a science that undertakes to do so has no need for an artificial construction of this kind in order to attain to an understanding of trade unionism.

To explain the origin, the nature, and the results of workingmen's associations, it is sufficient to start from much simpler assumptions, without any admixture of value judgments such as underlie the theories we have described. In order to secure a sound basis for judging *all* existing combinations in economic life, those of the entrepreneurs as well as of the workers, one need only make two points clear. In the first place, under a system in which everyone enjoys the legal freedom to choose and practice his calling, people in the same walk of life always have the possibility of forming associations among themselves and of fixing upon a common price to be demanded for their goods and services instead of competing against and underbidding one another. Secondly, this possibility will become a reality as soon as conditions are such as to permit higher prices to be obtained by concerted action than by competitive action.

It can readily be seen that this way of approaching the question is altogether different from that involved in the theories previously discussed. The latter are not comparable to scientific hypotheses assumed for the sake of explaining facts that otherwise would remain incomprehensible. They are not merely working hypotheses, such as other sciences employ, but *dogmatic articles of faith,* designed to support an emotional attitude toward a certain state of affairs. They are of arbitrary origin and therefore unprovable, but for those who believe in them they do not need any proof. Yet at the same time an artful attempt is made to conceal their subjective character—and herein lies their great danger to science. A subjective value judgment is presented as the strictly necessary logical conclusion consequent upon an objective state of affairs. It is thus clothed with a higher authority than is properly due to it. Tricking out subjective value judgments, in the form of a proof, with a kind of objective necessity is a stratagem often practised in the arena of political combat. Indeed, it is one of the principal methods of carrying on this kind of struggle to represent the aims toward which one aspires and the principles that guide one's judgment as derived from the very nature of things.

The greatest and boldest in this field have been the champions of so-called scientific socialism, with the doctrine that forms the essential foundation of their theoretical system, viz., that labor is the sole source of value, and that the value of commodities tends to be fixed by the cost of the labor required for their production. This socialist theory of value, as well as the fanatical vehemence of the whole struggle that has been waged in its behalf, can be understood only if one sees clearly its political function. It has the practical task of proving that what ought to be, as aimed at by socialism, objectively results, of necessity, from what is. The basic idea of all socialism is, of course, to compel economic life to conform to ethical standards, or more exactly, to achieve by force of law the realization of the ethical principle that everyone's income shall strictly correspond to the extent and the social importance of the labor he has performed. The older socialists, especially those of England and France, had generally proclaimed this quite openly as their social ideal and had based it solely upon ethical considerations. The so-called scientific socialists of Germany, on the other hand, have attempted, by means of their labor theory of value, to represent the ethical principle underlying their demands as a principle operating with objective validity in economic life itself. It is clear that if this attempt were to succeed, the idea of socialism would receive support of immeasurable value. The demands of the socialists would then no longer seem to be founded solely upon the subjective desires and opinions of men, but would appear in the light of a claim springing, as it were, from the very nature of things.

What the labor theory of value was designed to perform for the propagation of socialism in general the socialists of the chair have undertaken to achieve on a smaller scale in many other fields. Their doctrines have been developed not so much in the effort to explain economic phenomena and to understand their interrelations as in the desire to give value judgments and demands for political action in the economic sphere a kind of objective foundation by representing them as being necessarily required by the nature of things as they are. When the facts themselves are thus represented as demanding not only the specific goals of action, but the moral standards by which they are to be judged, both receive an added dignity. This way of supporting one's demands virtually guarantees one against any embarrassment. One can always find real or alleged facts useful to one's purpose as long as one is prepared to do a certain amount of violence to other facts. No one is generally more resourceful in finding arguments to justify these proposals or, it must be added, at the same time less critical of their true foundation than *homo politicus*. He is quite ready to accept and support enthusiastically the most questionable and even absurd theories as long as they lend themselves to making what he wants appear as right and necessary. It would be quite unjust to charge that those who concoct pseudoscientific theories of this kind are guilty of knowingly suppressing the truth. It is not their morality, but only their capacity for critical judgment, that is at fault.

Now we are far from wishing to oppose here the demands which these pseudo theories were developed to justify and which today play such an important role in political economy, or to reject them simply because of the incorrect factual foundations upon which the arguments adduced in favor of them to a great extent rest. That problem does not concern us here at all. This is not the place to take a position either for or against demands for political action in the economic sphere. It is not, in our opinion, the task of science to render a decision one way or the other on such questions. What we ask is only that science should not be cluttered up with theories that have nothing at all scientific about them, simply for the purpose of giving greater weight to demands for political action in the economic or the social sphere; for it is precisely through such theories that true science, i.e, the knowledge of real relations, is quite often falsified. Moreover, the practice of advancing such pseudo theories may yet prove a powerful boomerang against the very proposals that they were supposed to support. Truth has a way of always coming to light in the end, and once it becomes widely known that the theories by which our social reformers today seek to demonstrate the alleged objective necessity of their demands are quite fallacious, their entire program will be in danger of being thrown overboard. This can never happen to one who supports his proposals by basing them on purely political grounds, namely, the will of the people who back them, for that is the true source from which they spring.

The conceptions of trade unionism that we have here discussed and the doctrine of the allegedly prejudicial position of the isolated workingman in negotiations over wages also belong to this class of pseudo theories. In their obvious endeavor to represent workingmen's associations and labor unions as politically and socially desirable and hence as worthy of being furthered by all possible means, such theories have in no way advanced our actual understanding of these matters. On the contrary, they have rather hampered and impeded it. They make it difficult to classify workingmen's associations correctly from an economic point of view. For there is no doubt about the fact that these coalitions, like those of the entrepreneurs (cartels, syndicates, gentlemen's agreements, etc.) must be classified essentially as attempts to form monopolies.

I purposely speak of them as "attempts," and not as monopolies proper, since not even the best organized employers' or workingmen's associations will ever succeed in forming a perfect monopoly. But between monopoly in the strict sense and absolutely free competition, there are many intermediate gradations. These originate from the coalition of people in the same walk of life who, for the purpose of obtaining better prices, agree to a more or less far-reaching limitation on the competition among them. As these coalitions differ both in cohesiveness and in the extent to which they place limits on freedom of competition, they give rise to phenomena that are very different in their economic effects. At one extreme are associations that can obtain prices that are not essentially different from those prevailing under conditions of absolutely free competition; at the opposite extreme are combinations that have succeeded in attaining a position that is virtually monopolistic and in commanding prices corresponding to it. This is as true of the cartels formed by the entrepreneurs as it is of the trade unions formed by the workingmen. In spite of all external differences, both agree perfectly in principle, not only in their ultimate aims, but also in the means chosen to attain them; and a deeper study would therefore have to group both in the same class of economic phenomena.

The fact that this is not generally done today is chiefly due to purely political considerations. Those who find employers' associations beneficial and useful are often of the opposite opinion in regard to labor unions and think that placing both on the same level would be prejudicial to the former and would tend to present them in an unfavorable light. The proponents of labor unions, on the other hand, are afraid that they will prejudice their case if they emphasize the unions' essential kinship with cartels and trusts, whose influence on prices is often unfavorably judged by public opinion. Thus, even though from quite opposite motives, the two hostile camps find themselves in full accord in wishing to keep in the background the essential similarity in the aims and the whole economic structure of the two types of associations, despite the fact that a comparative approach of this kind would considerably facilitate the correct understanding of both phenomena.

It is obviously a political consideration also, viz., the fear of arousing adverse public opinion, that frequently prevents the socialists of the chair, in their description of trade unions, from giving any prominence to their monopolistic character (in the aforementioned sense of the term "monopoly"), which is strictly essential for the correct understanding of their economic foundations, although authors of the same persuasion have not hesitated to use this term in their description of employers' associations. The word "monopoly" is in itself quite neutral, merely denoting conceptually a definite economic fact, but in *political* discussions it immediately evokes undesirable connotations. Any association of this ominous word with the fundamental principle of trade unionism could easily bring the whole labor movement into disrepute; it could even raise doubts about the correctness of the doctrine that the isolated workingman is in an especially unfavorable position in negotiations over wages. Hence the socialists of the chair use this dangerous word only with the greatest caution in describing the activities of the trade unions—if, indeed, they do not prefer to avoid the word altogether. One will find many descriptions of workingmen's associations written by socialists of the chair that are entirely devoid of any reference to the fact that all trade unions exhibit exactly the same monopolistic tendencies as all cartels do, although the results achieved by such combinations differ very widely, depending upon the particular circumstances of each case and the means employed. And yet only the concept of monopolistic tendencies provides the key to a full understanding of the position of these associations in the economic system.

However, Zwiedineck-Südenhorst, in his above-mentioned *Sozialpolitik,* constitutes a laudable exception in this respect. He calls the child by its right name and openly recognizes that the labor movement ultimately aims at the establishment of a monopoly of labor, even though the immediate target may be the raising of wage rates, a reduction in the hours of labor, or some other important goal.[12] Herkner, on the other hand, deals with this fact, which is so important economically, as if it were of secondary significance, only toward the end of his dissertation on professional workers' associations.[13] In his work the monopolistic tendencies exhibited by labor unions are represented not as their essential characteristic (for an author for whom the very word "monopoly" always has a political connotation it might even be difficult to express such an idea), but merely as a phenomenon of degeneration in an institution in itself beneficial. Fortunately, this form of degeneration appears only in rather rare cases and especially in foreign countries; the German workers (thank Heaven!) are better men. Even agreements restricting the number of apprentices to be employed in German printing establishments do not appear in his eyes as monopolistic in tendency, but rather as a mere legal struggle against an abuse. And then he continues: "One must distinguish this legal struggle from the monopolistic tendencies in the direction of the guild type of association that prevail here and there in England and America."

Apparently, in Herkner's view, one may speak of monopolistic tendencies only if the problem dealt with concerns interference in an inadmissible way with access to employment. In characterizing the practices of trade unions, on the other hand, which require that the employer hire only organized workers, he eschews the term "monopolistic" entirely and expresses himself very cautiously in regard to the significance of successful efforts in this direction on the part of the workers. After having dropped a few adversely critical remarks concerning compulsory membership in the union, he continues: "It is, moreover, quite obvious how a union can increase its power when it controls the opportunities for employment and has succeeded in applying the principle of the closed shop, whereby only members of the union are able to find a job." In regard to trade unions that, insisting upon this principle, have sought to restrict the liberty of the employer in the selection of his workers, Herkner has nothing to offer but a few words, half critical, half apologetic:

It sometimes happens that an attempt is made to interfere at least with the exercise of the employer's right to discharge workers. For instance, the demand is made that when workers are to be laid off, the first to go should be the younger men, who can more easily pull up stakes, rather than older, married men, whose productive capacity is lower.[14] Although the aims of such a policy may be commendable from a humanitarian point of view, it is so little compatible with the conditions under which private enterprise can operate as to give rise very easily to powerful reactions on the part of employers to break the so-called "tyranny of the trade unions."

As can be seen clearly from the foregoing statements—and this is the point to which, as we have said, we wish to call the reader's attention—Herkner is quite incapable of writing dispassionately about trade unionism: he must continually adopt toward it an attitude of either praise or blame. He constantly injects value judgments into his discussion of this subject, as if he found it impossible to think in other than political or ethical categories. And this holds true not only for the sections of his *Arbeiterfrage* devoted to associations of professional workers, but for the entire book from beginning to end. There is scarcely a page that does not contain explicit or implicit value judgments. The book fairly swarms with them. The conclusions arrived at by reasoning that avails itself of value judgments in this way cannot, in our opinion, be considered the result of an unbiased scientific inquiry.

But it would be doing Herkner an injustice to suggest that he is the only one who makes use of this method of constantly dealing with economic phenomena in political terms. On the contrary, there is today a whole group of German economists of whom it might more accurately be said that they are in every respect politicians, for they are not known to have made any contribution whatsoever to science. If, then, we reject Herkner's *Arbeiterfrage,* and along with it the works of many other authors, on grounds of principle, we do not do so because Herkner's value judgments tend to show a special partiality in favor of trade unionism.[15] Once again we wish most emphatically to forestall such a misunderstanding of our purpose. What we object to, as completely out of place in a scientific work, is *every* variety of value judgment concerning trade unions, whether predominantly favorable, like Herkner's, or condemnatory, like that of Alexander Tille, which we have elsewhere rejected. In presuming to judge trade unions in terms of the moral categories of "good" and "bad," science transgresses its own limits and enters the domain of politics. As we have demonstrated, this constitutes a danger to science itself. It makes insight into the true nature of trade unionism more difficult and gives rise to all kinds of theories that have no claim to a place in science, since their purpose is not to explain phenomena, but to justify definite value judgments about them.

A great number of pseudo theories of this kind, however, are to be found in present-day political economy. They constitute no small part of the subject matter of the lectures that, under the heading of economic theory, are delivered today at the German universities. These pseudo theories have proliferated so luxuriantly in the economic doctrines of the socialists of the chair as to have quite grown over and choked off the real theory. In spite of their professed hostility to theoretical inquiry, in the sense of classical economics—the reasons for which will be discussed later —the socialists of the chair have had no qualms whatsoever about incorporating into science theories of the kind we have mentioned. Indeed, so fertile have they themselves proved to be in developing such theories that all those misgivings about the assumption of an abstract *homo oeconomicus* that played such an important role in their attacks on classical economic theory have quite disappeared, and they no longer shrink from the most audacious theoretical constructions and assumptions.

So much for the political propaganda that figures so prominently in the treatment of economics in Germany today! To show that the economic doctrine of the socialists of the chair is shot through with value judgments we have chosen as our principal example their way of dealing with the topic of trade unionism. However, we wish to emphasize that many specialists in so-called applied economics have considered this same topic in connection with the question of the *right* of the workers to organize into unions. If we enter into this question here at all, it is only because these value judgments on the labor-union movement are in the last analysis designed to criticize the way in which income is distributed in the present economic system, that is, to make it appear, at least in the case of the worker who enters into wage negotiations on an individual basis, as unjust and in need of some correction, to be brought about, of course, as a matter of distributive justice, by the intervention of the trade unions.

As a consequence of this now generally adopted way of approaching such questions, the expressions "too much" and "too little," which always imply a value judgment, are among the most frequently used in present-day German economics. Quite pertinent in this connection is the definition of economics that a humorous periodical published in Southern Germany recently put into the mouth of a Prussian *Referendar:* * "Political economy? What does that mean? Why, of course! It's when one measures the dimensions of the workers' apartments and then says that they're too small!" Although this definition does not, to be sure, state the essence of political economy itself, it certainly does correctly grasp and express an essential tendency in the approach to economics prevailing in Germany at the present time.

And it is this tendency too that explains the marked preference exhibited in that country today for scientific monographs, especially on such subjects as the condition of the working class, the current housing situation, etc. The authors of such dissertations are, of course, not loath to avail themselves of the opportunity that they provide for making use of such expressions as "not enough" and "too much," as well as "good" and "bad." In the description of factual conditions it is customary to intersperse judgments on them from the point of view of some ideal. Such value judgments play an important role even in some of the studies sponsored by the Verein für Sozialpolitik.

Under these circumstances the question must be raised: Can such a critique of actual conditions really be the task of science? Is it intrinsically competent to perform a task of this kind? And what consequence must such an extension of its scope have for science itself? **

NOTES

1. Translated into German by C. Hugo (Stuttgart, 1898). According to Schmoller, this book marks the beginning of the scientific treatment of the problem of trade unionism. But this is passing a rather harsh judgment on those economists who, like Brentano among others, had already published, prior to the Webbs, greater works on the same subject. As

* A *Referendar* in Germany is a junior barrister who, after having passed his first state examination, is preparing to qualify for the post of *Assessor,* i.e., the position of an assistant judge. [Translator's note.]

** The questions raised at the end of this section, although already touched upon incidentally in it, were more fully considered in the following chapter of Pohle's book. [Translator's note.]

will be seen from the analysis presented in the text, the Webbs' treatment of trade unionism, though it doubtless furthered our understanding
of its nature considerably, still gives rise to grave misgivings from the
scientific point of view.

2. *Industrial Democracy* (Longmans, Green and Co., 1897), II, 674.

3. In comparison with many of the theories current in German economics,
which would simply lay the blame on the entrepreneur for the pressure
that weighs upon the worker, the Webbs' interpretation, it must be
admitted, represents a great progress, since they correctly point to the
consumers as the ultimate source of this pressure. At least the Webbs see
as far as the last link in the chain, even though they are apparently
unaware that it is a closed chain.

4. Quoted from the fifth edition, pp. 6 ff. However, it is not the intent
of this quotation to make Herkner appear as the first to propound this
theory. That honor is rather due to Brentano, and that is why we find
the doctrine repeated by nearly all his disciples. On the other hand, it
has to be expressly emphasized that Schmoller does not adhere to it and
proceeds in general with great caution in his judgment of trade unions,
which, according to him, are in urgent need of legal regulation. Schmoller even attempts to give the theory of Brentano and his school as to
the effects of the individually negotiated labor contract an interpretation
that would blunt its edge considerably. He states: "In saying that the
formally (i.e., legally) free contract is made actually free only by the
trade unions, Brentano means that this contract becomes more nearly
perfect, more just, more conducive to the improvement of the conditions
of the working class." (See Schmoller's *Grundriss*, Part 2, p. 272.) If this
were indeed all that Brentano's doctrine meant to assert in regard to
labor relations in the present economic system, if it were frankly and
honestly presented as nothing more than a demand made in the interests
of the working class, then, of course, all the venom would have been
removed from its sting, and it would have to be judged quite differently.
Unfortunately, however, this novel interpretation of the meaning of the
theory quoted above is hardly consonant with the wording used by the
majority of Brentano's followers.

5. The case of a price formed under a monopolistic influence has been
omitted in both instances in order to avoid complicating the problem
unnecessarily.

6. Zwiedineck-Südenhorst, for example, in his *Sozialpolitik* (Leipzig, 1911),
p. 171, also adheres to this opinion, although just the history of the
changes that have taken place in the wages of German miners during the
last generation should have been enough to have taught him differently.

7. Leipzig: B. G. Teubner, 1911, p. 177.

8. Leipzig: G. A. Gloeckner, 1910, p. 153.

9. Equally representative of the type of theories that constitute apologetics
rather than science is the doctrine of labor relations there criticized by
Löwenfeld, by which Loening seeks to justify the imposition of criminal
sanctions for breach of contract on the part of the workers. *Ibid.*, Vol.
III, pp. 383 ff.

10. *Ibid.,* p. 184.
11. It is for this reason that we have here too abstained from making a complete criticism of these theories in so far as they have any general claim to being considered from a scientific point of view, i.e., in regard to the correctness of the factual assumptions from which they start. A complete criticism would above all still have to examine the assertion that constitutes merely the final link in the chain of reasoning by which the socialists of the chair prove that the isolated worker suffers a handicap in bargaining with his employers over wages, namely, the doctrine that there is a continual oversupply of labor in the market, or, in other words, that the normal state of the economy is such that more workers seek employment than are really needed. However, this is not the place to enter further into a discussion of the manner in which that doctrine misrepresents facts that are in themselves correctly observed.
12. Pages 178-179.
13. In the section entitled "Access to Employment in the Industry and Compulsory Membership in the Union."
14. Even the ablest champion of trade unionism could surely not have chosen a better example of the unions' infringement on the rights of the employer.
15. Herkner's judgment as a whole in this respect is without any doubt predominantly favorable, even though he does not fail to emphasize the grave dangers of all kinds, economic and political, that are to be apprehended from the further development of associations of professional workers. Such concessions and qualifications on his part merely serve to throw into sharper relief the decisive judgment of approval that follows and to give the whole an appearance of objectivity. Herkner himself sums up his opinion with the statement that trade unions in important respects fulfill a great cultural mission, and he even has a word of apology for those aspects of trade unionism that he characterized as unsatisfactory. Indeed, when discussing the trade unions, he obeys, on the whole, the rule prescribed by the catechism in reference to the Eighth Commandment, that one should speak only well of them and place the best construction on everything. After referring to the serious dangers to be apprehended from the exercise of the rights that have been granted to trade unions, he immediately continues: "It is by no means surprising that mistakes of various kinds should have been made by organizations composed of the lowest and least educated classes, whose power up to now has not been sufficient to enable them to learn the art of using it wisely. One will be less ready to condemn labor unions when one considers that employers' associations (cartels, trusts, etc.) as well as special organizations set up to safeguard their interests have also frequently been the objects of highly justified criticism."

4

The Nationalization of Credit*

Ludwig von Mises

Arthur Travers-Borgstroem, a Finnish author, published a book entitled *Mutualism,* of which a German translation appeared in 1923. It deals with problems of social reform and culminates in the idea of the nationalization of credit. With the immediate object of organizing a prize competition for the best work on this subject, he had an endowment fund established under his name in 1917 at Berne. The jury, composed of professors (Dr. Diehl, Dr. Weyermann, Dr. Milhaud, Dr. Reichesberg), bankers (Dr. Milliet, Dr. Somary, H. Kurz) and others, awarded the prize to a paper submitted by Dr. Robert Deumer, Director at the Berlin Reichsbank. His essay has been published in book form by the Mutualist Association in Finland.[1]

This history of the book's origin explains why only the problem of how, and not whether, credit is to be nationalized constitutes the author's theme. Dr. Deumer submitted to the committee a proposal, elaborated down to unessential details, envisaging the nationalization of all enterprises and concerns that carry on credit and banking transactions in Germany and the establishment of a government credit monopoly. However, this project does not concern us here. It certainly has no prospect of being realized in the visible future, and if anything of this kind ever should be planned,

* "Verstaatlichung des Kredits," *Zeitschrift für Nationalökonomie,* I (Vienna, 1929), 430-439.

conditions by then will doubtless have changed to such an extent as to render Deumer's proposals quite inappropriate. It would therefore be pointless to enter into a discussion of such details as §10, line 1, of his proposed "Draft of a Statute for the Nationalization of Credit and Banks," which runs as follows: "Whoever, after the nationalization of credit has been put into effect, carries on any banking or credit transactions whatsoever shall be subject to a fine not exceeding ten million gold marks or to imprisonment for not more than five years, or both." [2]

The only features of Deumer's work that are of general interest are the reasons he adduces in favor of the nationalization of credit and his ideas on the possibility of carrying out the proposed reforms without losing any of the advantages that "commercial" enterprises have over "bureaucratic" management. In dealing with these problems, Deumer merely reiterates opinions that can be said to be shared, and perhaps even unquestioningly accepted as correct, by the great majority of people today. If one concurs with the ideas of Deumer, Travers-Borgstroem, and the mutualists, one must consider the nationalization of credit and every other measure leading to socialism not only as desirable and practicable, but as urgently necessary.

General approval has greeted all criticism of the free enterprise economy based upon private ownership of the means of production, such as has been so effectively presented in Germany by the socialists of the chair, in France by the solidarists, in England by the Fabians, and in the United States by the Institutionalists. This explains the favorable reception which public opinion has accorded all proposals that tend to restrict the sphere in which private ownership and the spirit of enterprise can have free play. The reason why more of these proposals have not so far been put into effect is certainly not to be sought in the fact that the literature on economic policy and the political parties stand opposed to them. This is by no means the case. It is rather that the nationalization and municipalization of enterprises and all the etatist and interventionist encroachments upon economic freedom have brought about, instead of the anticipated favorable consequences, only financial failures and grave disturbances in production and marketing. Ideology, however, has so far taken no notice of these practical failures of socialism and interventionism. Now, as ever, it insists on holding public management in high esteem and private enterprise in low esteem. Now, as ever, the belief prevails that only malevolence, selfishness, and ignorance can oppose such projects for reform, while any unprejudiced person must thoroughly approve of them.

Under such circumstances an analysis of the fundamental ideas underlying Dr. Deumer's book seems appropriate.

1. *Private Interest vs. Public Interest*

Actually, says Deumer, banks serve private interests; they serve the public interest only in so far as the latter is not opposed to the former. The banks finance, not those enterprises which seem the most suitable from the point of view of the national economy, but those which promise to yield the highest profit. Thus, for instance, they extend credit to "a brandy distillery or some other manufacturing enterprise superfluous in the framework of the national economy." But, in doing so, the banks "act, from the point of view of the general economy, not only in a useless, but even in a detrimental way." For

banks, by fostering enterprises whose products are not in necessary demand, actually stimulate superfluous consumption and thereby further weaken the people's purchasing power for goods more important for their cultural and rational needs. Besides, by granting these credits, banks deprive economically necessary enterprises of capital, a procedure that, even if it did not result in restricting production, may in any case contribute to increasing the price they have to pay for credit and thereby the costs of production of a commodity that is important for the community.[3]

In reasoning thus, Deumer fails to recognize that in the capitalist economy capital and labor are distributed among the different branches of production in such a way that everywhere, without prejudice to the difference in the risk premium, equal returns on capital are obtained and the same wage paid to equal kinds of labor. One makes neither higher nor lower profits by the production of "superfluous" goods than by that of "useful" goods. The employment of capital and labor by the different branches of production is ultimately determined by the behavior of the consumers in the market. If an increase in the demand for an article brings about an increase in prices and profits, new enterprises will be established and the already existing ones enlarged. It is with the consumers, therefore, that the decision rests whether this or that branch of production should be provided with more capital. If they want more beer, more beer will be brewed; if they want to attend more performances of classical drama, the theaters will present more of these and fewer frivolous vaudeville shows, farces, and operettas. Not the stage managers, but the taste of the public is responsible for the fact that "The Merry Widow" has been produced far more frequently than Goethe's "Tasso."

Deumer's taste deviates from that of the masses. He finds that men would do better to distribute their expenditures in a different way. He is not alone in this opinion. But, from his point of view, which is at variance with that of the masses, Deumer draws the conclusion that in order to give a different direction to consumption, a socialist planned economy has to be established by the nationalization of credit. We cannot agree with Deumer on this point.

A socialist economy, guided according to a uniform plan by a central authority, may be conceived of either as democratic or as dictatorial. If it is democratic, i.e., if the central authority depends on the will of the people as evidenced by ballots and elections, the procedure will not differ from that of the capitalist economy: it will produce and place at the disposal of the consumers just what the masses like—alcoholic beverages; tobacco; trash in literature, on the stage, and in the cinema; and fashionable gewgaws of all kinds. In the capitalist economy, however, the varieties of taste of small groups are also taken into account: enterprises also produce goods that are demanded, not by all the consumers, but only by some of them. The democratically controlled planned economy, since its direction depends on the *majority* of the people, will not have to pay heed to such special desires on the part of the minority. It will have to accommodate itself exclusively to the tastes of the masses.

But even if the planned economy is directed by a dictator, who, without considering the wishes of the people, does as he himself sees fit and proceeds to clothe, feed, and house them as he thinks best, we still do not have any guarantee that what "we" think right will be carried out. The critics of the capitalist order of society are always inclined to believe that in the socialist community they dream of only what they themselves approve will be put into effect. Even though they may not go so far as to envision themselves as future dictators, nevertheless they at least hope that the dictator will not do anything without first consulting them. In this way they arrive at the customary antithesis between profitability and productivity. Economic activities that commend themselves to their own necessarily subjective judgment they call "productive," and they reject the capitalist order of society, where conditions are different in that considerations of profit require taking into account the wishes of the consumers, the real masters of the market and production. These critics forget that a dictator may proceed in a way that is totally different from the one they would have him take. They forget, too, that there is no guarantee that he will actually direct his efforts toward the "best" ends or that, even if he were to do so, he would be able to find the most appropriate means of achieving them.

A still more serious question is whether a dictatorship by the "best" or by a group of the "best" could maintain itself against the will of the masses. Would the people, in the long run, put up with an economic dictatorship that did not give them what they themselves wanted to use and consume, but only what the rulers thought useful? And will not the masses ultimately succeed in inducing the producers to take their wishes and their tastes into consideration, so that the very situation that the reformers wanted to eliminate will finally recur?

Many of us will agree with Dr. Deumer's subjective judgment that our fellow citizens are often msiguided in their habits of consumption. Whoever is of this opinion should try to convince his fellow citizens of the error of their ways. One may enlighten them concerning the detrimental influence of an excessive consumption of alcohol and nicotine, the cheap sentimentality of the cinema, and many other things. If one wishes to promote the diffusion of good literature, one would be well advised to follow the example of Bible societies, which, at a substantial sacrifice, sell their Bibles at low prices and display them in restaurants and similar places. But, if all this is judged to be insufficient, the last expedient that remains—and one should beware of cherishing illusions on this point—is the forcible imposition of our own will on our fellow citizens. The orientation of production according to profit means, in reality, its orientation in accordance with the wishes of the consumers, on whose demand depend the prices of commodities and therewith also the returns on capital and enterprise. On the other hand, an orientation according to the "productivity of the national economy" would mean, if it deviates from the wishes of the consumers, an orientation prompted by a will antagonistic to theirs: the authoritative order of a dictator or of a board of dictators.

There is no doubt that in the capitalist order of society a part of the national income is absorbed in the consumption of luxury goods by the rich. But even aside from the fact that this part, owing to its relative insignificance, cannot bring about any really important displacement of production, the luxury consumption of the well-to-do plays a dynamic role that makes it one of the most powerful propulsive forces of economic progress. Every innovation enters into life as the "luxury" of a small number of wealthy individuals, but once industry and the consumers have learned to adopt new ways, it becomes one of the obvious "necessities" of the masses. Think, for instance, of our clothing, the lighting equipment and bathroom fixtures in our apartments, the automobile, and tourism. Economic history shows how yesterday's luxury has become today's necessity. Many of the goods that in capitalistically backward countries are considered as luxuries become in capitalistically developed countries the common property of the masses. In Vienna the possession of an automobile is regarded as a luxury—and not only in the eyes of the tax collector; in the United States there is a car to every four or five inhabitants.

Critics of the capitalist social order, if they plan to improve the conditions of the masses, should hesitate to make any reference to luxury consumption, since so far no one has succeeded in invalidating the assertions of theorists and the experiences of practical men that only capitalist management warrants the highest conceivable productivity. If, however, in the planned economy they are aiming at, less will be produced than under capitalism, then naturally they will not succeed in providing the masses with a better way of life than they enjoy today.

2. *Should Nationalized Banks Be Managed Commercially or Bureaucratically?*

There is a general opinion that the reduced efficiency of public management is to be ascribed to its bureaucratic method of conducting its affairs. In order to make national, municipal, and other publicly operated enterprises as successful as private enterprises, they should, we are told, be organized and directed according to commercial principles. For many decades now strenuous efforts have been made to increase their productivity by "commercializing" the management of their business. With the extension of socialism and the consequent growth in the activity of the state and the municipalities, this problem has gained in importance, but we have not yet come even a single step nearer to its solution.

Deumer too considers it indispensable that "the banking monopoly of the state be administered according to *commercial* principles" and submits a series of proposals for attaining this end.[4] All these proposals differ scarcely in any way from those that have recently been suggested and, as far as possible, put into effect with this object in view, viz., schools and examinations, the promotion of the "fittest," sufficient payment to employees, and opportunities for the leading officials to share in the profits. However, Deumer is as far from seeing the essence of the problem as are all the others who are struggling to find some way of reforming and rendering productive the inevitably unproductive system of public management.

The "commercial" element is by no means to be conceived as a form of organization that one could simply graft on to the government's administration in order thereby to neutralize its bureaucratic features, as Deumer, following the prevailing opinion in this respect, seems to believe. What is usually designated the "commercial" element in the conduct of affairs is the very essence of the pursuit on the part of private enterprise of nothing else than the maximum possible profit, and what is usually designated the "bureaucratic" element is the essence of the pursuit on the part of public management of ends determined by considerations of the "national economic interest." There is no possibility whatsoever of "commercializing" the government administration of business, not even by superimposing upon it as many as possible of the incidental and external features of private enterprise.

The entrepreneur operates on his own responsibility. He suffers losses if he does not succeed in producing economically, i.e., at the lowest cost in expenditure of capital and labor, what the consumers feel they need most urgently. The final result of such losses will be that his wealth, and with it his power to decide upon the utilization of the means of production, will pass into the hands of more efficient men. In the capitalist order of society there prevails a tendency to transfer control of the means of production to those who have the talent to use them in the most appropriate way for the satisfaction of the consumers' wants. Public management, however, is in the hands of men who are not themselves held responsible for its resulting success or failure.

But, it is said, the same holds true of the leading officials of big private concerns. It is therefore to be assumed that these too must be managed as "bureaucratically" as the nationally and municipally operated enterprises. However, to argue in this way is to overlook the fundamental difference that exists between public and private management.

In private, profit-seeking enterprise every department and every branch is controlled by bookkeeping and cost accounting, which rest upon the same principles. Unprofitable departments and branches have to be reorganized or closed. Employees and directors who do not give practical proof that they meet the requirements demanded by the nature of their jobs—i.e., those who are unable to carry out, with the expected success, the duties with which they have been entrusted—have to be dismissed. In the final analysis the whole business is controlled by accounting, which reckons everything dispassionately in dollars and cents. What is decisive is monetary calculation and nothing else. Every undertaking of any kind whatsoever aims at the highest attainable profit. The only order given by the owners (i.e., in the case of corporations, by the shareholders) to the managers of the enterprises and transmitted in turn by them to their assistants is: Make a profit!

But the situation is altogether different in the bureaus and boards that are charged with the sovereign administration of the state. In regard to the tasks whose fulfillment is entrusted to courts and other authorities there is no criterion of quantitative measurement such as exists for the economy oriented toward the prices of the market. For this reason the supreme administration of state business cannot define and circumscribe the tasks of subordinate officials in the same simple way as the entrepreneur can in dealing with his functionaries. In order to maintain uniformity of administration and to prevent the power to make decisions from being delegated by the top authority to the executive offices of lowest instance, what the latter are and are not to do has to be regulated in the most minute detail by official instructions and directions of all kinds that provide for every conceivable contingency. It then becomes the duty of each official concerned to follow these instructions. For the bureaucrat, what matters ultimately is not so much success or failure in the carrying out of his assigned task as whether or not he is formally justified in his conduct by the regulations. This insistence on procedure in due conformity with official regulations, particularly in everything that concerns the hiring, management, and promotion of personnel, is what we call bureaucratism. Bureaucratism does not originate from shortcomings and defects in the organization nor from any insufficiency on the part of the officeholders; it is the essence of any management that does not take profit into account.

When the state and the municipalities expand their functions beyond the sphere of police and judicial action, bureaucratism becomes a fundamental problem of social organization. Even if a publicly managed enterprise is conducted exclusively on a profit basis, it cannot but be administered bureaucratically. An attempt has been made to eliminate bureaucratism by having the managers share in the profits. But since they could never bear any losses that might be incurred, such a method all too easily encouraged reckless speculation; and if, in order to prevent this, one requires the more important decisions to be ratified by resolutions on the part of certain superior authorities, boards, and advisory councils and to be subject to the judgment of specialists and experts, one simply succeeds thereby in extending even further the whole bureaucratic system of procedural formalities.

Usually, however, one demands of publicly operated enterprises that they should not aim at profit alone. Indeed, it is precisely for this reason that it is deemed advisable to place them under public management. Deumer too expects the nationalized banks to orient themselves more to the point of view of the public welfare than of private gain: accordingly, they should invest their funds, not where the highest profit might be obtained, but, in disregard of such considerations, where it would be desirable in the national interest.[5]

We have no intention of entering further into the other consequences of such a credit policy (e.g., the continued support of uneconomically operated plants); we are concerned only with its effects upon the management of nationalized enterprises. If the national board of credit or any of its branches reports a deficit at the end of the year, it will be in a position to say: "From the point of view of profitability, which takes into consideration private interests alone, we admit that we have not been very successful in our operations. But it should be noted that the decrease in productivity that commercial accounting discloses is counterbalanced by services we have rendered to the national economy that cannot, to be sure, be made visible in the account books: what we have done, for example, in the interest of preserving small or medium-sized business and for improving the material conditions of the 'loyal' elements of the population, etc., cannot be expressed in terms of money." Under such circumstances calculation in terms of profits and losses no longer has any importance for the enterprise; and if the operations of the supreme board and of the heads of departments are really to be kept under control, one must have recourse to the old methods of bureaucratism: the subjection of business management to strict procedural regulations and the filling of all positions with persons prepared to follow them.

Indeed, try as we may, we shall not succeed in finding any way of organizing publicly managed enterprises that could prevent them from becoming enmeshed in bureaucratic red tape. It will not do for us to seek to allay our qualms on this point with the comforting assurance that in the last few decades many large corporations have also been "bureaucratized." This bureaucratization is not, as is erroneously maintained, a consequence of their size. Even the biggest concern, so long as it is operated exclusively on a profit basis, is proof against all the dangers of bureaucratism. Only if considerations other than those of profit-seeking are forced upon it will it lose the essential properties of capitalist enterprise. It is the etatist and interventionist policy prevailing today that has compelled big companies to bureaucratize themselves to an ever-increasing extent. For example, they have been forced to place at their head, instead of efficient businessmen, socialites with good connections in leading circles; they have been obliged to enter into unprofitable business transactions in order to please influential politicians and parties or the government; they have been required to continue operations in businesses that they preferred to liquidate and to take over companies and plants for which there was no need. The mixing of politics with business is detrimental not only, as is commonly observed, to politics, but still more so to business. The thousands of factors of all kinds, alien to the enterprise, that many big companies nowadays have to take into consideration have implanted in them the seed of bureaucratism. But this by no means justifies proposals that, by nationalizing banks, would completely bureaucratize and regulate the whole of production. What would be the situation of the present German economy if credit had been nationalized in 1890, or even in 1860? Are we aware of the possibilities for further development that we would cut off if we nationalized it today?

3. *The Danger of the Overexpansion and Immobilization of Credit*

What has been said so far refers to any attempt to transfer enterprises from the hands of the entrepreneurs into those of the state, and particularly to the nationalization of banks, which would be scarcely distinguishable in its effect from full socialization. However, the nationalization of credit gives rise to special problems that should not be allowed to pass unnoticed.

Deumer endeavors to prove that the credit monopoly enjoyed by the state could not be abused for fiscal purposes. But the dangers to be apprehended from the nationalization of credit are not to be sought in this area; they concern, rather, the problem of the formation of the purchasing power of money.

It is generally acknowledged today that bank deposits subject to check are equivalent to banknotes in their effect upon the purchasing power of money. Deumer, moreover, specifically suggests that the national bank issue "guaranteed treasury certificates, or checks for clearing purposes only," which would never be redeemed in cash.[6] This means, therefore, that it would be possible for the national bank to indulge in inflation.

Public opinion always clamors for "easy money," i.e., low interest rates. However, in opposition to this demand, the cornerstone of the policy of the central bank consists in concern for its own solvency and the consequent maintenance of the parity price of the domestic currency against foreign money and gold. The national bank, once exempted from the obligation to redeem in cash its certificates and checks for clearance purposes only, will be free to expand its credit in accordance with the wishes of the politicians. It will be too weak to hold back the tide of credit seekers. Indeed, the nationalization of credit is proposed precisely for this purpose: to meet, as Deumer says,

the complaints of the smaller industrial enterprises and of many commercial firms that only under great difficulties and at much sacrifice do they succeed in obtaining credits at all, and that these are such as to prove scarcely sufficient to cover their most urgent requirements.[7]

Even a few years ago it would still have been necessary to set forth at some length the consequences of an excessive expansion of credit. Today one may spare oneself the pains. Thanks to the work of enlightenment carried on by several economists and to the fact that American and English experiences and doctrines are no longer unknown even to the Germans, the relationship between the expansion of credit and a rise in the prices of commodities and foreign exchange has nowadays become a matter of common knowledge. It would therefore be supererogatory to discuss these problems in detail.

Summation

It is clearly evident from Deumer's book that etatism, socialism, and interventionism have run their course. Deumer is unable to advance in favor of his proposals anything but the old arguments, already refuted a hundred times, of the socialists of the chair and the Marxists. He ignores the criticism that has been leveled against these arguments. Nor does he take into consideration the problems that recent experiences with socialism have made manifest. He still takes his stand on an ideology that, hailing every act of nationalization as one step further along the road to utopia, has been shaken to its very foundations in recent years.

Deumer's book, therefore, will not have any political consequences. For the sake of the author, who has displayed the utmost diligence, acumen, and technical knowledge in the presentation of his ideas, one may regard such a negative prospect as a misfortune, but in the interest of healthy progress in the economic recovery of Germany, this can only be a cause of gratification.

NOTES

1. *Die Verstaatlichung des Kredits (Mutualisierung des Kredits).* Gekronte Preisschrift der Travers-Borstroem-Stiftung in Bern. Berlin. 8°, xii + 371. Duncker & Humblot, Munich and Leipzig, 1926.
2. P. 335.
3. P. 86.
4. P. 210.
5. P. 184.
6. Pp. 152 ff.
7. P. 184.

5

The Place of Mathematical
Reasoning in Economics *

PAUL PAINLEVÉ

It is the natural course of development of the sciences to pass from a qualitative and descriptive state to a quantitative and causal state. Astronomy, for example, consisted at first of nothing more than picturesque and rather vague remarks on the aspects of the constellations and on the position, form, and color of the sun, the moon, and the planets. But as soon as the first precise instruments of observation had been introduced and the relative movements of the stars exactly plotted, astronomy became a *quantitative* science (i.e., one capable of measuring and expressing in numbers the phenomena that it studied), although still remaining purely *descriptive*. Only later did it concern itself with the *causes* of the precise phenomena that it was able to observe; and once it had discovered their causal order, astronomy became capable of predicting the future of the heavens. In this way the astronomy of position developed, that is, that branch of astronomy which is concerned only with the position of the stars, independently of their internal physical transformations, and which is the perfect type of quantitative and causal science.

The method of this science consists in considering each element of the different heavenly bodies, summing up the attractions that

* *Préface* to *La théorie de l'économie politique* (Paris: V. Giard and E. Brière, 1909), the French translation by H.-E. Barrault and Maurice Alfassa of the third edition of *The Theory of Political Economy* by William Stanley Jevons.

any two of these elements exert upon each other, and thus calculating in the utmost detail the positions that the sun, the planets, and their satellites will occupy in one hundred years, two hundred years, etc.

But the other sciences are far from having attained such a state of perfection. Physics, which has come closest to it, is still half qualitative, and chemistry more than half. Nevertheless, in these two sciences there are very important kinds of phenomena of a highly complex nature that, precisely because of their complexity, admit of the development of a quantitative discipline, imperfect, to be sure, yet singularly fruitful. These result from a colossal multiplicity of complicated and confused phenomena on a small scale, of which our senses perceive only their combined effects. Since the capricious irregularities of these elementary phenomena in some sort cancel one another out, we can exactly calculate their total result without entering into details. A science of this kind, which can be called *statistical,* is theoretically less perfect than astronomy, but because it is simpler, it can be more important for practical purposes. Ignoring phenomena that do not affect us, it provides us with precise and easily acquired information about those which are of interest to us. The kinetic theory of gases is an example of a statistical science. This form of quantitative science plays an essential role in all the recent developments in physics.

In other cases the phenomena do not lend themselves to this kind of statistical integration, but science nevertheless imposes upon them certain precise laws, by no means sufficient to determine them, but which at least they must always obey. Such laws trace out a sort of rigid channel for the undulating flow of those phenomena which have not yet been reduced to quantitative rule. The principle of the conservation of energy and that of Carnot-Clausius are types of these laws.

Consider, for example, a steam engine that, through a series of intermediate connections, operates some implement. However well the wheels of the engine may be lubricated and its connecting parts arranged, the motive power of the steam always exceeds the power transmitted to the implement it operates, and the excess energy so dissipated is transformed into a proportionate quantity of heat, which causes the machine's lubricants to melt. This is what we learn from the "inequality" principle of Carnot-Clausius and the principle of the conservation of energy. No doubt information of this kind is insufficient to enable us to understand exactly all that is going on in the machine, but it is of importance nevertheless. If the power required by any implement exceeds that which the steam is able to produce, we at least know without further discussion that the machine cannot work.

We may thus distinguish three different types of quantitative sciences: perfect, statistical, and imperfect. In the latter cases the phenomena are subject to numerical laws, but are not determined by them. These considerations are not useless, for they help us to get some idea of what political economy can expect from quantitative reasoning or, if one prefers, from mathematics.

Let us imagine a brain so comprehensive and so well informed as to know precisely the actual economic state of the entire world: its products, means of transportation, and commercial organization. Let us further assume that this brain is equally conversant with the psychological state of each individual and with the exact laws of interaction between each individual and his environment. Now if such a brain were to possess, in addition, an unlimited power of deduction, it would be able to calculate the economic phenomena that will take place over the entire world tomorrow, the day after tomorrow, etc. A science so constituted would be as perfect as astronomy. But it is hardly necessary to add that the hypothesis that we have assumed is fantastic. Is it not evident that political economy will always be impotent when confronted with phenomena that require it to take into account the capricious behavior of each individual human being? The only quantitative form that economics could possibly assume is the statistical form. In other words, economics can deal only with phenomena in the mass, upon which individual deviations have no influence, whether because they do not occur at all or because their mutual contrarieties cancel one another out.

But even in statistical form a quantitative science could base its reasoning only on measurable, well-defined magnitudes. Consider, for example, the concept of length. Once we have accepted the meter as our standard, we are able to measure the length of a ruler or the dimensions of an object at any given moment without knowing anything else but the object in question and the standard of length. Let us now assume an analogous concept in economics: that of value; and let us adopt as the unit of value, the value of a gram of pure gold. Can we, on the basis of a mere examination of an object, for instance, a lot of fish, indicate its value at any given moment? Or, more precisely, is there, like the standard of length, a generally recognized and accepted definition of value such that the value of an object at any given moment can be immediately measured in the same way as its dimensions, its weight, etc., as soon as we know the object, the unit of value, and nothing else?

It is easy to understand that such a definition cannot exist. Imagine an island whose population lives exclusively on fish and where the entire catch is in the hands of but two fishermen. Let us further suppose that these fish have to be consumed within twenty-four hours, that the combined haul of both fishermen is just sufficient to nourish the island today, and that tomorrow it will be twice as plentiful. Will the value of two identical lots of fish be the same today and tomorrow, or will it be half as much tomorrow as it is today? Everything depends upon the agreement between the two fishermen. If they form a cartel, they are the masters of the market, at least within the limits of the population's ability to go without fish: they can maintain a fixed price, independent of the vicissitudes of the catch; or they can agree to throw the surplus fish overboard. If, on the contrary, they enter into a competitive struggle with each other, then tomorrow, when each seeks to underbid the other in selling his fish, the price of fish will fall almost to nothing.

Of course, it would not be at all absurd to define the value of different objects once and for all, and we can imagine an infinite number of such definitions. But each of these definitions would be of purely academic interest, without any relation to value in the common acceptation of that word and hence without application to reality.

Very well, it may be said, let us give up the idea of a theoreti-

cal definition of value that would have the same significance as
that of length. This will still not make it impossible to determine
correctly the price of a commodity in a given market at a given
hour. Expressing as it does an essentially transitory and local
evaluation, the price will vary according to the circumstances of
time and place, and it is these variations that we shall be able to
study.

But the difficulty is merely postponed. How are we to evaluate
the different elements that have an influence upon the formation
of a price? I open Jevons' treatise to the chapter on exchange.
Jevons considers two groups of merchants, A and B, of whom the
first possesses the quantity a of wheat, and the second the quantity
b of beef. These two groups trade with each other. Jevons represents by Φ_1 (a) and Ψ_1 (y) the utility which the quantity a of
wheat and the quantity y of beef have for A, and by Φ_2 (x) and
Ψ_2 (b) the utility which the quantity x of wheat and the quantity
b of beef have for B. He shows that exchange between A and B
comes to a standstill, or, in other words, that economic equilibrium is established, when the conditions of the following double
equation are fulfilled:

$$\frac{\phi_1(a-x)}{\psi_1(y)} = \frac{y}{x} = \frac{\phi_2(x)}{\psi_2(b-y)}$$

But how shall we define *quantitatively* the *utility* that such
commodities have for A and for B? It is easy to conceive of a great
many cases in which the utility of a commodity will not depend
only upon its quantity.[1] And even if it did, we must realize that
the utility of a given commodity, as Jevons conceives it, decreases
for A whenever there is an increase in the quantity a of that commodity already possessed by A. But if we want to define this
utility by a function like φ (a), our own good judgment leaves us
the choice among an infinite number of functions, all subject to
but one restriction, namely, that of decreasing with a. Shall we
say that from all these functions we shall choose the one that
results from the statistics of the market? But in that case we are

no longer dealing with a theory, but merely with a factual report in the guise of a theory.

The same observations apply to most of the other economic concepts (labor, etc.) which are introduced in quantitative form into Jevons' equations. As for the *dimensions* of these so-called magnitudes, it is premature to speak of them. In physics a magnitude has defined dimensions only if the standard for measuring it is itself well defined; in other words, once the fundamental units have been chosen upon which the magnitude depends, the number of such units measuring it is bound to be well determined. If one changes the fundamental unit in a certain relation (for instance, if one replaces the meter by the centimeter, or the second by the hour), the numbers measuring the quantity in question and all the quantities of the same nature are multiplied by a certain constant factor that indicates the dimensions of the quantity. Only on the day when we can define an economic magnitude as exactly as we do a unit of length shall we be in a position to speak with precision of its dimensions.

In the same way, the likening of the laws of economic equilibrium to the mechanical principles of static equilibrium has thus far had no more import than a figure of speech.

Thus, the first aspect under which mathematical economics presents itself—as a mode of reasoning referring to things that are not quantities because they are not measurable—is hardly encouraging.

But the very severity of this judgment puts us on our guard against accepting it as conclusive. We well know, for example, that our desire for or need of any product continually changes in accordance with the quantity of this product already in our possession. How can we take this continual variation into account, and what secret truths are hidden behind the incoherences and obscurities that detain and impede our access to them? Let us try to get some idea of them.

In the first place, there are certain classes of economic phenomena to which the objections I have just formulated do not apply. For instance, all kinds of *insurance* are essentially a precise application of the calculus of probability. In the same way, the broader movements of credit and the gross fluctuations of the stock exchange can be subjected to mathematical reasoning, although here psychological considerations, albeit in "statistical" form, do play a role.*

Or consider the fundamental problem of *monopolies*. Let us imagine an industrial cartel dominating, for example, the production of a perfume and seeking to fix its price in such a way as to realize the maximum profit. Reliable statistics indicate that at the price p the quantity of the product in question that is sold annually is a certain function, $\Phi(p)$, say A/p^2, where A designates the yearly sales when $p = 1$. On the other hand, the cost of production is d. The annual profit will be:

$$(p - d)\psi(p) \quad \text{or} \quad (p-d)\left(\frac{A}{p^2}\right)$$

Now p has to be chosen in such a way as to make this quantity as high as possible. The mathematicians tell us that for this purpose we should cancel the *derivative* of the preceding expression (in relation to p), and this gives us: $p = 2d$. Quite elementary mathematical reasoning could, in this case, have replaced the derivation. But, in fact, we have simplified the problem. The cost of production d itself depends upon the quantity annually produced, that is to say, upon $A;$ hence, it is also a certain function of p that increases along with p. If one takes this fact into account, the problem of finding the optimum price becomes more complicated. In the same way, let us assume that the cartel in question dominates the market in two kinds of perfume that are to some extent in competition with each other, and let p' and d' be, respectively, the sales price and the cost of production of the second perfume. Then the annual sale of the first perfume depends at the same time upon p and p'; for instance, statistics show that it is equal to Ap'/p^2. Hence the cost of production will also depend upon p'/p^2, and the same observations will apply to the second perfume. Thus, the total profit will appear as a rather

* As collective or mass psychology. [Translator's note.]

complicated expression of p and p', of which the differential calculus will immediately furnish us the maximum when elementary reasoning fails to give us the result.

Here, then, we do encounter classes of economic facts where the introduction of mathematics is incontestably useful; but this usefulness is, alas, as slight as it is incontestable. If we are to expect from mathematics nothing more than actuarial calculations and similar services, its role will be singularly subordinate for a science that is rather accustomed to occupy a position of supremacy. In the household of political economy it would then resemble a part-time servant who is engaged to perform heavy work, but is never consulted regarding the general management of the house. Now is it conceivable that for results as limited as these, thinkers as vigorous as Cournot and Walras meditated for so many years? Were they dupes of an illusion in believing that they had laid the foundations of a new science?

Let us once again consider the theory of exchange and examine the formula of Jevons quoted above. It has quantitative significance only if I admit for each of the groups of merchants, A and B, who confront each other in the market, and for each of the two commodities, wheat and beef, a hypothesis such as the following: when B, for instance, possesses the quantity x of wheat, the utility[2] which his purchase of another quantity of wheat has for him depends only on the quantity he already possesses, that is to say, on x, and can be characterized for each value of x by a certain number, say $\Psi_2(x)$, which decreases when x increases. The two equations on page 124 then quantitatively define the state of equilibrium in the market, but they show us, in addition, the reciprocal and continual repercussions of a and b upon prices, the tendencies in the variations in price before equilibrium is established, etc.

Now, from this whole mathematical discussion, let us retain only the qualitative tendencies which it has brought into relief and which subsist no matter what the functions Φ_1, Ψ_1, Φ_2, Ψ_2 may be, provided only that these functions vary inversely with the quantity upon which they depend. We thus make evident, in a rudimentary and simplified manner, the entire complexity of a market, the continuous interplay of intersecting influences that change the state of the market at every moment, and the tendencies in its incessant variations. In a word, mathematical reasoning serves us only as an auxiliary and temporary instrument in deducing more conveniently and reliably qualitative consequences from qualitative premises. In the intermediate process we may find it necessary to present in quantitative form data that are, after all, essentially qualitative, but once arrived at our destination, we can throw off such borrowed vestments.

It should be noted that similar observations may be made about certain branches of mathematics proper. Thus, in the theory of probability there are an infinite number of cases in which the classical definition of probability may be found inadequate, while the definitions suggested by common sense prove to be too vague and open to an indefinite variety of interpretations *of the same tendency,* depending upon an arbitrary function. But in this case the following remarkable circumstance presents itself: whatever definition one adopts from among the many that are *possible,* the conclusion is always the same; for example, that the probability of a certain event is zero.

But, it may be said, if that is the case, what is the advantage of introducing mathematical reasoning? Since we are concerned only with qualitative results and not with anything numerical at all, why not use ordinary language?

This objection would be justified if our capacity for deductive reasoning in ordinary language were not incomparably weaker than it is when we use mathematical language. I should like in this case to compare mathematical reasoning to a stony path leading to the summit of a mountain. We have the choice among an infinite number of such paths, all leading approximately to the same point of vantage; whereas if we take no path at all, we remain at the foot of the mountain.

The application of quantitative reasoning, conceived in this sense, is all the more legitimate inasmuch as the most important service for which we have hitherto been indebted to mathematical economics consists, I repeat, in having made evident the extreme complexity of economic phenomena and in having dispelled the oversimplified and optimistic illusions of certain orthodox theories. By means of its artificially precise laws mathematical economics traces out for us the pattern of social facts in an extremely simplified and virtually disembodied outline, which, nevertheless, throws into relief, in a fascinating way, the whole complex network of influences and causes and their indefinitely reverberating mutual repercussions. Now if this is the outline, what, then, is the reality?

One is no doubt tempted to think that, according to Renan's formula, such a science preserves more of error than it offers in the way of truth. But, in a study dealing with innumerable and confused facts, the service it renders is by no means insignificant in helping us to foresee the difficulties, in specifying their nature, and in introducing scientific method and criticism by means of quantitative reasoning, however imperfect. Besides, the usefulness of mathematical economics is evidenced not only by its positive results, but also by the influence that it has had upon the whole spirit of sociology.

Moreover, it should be observed that even if economic phenomena cannot be brought under the absolutely strict laws of the exact sciences, one can still distinguish, just as one can in highly complex physical phenomena, certain general and precise laws of the kind previously mentioned, to which these phenomena are subject without being completely determined by them. Such laws are comparable, for instance, to the principle of the conservation of energy, which the functioning of every machine, however complicated, obeys. Thus, the return that capital always requires (at least in the existing economic system) is not altogether without analogy to the loss or dissipation of power in a machine, and its consequences can in the same way be followed and studied mathematically through the most diverse economic transformations.

These are, to be sure, grossly simplified and artificially *quantified* models of real phenomena, but by means of them one can bring into sharp relief a whole complex network of reciprocal and continuous economic influences and causes, together with their *qualitative* tendencies. In this way the method and the spirit of science are introduced, in a more precise form, into political economy and into the different branches of the contiguous science of sociology. Finally, among the *quantitative* consequences to be credited to the achievement of this new science, which one could call mathematical economics, are the systematic interpretation of statistical data, the clear distinguishing of certain general laws, and the numerical study of some very special classes of facts.

May one hope for something more from this science? The economists of today are torn by opposing tendencies. Some are proponents of absolute freedom and unhampered competition; others, with Renouvier, qualify such policies as "economic cannibalism." Will the time ever come when the same general acceptance that is today enjoyed by geometry will be won by a really scientific economics, which will fix the value of every object of exchange so indisputably that the logic of its decisions will never be challenged either by the intellect or by the will of any man?

Such hopes are chimerical. A definition of the intrinsic and absolute value of any object, no matter what, is, as we have said, impossible. All attempts to arrive at such a definition—whether it rests upon the labor-time required for the production of the object or upon its utility, etc.—have always failed and are doomed to fail. And even if such a definition should some day be found and science were to declare it the *just* one, there is no mathematical reasoning whatsoever that could impose the idea of social justice on those who do not possess it or who refuse to bow to it.

Nevertheless, the social influence of scientific economics is incontestable. It is owing to this influence that the most determined champions of unrestricted liberty, those for whom the economic crushing of the weak by the strong was a sacred law, have moderated their doctrine. How can this influence be explained?

The reason is that most people are not at all moved by theoretical arguments, of whose real importance they are ignorant, but are quite ready to accept established conclusions once these bear the stamp of verification.

Consider, for example, the fundamental argument of Marxism. Thanks to the rate of interest, once a sum of money is acquired, it continues to be remunerative forever; capital, the fruit of accomplished work, demands from the community an indefinite return. This argument, for the understanding of which no mathematics is required, suffices for some people to declare the capitalistic system iniquitous and revolting. Others, not at all shocked, dream of nothing but of drawing profit from it. But the great majority of those who take the trouble to reflect upon this question adopt the attitude of Dr. Pangloss: since the customary practice of charging and paying interest seems to them inevitable, they hold that it cannot be injurious and must correct itself by its own excesses. Yet it is easy to imagine that once capital has exceeded a certain limit it must, in spite of all causes tending toward its dissipation, automatically reproduce itself and go on increasing, thought this limit may be so high that, in fact, it will never be reached.

Now let us assume that tomorrow a very learned economist makes a precise analysis of the development of private fortunes in some country during the last thirty years. A task of this kind, to be carried out successfully, would require all the resources of scientific method and mathematics. If, as a result of this analysis, it should be found that the influence of interest is even more than counterbalanced by opposing factors (taxes, the division of inherited property, etc.), and that wealth is to be found ever more widely distributed, our Dr. Pangloss and his followers would be right. But if the opposite should be found to be the case, if capital has automatically increased in considerable proportions and has concentrated itself in the hands of a small number of people, then they are wrong and, once convinced of the facts, they become resolute *interventionists*. Thus, the same argument, which in its abstract form impresses only a few "pure" thinkers, imposes itself, by its real, mathematically verified consequences, on the minds of the majority.

Analogous observations could be made concerning the results of free competition, the lowering of wages by overproduction, etc. All these are problems in which the consideration of *real* consequences will have a much greater influence on public opinion than the theoretical value of arguments. But, I repeat, these consequences cannot be appraised with any certainty without the aid of scientific methods.

That is why all who wish that first a little light, and then a measure of justice, may be brought into the frightful confusion of modern economic life must be interested in the development of mathematical economics, even though it may bristle with difficulties at first sight. Jevons' book, which its distinguished translators, Messrs. H.-E. Barrault and M. Alfassa, have asked me to introduce to the French public, is one of those which, by their clarity and elementary character, have made the greatest contribution to the diffusion of this new science and of its influence. Less profound but more readily comprehensible than the treatises of Cournot, Walras, or Pareto, it may be recommended to all who, without possessing a thorough background in mathematics, wish to be initiated into the rational science of economic phenomena. They will find here the elements of this science set forth in a very simple manner by a lucid and well-balanced intellect sincerely in search of the truth.

NOTES

1. If A possesses the quantity y of beef, his need of bread will be less than it would be if he did not possesss any meat at all; the utility that the quantity x of wheat has for him depends not merely upon x, but also upon y. Besides, Jevons' equation supposes that the ratio of exchange (or the price of beef expressed in wheat) remains constant throughout all the vicissitudes of the market.

2. Mathematical economists, it is true, have striven to construct a theory of exchange upon purely positive data. (See especially Pareto, *Manuel d'économie politique,* Appendix.) But (aside from mathematical objections) such a theory, however interesting, is open to the same objection that we have already pointed out here, at least as soon as one no longer restricts oneself merely to reporting the statistics in scholarly fashion, but pretends to derive the facts quantitatively by way of their causes.

6

A Letter to the Advocates
of a Controlled Economy*

Jacques Rueff

I

Agreement in Regard to Ends

I address this letter to you because we have different views on some rather important issues.

For several months the pressure groups you have formed have insistently importuned the government to take action to bring prices down.

If in fact many items have been freed of price control, this was always done against your opposition and only because it was no longer possible to maintain the fiction that their prices were really fixed. But the prices of raw materials, of the principal forms of energy, and of many products of industry, as well as wages, are still fixed in France by the government.

Several weeks ago it even happened that some controls which had previously been lifted were re-established.

In England wages and the prices of all important goods are regulated by the authorities.

* Épitre aux Dirigistes (Paris: Gallimard, 1949).

In the United States radical opinion demands the return to price controls in large sectors of the economy.

This situation cannot be considered as merely temporary. Hostility to uncontrolled prices will become even more vehement if tomorrow they begin to move in the opposite direction. Then the same voices that today demand that the rise in prices be brought to a halt will clamor for measures to prevent prices from falling.

Thus the opinion that you defend is very widespread.

I believe I am not mistaken in thinking that your chief motive in advocating a controlled economy is your concern—eminently estimable in itself—for protecting and, as much as possible, raising the standard of living of the wage earners.

Your attitude is certainly logical. In the past it was always the increase in prices that thwarted your efforts to improve the conditions of the masses. Fundamentally, the object of your aversion is a factor inherent in the mobility of prices, namely, the process which tends to equate the total purchasing power in the hands of the consumers—whatever nominal wage rates may be—with the total value of what is for sale in the market and which thereby prevents any social policy, however nobly inspired, from giving away what does not exist.

However, your hostility to the mechanism of the pricing process is based on even more general principles. You are profoundly and sincerely shocked by a system that leaves the structure of the social order at the mercy of what you regard as blind forces. You want society to be consciously directed toward the ends that you propose to assign to it.

I believe, on the contrary, that our policy should keep to the path that events, in spite of you, have compelled it to take and that we should aim at decontrolling prices just as rapidly as possible.

I am not unaware of the repercussions of such a policy. I realize that during the delicate period of transition—which we are, in fact, passing through right now, though we hardly know it—

certain precautionary measures are required, which I have out-lined in the fourth chapter of my *Dilemme Français.**

Many of you attribute my attitude to a cruel indifference to the human side of economic phenomena.

But, contrary to what you may think, I am entirely and pro-foundly in agreement with you in desiring and advocating an increase in the well-being of the masses. I believe it to be one of the chief objects of economic policy to give the people, and particularly the most indigent classes, those conditions of life—liberty, well-being, security—which the respect that you and I and all men of good will have for the human person properly demands.

I believe that a society of human beings left to itself—or rather to the individual men who compose it—would be intolerable. The history of civilization reveals a perpetual effort to achieve liberty and progress. All the decalogues, all the moral codes, all the teachings of religion and philosophy have constantly aimed at counteracting the tendencies of human nature when left to its own inclinations and at substituting for undisciplined impulse an order more in conformity with the great ideals that fill our hearts.

I share with you the belief in the existence of an inherent prin-ciple of order in the various forms of human sociality. Like you I consider that the problem is not that of leaving the world as it is or as it was, but of creating a social order as acceptable as possible to the conscience of the majority of mankind.

Like you, therefore, I believe that the authorities should "inter-vene" in order to make the world what we want it to be.

But where we differ is in the choice of the method of interven-tion. Yours consists in fixing prices; mine, in the rational correc-tion of the effects of allowing prices to fluctuate freely.

I am firmly convinced that your method leads inevitably to results directly opposed to those that you wish to realize. You desire order, liberty, and prosperity; but what you have is chaos, slavery, and poverty.

* See p. 105 of the same volume in which the essay here translated appeared. [Translator's note.]

I assure you that the future consequences of your policy must be no less deceptive than those it has always had in the past. Yet I can also assure you that the results you desire to achieve are within your reach and that you can easily attain them, provided only that you are prepared to adopt the appropriate methods.

The stakes are enormous. The entire future of human civilization is in the balance. It seems impossible that earnest and generous people like you should refuse to submit their views to a serious discussion. It is to such a discussion that I invite you.

The rational bases of my conviction can easily be demonstrated. Give heed to what I have to say. If I am wrong, say so; but if I am right, urge your governments to take the path that leads to the goal you wish to attain.

II

Liberty and Prices

You want both order and liberty at one and the same time.

By fixing prices at a level different from that at which they would have spontaneously established themselves, you can have only disorder and slavery.

Let us first consider the conditions of economic freedom: freedom to buy and to sell and to choose one's calling, one's place of residence, and the manner of employing one's resources.

In our system of production for the market, most economic activities are ultimately oriented to supply and demand. But supply and demand merely express tendencies. If exchange is to take place, these tendencies must find their respective counterparts in the market. Now this condition is fulfilled for the entire supply and demand in the market only when, under all circumstances, and no matter how unpredictably the buyers and the sellers may behave, the total demand expressed in money is equal to the total value of what is offered for sale.

This condition may appear to you as purely theoretical.

But is it just theory, or simply common sense, to say that the harvest will not be entirely sold if its value—that is, the price asked for it in the market—exceeds the amount that potential purchasers are prepared to pay for it; or, conversely, that some people will not be able to obtain the apartments they want if, at the present level of rents, the total value of the apartments available is lower than the total amount of income allotted to expenditure for residential rent? And is it really just a theory that some workers will not find the employment that they desire, and consequently will not be free to follow the calling of their choice, if in some lines of work the total value, at the level of prevailing wages, of the hours of labor offered in the market exceeds the amount of the resources that the entrepreneurs are prepared to devote to such expenditures?

Thus, the entire supply and demand in the market will become effective only in so far as their respective total values remain equal, for only then will the available supply be fully absorbed by the existing demand and the existing demand be fully satisfied by the available supply.

But is there any chance that, in fact, this equality will always be assured?

Theorists often forget, in dealing with total quantities, that supply and demand are the result of individual decisions made by people acting independently of one another without being concerned in the least about the possible repercussions that their actions may have upon the collective equilibrium.

Now these people are not abstract beings, but living persons, each of whom is endowed with a "personality."

To have personality means to confront life with a set of personal tastes and hence to feel in all circumstances certain preferences that, if you are free, determine your behavior.

Is this still just a theory? Is it not true that man, once he commits himself to action in the world, knows what he wants? Surely this has become abundantly clear to those (and many of you were among them) who have tried to induce people to use margarine rather than butter, to drink a beverage made from the acorn instead of coffee, to prefer labor in the mines to a white-collar job, or to invest in treasury bonds instead of spending their money on consumers' goods. How rarely have admonitions on the part of the authorities, even when backed up with the force of law, succeeded in getting milk to the market as long as it was more profitable to churn it into butter, or in providing meat for the consumer as long as its price did not cover the costs of production!

For among the conditions that affect the behavior of people the one that plays a decisive role is price, a factor that determines the sacrifices required of consumers as well as the reward offered to producers.

I ask you to give this point some thought, for it is essential.

Is it not true that a housewife who goes to the market with the object of buying meat will demand fish or eggs instead if the price of what she intended to buy seems to her too high?

Is it not true that the head of a family will demand a five-room apartment if he can obtain it for a rent of 20,000 francs, but will look for only three rooms if, as in the United States, he has to pay more than 100,000 francs a year for each room?

Is it not true that many of you would buy a Citroën if it were offered for sale at 100,000 francs, but prefer to leave it for the export market as long as you cannot obtain it for less than a million?

Is it not true that a young worker who would not consider going down into the mines for 100 francs a day will be willing to engage in that kind of work at a daily wage of 2,000 francs?

I know that it comes as a shock to many of you to realize that individuals, as long as they act freely, persist in behaving in this way. But do you think you can change human nature? In the periods when you were in power did it not remain what it has always been? And have not even your comrades in the camp of the enemy, after having changed the whole political and social structure to suit their wishes, been obliged to resort to a differentiation in wages in order to influence men's behavior?

I ask you to be objective, then, and to tell me if you do not think I am right.

If I am, you must admit that as long as consumers and producers are free to make their own decisions, price is the decisive factor that determines the supply of and the demand for every article in the market. It follows that in a free economy there is only one level of prices at which supply and demand are equal.

Now this uniquely determined level is precisely that at which all free prices spontaneously tend to establish themselves.

Consequently, every time you succeed in fixing, by means of the authority of the government, a price, a wage, an interest rate, or a foreign exchange rate, at a level different from that at which it would have spontaneously established itself, the supply in the market will not and cannot be at the same level as the demand— at least as long as human nature and the nature of things remain unchanged and as long as men are free to make their own decisions. Those buyers or sellers who cannot discover anyone willing to exchange with them in the market at the prices fixed by the authorities will find themselves unable to do what they nevertheless desire and are free to do.

Is this just a theory, or is it a fact?

If you wish to form an objective judgment of the consequences of economic controls, you have only to look about you. You will note that as soon as the price of a commodity is fixed, buyers start queuing up at the doors of the shops where it is sold. Does this not prove that some of those waiting in line to make their purchase run the risk of being turned away empty-handed when the supply available at that price is exhausted? In the same way, does not the shortage of apartments that follows upon every freezing of residential rents deprive some prospective tenants of the freedom to use their funds as they see fit? And similarly, has not the maintenance of wheat prices for several years now below the level at which they would have freely established themselves deprived many potential purchasers of the possibility of obtaining the grain they need not only for their own sustenance, but for that of their poultry or their pigs?

Note too what have been the results of freezing wages. In France since the liberation they have been kept below the level that they would have reached in a free market. Wage controls have created a general shortage of labor, and we are consequently witnessing the emergence of a black market in labor, where employers have sought clandestinely to raise the legally fixed wage rates. This clearly demonstrates that, despite all theories, the price that is permitted to establish itself freely is, indeed, the only price at which the market reaches equilibrium.

I am not wrong, then. The fixing of a price at a level different from that at which it would have freely established itself creates a disequilibrium between the supply of and the demand for the article in question. Those who, at the prices fixed by the authorities, cannot find in the market anyone prepared to buy what they have to offer or to sell what they are eager to buy are thus deprived of their freedom to act as they see fit.

There is no way of avoiding this consequence. For if, at the fixed price, the entire demand could have been satisfied and the entire supply absorbed, this means that the price would have spontaneously established itself at the level fixed by the authorities and there was no need in the first place for coercive measures to maintain it at that level.

If the price is maintained below its equilibrium level, demand exceeds supply. Then it is only a matter of chance if certain buyers succeed in establishing contact with someone with whom they can make a deal at the fixed price. Everyone else's freedom will be curtailed, just as it is in the case of those whom we see around us today vainly seeking to get things like butter, milk, or an apartment that are not to be had at the prices fixed by the authorities.

If the price is maintained above its equilibrium level, as was the case with wheat in 1934, only the lucky sellers will find the buyer they are looking for. The impossibility of selling, and consequently of continuing production, at the fixed price will render illusory the freedom of those producers who are forced to go out of business.

In both cases the fixing of prices by the government creates chaos.

But buyers or sellers who face the possibility of not being able to find anyone to trade with in the market will not remain inactive. They will have recourse to covert means of payment or to supplementary services in the attempt to obtain preferential treatment over their too numerous competitors. Thus, the inseparable concomitants of price control are the black market and a general decline in ethical standards.

There is but one way to bring the disorder to an end and to curb the spreading demoralization of society without at the same time eradicating the system of price control that has brought them into being, and that is to remove the discrepancy between supply and demand by resorting to measures that will forcibly reduce whichever one of the two is greater than the other.

If a ceiling such as is now in effect is imposed on the upward movement of prices, universal rationing must inevitably follow. Although theoretically free to dispose of their resources as they please, people will not be able to employ them without first obtaining official authorization to use them in the specific way they have in mind.

If, as was the case in certain prewar markets, limits are set to the downward movement of prices, the inevitable consequence must be the imposition of production quotas, the uprooting of vineyards, the destruction of coffee, the burning of wheat, acreage restrictions on sowing and planting, and the enforced reduction in the number of working days. Although still free theoretically, people will be able to produce or to sell only what has been officially authorized.

You will say that in both cases only economic freedom is affected and that this is not what interests you.

But you will be quickly undeceived.

Can there be any doubt that when the demand for labor permanently exceeds the supply, it becomes imperative, in the interests of safeguarding indispensable branches of production, to forbid workers to change jobs without official authorization? Great Britain has already gone through this experience. The Labor Government itself, in distinct violation of its own declared intentions, established in September, 1947, what amounted to a system of compulsory labor. Are workers whose place of residence, line of work, and specific job can be fixed by administrative fiat really free men? Were young people of an earlier day who had nothing but permanent unemployment to look forward to really free, when they knew that they could never find work in the occupation of their choice? What shall we say of those workingmen who—in order to avoid adding to the existing oversupply of labor—were not allowed to raise the standard of living of their families and to provide a better education for their children by performing at the end of their day's work some kind of remunerative labor or by drawing a pension and a salary at the same time? Were they free men? And what of those who, before they can start a family or set up a business, have to wait until the municipal authorities have assigned them an apartment or a shop? Are they too free men? As free, no doubt, as those who need official authorization to travel abroad or to have foreign books and newspapers sent to them!

Be candid. Is it not true that through price control we have created a society where purchasing power does not necessarily guarantee that one will be able to make any purchases, where the willingness and capacity to work is no assurance that one will be able to find work, and where liberty is little more than an empty form giving one the abstract right to do what in fact cannot be done?

In order to devise laws and regulations which will not only leave men free to do everything that they are physically capable of doing, but assure them of being able to act effectively and at the same time prevent this freedom from ever resulting in disorder, it is essential that the consequences of their unpredictable behavior be, at every instant, adjusted to the consequences of the unpredictable behavior of all their fellow men, to unpredictable changes in circumstances, and to the no less unpredictable progress of technology. Since you do not want this to be accomplished by compulsion, it can be brought about only by the mechanism of the pricing process.

Those who really want a society of free men cannot but be in favor of economic freedom.

III

Prices and Welfare

You want the whole population, and especially the most indigent classes, to enjoy the maximum possible well-being.

By fixing prices at a level appreciably different from that at which they would have spontaneously established themselves, you can succeed only in greatly reducing everyone's standard of living.

I believe you agree with me that neither production nor consumption are facts of nature. Yet I am sure that you underestimate the significance of this point.

To be sure, neither the nature of things nor the nature of man depends on us. But aside from them, everything that exists could just as well not have come into being, and whatever is yet to be is still indeterminate.

Look around you. Neither the farm that feeds you nor the house that shelters you was necessary. Practically everything available for your consumption, material as well as intellectual—and this means almost everything characteristic of what you call your universe—is the result of man's work. An immense effort of production has brought all these things into being. Now, out of all the possible goods toward the production of which that effort might have been directed, those actually produced, taken in their entirety, constitute a unique reality.

Whoever really wishes to understand the nature of our economic system must first of all examine the way in which the actual objects of productive effort are chosen from among the innumerable possibilities open to choice.

Production is the offspring of desire. It comes into being as soon as men feel, however obscurely, that the desirability of the product outweighs the undesirability of the effort necessary to obtain it.

But specialization very soon brought with it the system of production for the market, in which the compensation for the producer's effort was no longer the product itself, but the monetary equivalent that its sale procured.

In this system each consumer demanded everything whose consumption seemed to him sufficiently desirable to outweigh the sacrifice in his purchasing power necessary to pay the price, and each producer offered for sale whatever seemed to him to cost him in its production less than the amount of the increase in his purchasing power that he desired to obtain by the sale.

This formula is abstract. It shows how the mechanism of the pricing process selects from among the desires that fill men's hearts those that actually create a demand, at the same time that it brings into being the goods necessary to satisfy this demand.

By virtue of this double efficacy the mechanism of the pricing process plunges men into the world of reality and permits them to mould it to their hearts' desire.

Do you call this just a theory?

On the contrary, is it not true that the fixing of prices below their equilibrium level has everywhere increased the demand for goods, while at the same time hampering their production?

Do you deny that fixing the price of wheat at too low a level in terms of its importance to society has created an additional demand for it, while at the same time discouraging farmers from producing it?

Do you deny that the freezing of residential rents at a very low level in relation to the amount by which inflation has increased the income of tenants has eliminated any restraining influence on the demand for apartments and has so far penalized the construction of new houses as to reduce it to zero?

Do you deny that the fixing of foreign exchange rates below those that the market would have established has greatly increased the profitability of imports, and hence the demand for them, while at the same time reducing the exports by which purchases from foreign countries could have been paid for?

Finally, do you deny that men's wants, the conditions of production, and the state of technology are in perpetual evolution? For production to provide the maximum well-being with the minimum of effort, it must at every instant be adjusted to the situation of the moment. Just imagine the enormous number of changes that are going to be required by the general use of atomic energy, the numerous activities that will be eliminated, and the widespread depreciation of capital investments that will be brought about. Do you think that these transformations, which will affect innumerable particular interests, could take place if they were not imposed by the constant operation of the mechanism of the pricing process? Its action is necessarily efficacious because it continues right up to the very moment when the result it aims at is in fact obtained.

No doubt you will contend that what that mechanism, once its operation has been sabotaged by you, will be unable to do, you advocates of economic control will accomplish by conscious planning.

Let us admit, for the moment, that your planning is such that it gives people precisely what the mechanism of the unhampered market would have given them: a maximum of well-being. But will you deny that if you first fix prices above or below their equilibrium level, you create a situation in which producers and consumers will be motivated to behave in ways that are different from the roles assigned to them by the economic plan? For the plan to be put into effect, it will be necessary to require people to do what they do not want to do. Do you understand now why compulsion is the necessary adjuvant of any system of price-fixing? Is it really reasonable, if one wants men to perform certain acts, to begin by discouraging them?

The essential characteristic of the free market is that it does not need to compel men to serve the general interest, because prices are such as to inspire the desire to do so precisely in those who are best able to perform such services, while at the same time rendering it unnecessary to prevent men from doing what is contrary to the general interest, because prices are such as to forestall any desire in that direction.

In an unhampered market the crime of sabotage, which is indissolubly associated with every system of controlled prices, simply cannot occur.

We are thus forced to conclude that price control gives rise to scarcity by creating a desire for precisely the commodities whose production it prevents. It destroys the mechanism that has made it possible for men to fashion the world to their needs. It creates a universe whose structure results from purely accidental circumstances and which, no longer made to serve man's needs, must necessarily seem to him devoid of meaning.

The world that you blind planners have created is an absurd world. It requires to be overthrown in just the same way as a rotten tree requires the woodcutter's axe.

All those who really have at heart the welfare of mankind must necessarily be in favor of the free market.

IV

Price Control Is Not a Viable Social Policy

You favor price controls because experience has taught you that wage adjustments, in a period of rising prices, are always both tardy and insufficient. Freezing prices seems to be the only effective means of safeguarding the purchasing power of the workers.

In the short run you are right. Any reduction in selling prices without an attendant reduction in wages lowers entrepreneurial profits and transfers to the workers the purchasing power of which the entrepreneurs and shareholders are deprived.

Nevertheless, the effect of this process is rather limited. Entrepreneurial profits (i.e., the remuneration of entrepreneurs and shareholders) represent only eighteen percent of the national income. The downward movement of prices will very quickly reduce them to a level below which it will be considered impossible to let them fall for fear of bringing production to a complete standstill.

If prices are permitted to fall below that level, while at the same time wages remain unchanged—or, what amounts to the same thing, if, starting from this level, wages are increased, while at the same time increases in prices are forbidden—the enterprises will operate at a deficit, and the total volume of income distributed will exceed the value of national production.

Now there is one result that no policy, however well intentioned, can possibly obtain, and that is to enable people to buy what does not exist.

If ten million products are demanded at a time when the entire production offered for sale amounts, at the official prices, to the value of but five million, there can be only two possible consequences: either the doubling of prices, whether officially or on the black market, which will, in fact, raise the total value of the supply to the level of the demand; or, if price controls are maintained, the rejection of fifty percent of the demand, which will cause the would-be buyers who are turned away to queue up outside the doors of the shops in anticipation of forthcoming deliveries.

The market cannot supply what it does not have. This fundamental truth explains why all systems of price control have always had to resort to rationing whenever it was desired to put an end to the intolerable disorder of clandestine remunerations or of unsatisfied demand. Price control over a prolonged period is not conceivable without rationing.

Now rationing is nothing but a system of forced deprivation by which the government reduces purchasing power capable of absorbing, at their total market value, all goods offered for sale, to the prices that the authorities wish to maintain.

This procedure no doubt makes it possible to distribute money wages that—thanks to price control—can be made to appear, at least statistically, to have a high purchasing power. But such a policy authorizes this purchasing power to be used only in competition for the rations available.

Rationing permits the public authorities to practise an illusory generosity, for it enables the government indirectly to take back everything that the policy of price controls has given in excess of what it could legitimately provide.

By permitting appearances to be maintained and, when strictly enforced, by refusing to recognize realities, rationing renders demagogy inoffensive and makes of lying a system of government.

No doubt it will be said that in a period of scarcity price control and rationing, by reducing entrepreneurial profits, permit a greater part of production to be left to the poorer classes and thus make possible a more equitable distribution of privation. Price control is alleged to have an egalitarian tendency, and this indeed is what is held to constitute its specific social virtue.

It is true that price control does succeed in reducing the profits of big enterprises, whose books provide a precise picture of their condition and are easily open to inspection. Very often, in fact, these enterprises even operate at a deficit and can continue in business only with the help of direct or indirect subsidies.

However, for all the medium-sized and small enterprises, for the enormous cohort of middlemen, price control, which was supposed to reduce the margins of profit, has, in reality, immensely increased them. Under a system of controlled prices does one ever hear of middlemen becoming bankrupt, as they did when competition constantly pared profits to the breaking point and ruthlessly eliminated the inefficient? The facts to which I refer can be attested to best by those who know from experience how small the margin of profit was for milk distributors before the institution of price controls and what it has become since. And it cannot be otherwise. Since it is impossible for the authorities to make sufficiently fine adjustments in fixing prices to take account of differences in the cost of production in each enterprise, price control is bound to give to all a return great enough to allow those with the highest operating costs to survive. Even when it is effectively enforced, it is and cannot help being a paradise for the middleman.

But you well know that in fact enforcement will never be entirely effective. Whenever the price is maintained below its equilibrium level, the cunning and the unscrupulous contrive, for their own advantage, to possess themselves of articles in scarce supply by clandestinely paying the seller more than the legal price. In the black market thus established, the sellers acquire additional purchasing power. Be candid. Is it not true that the black market has completely upset the distribution of purchasing power that official prices sought to establish? If you have any doubts on that score, just look at what has been happening in the market in gasoline. Since the liberation it has been controlled, and cars are supposed to be on the road on a priority basis. The sight of the streets of Paris should be enough to forever convince every honest advocate of price control of the monstrous inefficiency of any system of enforced rationing. The profits realized in the black market in gasoline amount to twenty-four billion francs a year. The purchasing power of these billions permits those who receive them to withdraw the equivalent in goods from the total national production. If we assume that the rations allotted to each person have been exactly calculated for the whole population, then the twenty-four billions' worth of goods illegally withdrawn from the total national production by those engaged in the sale of gasoline on the black market will not be available to honor all the rationing coupons you have distributed. Some infants will be left undernourished; some mothers will be left waiting in vain for the rations you have promised them.

But sales in the black market to unauthorized buyers not only result in a skewed distribution of purchasing power; they also adversely affect the distribution of the products and thereby in effect nullify the provisions of the overall production plan. Try to imagine the extent to which production has fallen off in France as a result of the shortage in gasoline. Anyone who has attempted to build a house knows well enough that even though gasoline has been allocated on a priority basis, the only way to provide for the transportation of bricks and cement and for the visits of the architect is to enter into complicated, always time-consuming, and often clandestine arrangements. The scarcity of transportation has not only retarded production, but has prompted certain producers who have received special gasoline rations to reduce their production to the minimum in order to be able to resell as much of their allotment as possible in the black market. No really sincere person can have any doubt whatsoever that gasoline rationing has vastly diminished the productivity of the French economy since the liberation.

No doubt you will say that control and rationing have been poorly enforced. But men and systems are what they are. The most ardent advocates of control have been in power since the liberation. Have they done a better job than their predecessors? With all that power in their hands, have they seriously lessened the misery of the most indigent classes, have they prohibited the existence of scandalous inequalities, have they succeeded in preventing the system, under their direction, from giving rise to the depravity and disorder that have so far been its only results?

England, it is said, has managed these things better. It is true that insularity creates conditions particularly favorable to the discipline required by economic controls, that the liberal tradition of England has developed the typically British civic spirit, and that as long as the restrictions imposed on their economic freedom do not make them forget the healthy virtues of liberty, the English will be particularly suited for the discipline of a controlled economy.

But the periodic announcement of new measures of austerity proves that the system has borne in England the same fruits as it has on the Continent. Everywhere the first objective of control was to limit demand to the value of the goods actually produced and to equalize their distribution. This objective has been better attained in England than anywhere else. But the system has everywhere had the same secondary effects: it has weakened the incentives to production, prevented the constant natural adjustment of production to demand, and conflicted with the establishment and maintenance of economic equilibrium.

By these secondary effects, which diminish the quantity and utility of the goods produced, price control and rationing have reduced the people's standard of living, not to the advantage of the most indigent, but to the detriment of all.

It is the worst of all errors to believe that this policy gives to some what it takes away from others, for the goods that it has not distributed it has simply prevented from being produced at all.

Economic controls are egalitarian in appearance, but in reality they are Malthusian. They create scarcity and hence cannot be seriously considered as a viable social policy.

V

A True Social Policy

What you want, undoubtedly, is that man should be free in a world that has been made for him.

I hope that the preceding chapters have convinced you that if this is what you really want, you must also be in favor of a free market.

However, you are appalled by its consequences.

You do not accept the idea that human life should be directed by a blind mechanism geared exclusively to the pursuit of profit.

The respect you have for the dignity of man makes you want to compel men, even against their will, and to their material detriment, to safeguard their health and their capacity for intellectual, moral, and aesthetic development, so that they may be able to appreciate the beauty of the world and feel the joy of life.

You believe that the structure of society, the distribution of the population, and the determination of the order of priority of all human activities cannot be left to purely economic and momentary forces, ignorant of the past and indifferent to the future.

You are particularly opposed to allowing the distribution of the social product to be determined by a mechanism that measures the merits of each person in proportion to his economic productivity. The spirit of charity impels you increasingly to espouse the cause of others, especially of the unfit and the weak. You reject the idea that the sick, the old, or the very young should be refused satisfactions that their own incapacity renders it impossible for them to acquire. You want to shelter them from economic insecurity.

It is for all these reasons that you are wholeheartedly and profoundly hostile to the mechanism of the free market.

But I tell you and affirm with all the force of my conviction that you are wrong and that the methods you favor can only bring about the contrary of what you wish to attain.

Surely no man who has any feeling for his fellow men would want our society to be at the mercy of some of the forces that would be free to operate in an unhampered market. For groups of men to become societies, intervention is necessary. But for this intervention not to be destructive of the very conditions that are essential to the dignity of man, namely, liberty and abundance, it must in no way jeopardize the free mobility of prices.

A true social policy is one that intervenes in economic life in order to make it what we want it to be, but only in ways compatible with the mechanism by which prices spontaneously adjust themselves to the supply and demand in the market.

In what follows I shall enumerate the measures that a truly liberal policy of interventionism would have to take.

Essentially compatible with the mechanism of the pricing process are all acts of intervention of a legal or regulatory nature and all administrative policies that do not prevent prices from freely settling at a level in keeping with the conditions that such measures establish.

The measures in question fall into three categories: those affecting the conditions within which they operate—in other words, the institutional framework of social life; those that directly modify the causes determining the formation of prices; and those that correct the effects of prices.

Interventionist measures of an institutional nature are, in general, not very interesting to you because their action is too indirect or remote to attract public attention. They are, nevertheless, the most effective means of putting into force the policy that you favor.

You desire price stability and security of employment. You also favor large plans of investment for modernization and plant equipment. But in the absence of an extensive fund of savings, all of this is nothing but empty talk. The structure of the monetary system and the conditions under which it is administered constitute a better foundation for an effective social policy than the authoritarian measures by which you seek to establish directly the conditions you wish to see prevail.

Now the monetary mechanism has been progressively deprived, in the course of the last thirty years, of all its regulatory powers.

The first task to be accomplished in all the countries of the world is a return to sound money.

But to embark upon a program of large investments for the social purposes you have in mind, for rapid progress, especially in the construction of houses, and for the policy of electrification and irrigation that the country is expecting, it will not be sufficient to restore monetary stability and thus to regenerate the spirit of savings and capital accumulation. It will also be necessary to revise the law of contracts, to change the provisions of the codes that provide penalties for their violation, and, above all, to reorganize the courts that have the function of interpreting and enforcing them.

You denounce combinations in restraint of trade as instruments of social pauperization. But in nine cases out of ten it is you who make them possible, if you do not actually create them. Do not forget that in 1936 there was a government that proposed and a parliament that passed a law that prohibited not only the creation of new shoe factories, but even the opening of simple cobblers' shops. Expunge from our statute books immediately all provisions capable of creating or fostering monopolies. Enforce the laws that prohibit and penalize every maneuver tending to jeopardize the free movement of prices in the market.

If you wish to raise the ethical standards of business, change the law that limits the liability of corporations and hold their executives personally responsible for their management, provide stricter safeguards to ensure veracity in the drawing up of balance sheets, and penalize with a rigor comparable to that of British legislation any inexact or simply biased declaration made by the board of directors.

And above all, do not forget that a society of free men requires of its members a high standard of personal ethics and good citizenship. To restore these qualities you have to suppress in our economic system anything that makes the fortune of the individual dependent not on his application to his work, but on his ability to cheat and his aptitude for corruption.

I cite these examples, not in order to provide an exhaustive list of the innumerable forms of intervention of an institutional nature that are urgently required for the reconstitution of a system based upon the mechanism of the free market, but in order to show you that such a system, far from embodying the principle of "laissez faire" that its detractors denounce, requires a vigilant and strict authority to prevent anything from being done that might jeopardize its functioning.

The mechanism of the pricing process, when liberated from the parasitic influences which corrupt it, will make it possible for every one of us to use his legal rights in whatever way he likes.

But you believe, as I do, that individuals do not necessarily always prefer what is best and that in certain cases society should substitute its own judgment for theirs.

For example, you do not want the hours or conditions of labor to be such as to undermine the dignity or the health of the worker: he must still be able to enjoy a personal life of his own and with his family, even if he himself is prepared to sacrifice such considerations for the sake of advancing himself materially. You may make whatever regulations you like concerning the hours and conditions of labor, including women's and children's, and the system of lay-offs, discharges, and vacations. Such measures of intervention merely affect the supply of labor and create a situation analogous to that which would exist if the population were less numerous, but they do not prevent the mechanism of the pricing process from establishing an equilibrium corresponding to the changes thus brought about in the supply.

In the same way, you wish to protect enterprises that competition would eliminate, or to avoid, for political reasons, the lowering of certain prices. By imposing customs duties on those imports that you consider injurious to the domestic economy and excise taxes on products that would replace those you wish to protect, you create a situation analogous to that which would have existed had transportation costs been higher or presently employed techniques not yet discovered; but you do not prevent the mechanism of the pricing process from establishing an equilibrium corresponding to the increased costs of production thereby brought about.

All such forms of intervention are compatible with the mechanism of the free market, since they affect only the causes determining the formation of prices, but permit prices to determine themselves freely under the conditions thus established.

Nevertheless, all these different kinds of intervention still fail to meet the major objection that you have against the mechanism of the pricing process, namely, that once the causes determining the formation of prices have been fixed, the distribution of the social product is entirely removed from the sphere of conscious action. The competitive pricing process of the unhampered market excludes all considerations of equity in determining the amount that the participants in production are to receive as income and would oblige us to acquiesce in a policy of poverty that would, in effect, pauperize men, and especially the most indigent classes, whose interests you have chiefly at heart.

These objections assume particular importance whenever some disaster suddenly diminishes the quantity of products available. It then becomes utterly intolerable that the freedom of prices to adjust themselves to the diminished supply should prevent you from shifting the burden to the shoulders of those who are best able to bear it.

Because you are men of good will, you advocates of economic controls consider this as the irrefutable condemnation of the policies of liberalism. For this reason I propose to consider it in the fullest possible light.

What you expect from price control is, essentially, the possibility of safeguarding the purchasing power of the wage earners by transferring to the latter all or a part of the purchasing power accruing from profits, dividends, interest, and rents.

But what you can obtain indirectly by acting upon prices you can obtain directly, taking as your point of departure the situation created by the competitive pricing process of the unhampered market. By a combination of taxes and subsidies, in kind or in money, you can, in effect, redistribute the national income as you please.

Does not such a procedure of itself bring about important displacements of resources? Family allowances, welfare aid in all its forms, free schooling, all serve to transfer purchasing power quite as effectively as, and far more equitably than, for example, indiscriminate controls on residential rents. Can one imagine a more powerful instrument for equalizing the distribution of wealth than inheritance taxes?

The field of application of this technique of redistribution can be extended without limit. The government of Belgium has recently applied it in a new way. With the object of removing certain limitations on prices, it has granted "compensatory indemnities" to those whom it wishes to protect from an increase in costs. Rent allowances commit us to the same policy. Loans made at specially reduced interest rates for investments that the government wishes to foster—housing construction, for example—offer the same possibilities. There is, in fact, no form of discrimination, including the raising of the wages of certain groups of favored workers, that cannot be practised by way of subsidies.

Nevertheless, in order to prevent these acts of intervention from disappointing those whom they are supposed to favor, they have to be practised within the framework of a balanced budget, for otherwise the rise in prices would indirectly offset the improvement in living standards that the subsidies were designed to bring about.

The procedure of direct redistribution thus finds its upper limit in the amount of the resources that can be set free by the fiscal system. It cannot give without taking, or rather, without showing that it takes. This is the principal respect in which it differs from price control. But, unlike the latter, what it promises to give, it gives in fact. Consciously applied, it is the policy of effective liberality: within the limits of the resources currently available or capable of being borrowed, it permits one to correct in whatever way one likes the effects of the operation of the competitive pricing process without in any way threatening to impair its mechanism.

You will no doubt reply that in a liberal regime the necessity of leaving some incentive to productive effort sets a limit to what can be accomplished by purely fiscal means and thus narrows the effective scope of the social policy compatible with the mechanism of the pricing process. But a policy of price control, if one means to put it into effect anywhere outside of a concentration camp, is quite evidently subject to the same limitations.

Now make your decision. If what you desire is a truly effective policy of social legislation, you can obtain quite as much without jeopardizing the freedom of the market as you can by means of a system of price controls.

But in a free market economy you will have both liberty and prosperity at the same time, whereas a controlled economy will bring with it only disorder or slavery and will leave nothing but penury to be distributed.

Whoever desires a truly effective policy of social legislation cannot but be in favor of a free market economy.

VI

Social Liberalism: A Formula for Unity Among Men of Good Will of All Parties

You are no doubt well aware that the system under which we are living cannot endure.

It is a system that in England has kept a million unemployed for fifteen years, that has burned wheat and coffee, that has upset the balance of international exchange, that compels the French to live in hovels of unparalleled wretchedness, that can find no other remedy for scarcity than the distribution of privation, and that, above all, imbues the less favored classes with a sense of useless and unjust frustration, while at the same time it leaves the privileged classes with a bad conscience because of their illegal and ill-gotten gains. Such a system is a rotten ruin, doomed to collapse.

Now, do you doubt that we alone are responsible for this enormous disaster to world economy and civilization? To be sure, both world wars profoundly modified the structure of the economy of every country. But these upheavals brought disorder in their wake only because—sometimes by error, often by demagogy, but always with the approval of public opinion—we destroyed the mechanism that once, by virtue of the competitive pricing process of the free market, impelled men to want to do of their own accord what the general interest required; and we have replaced it by certain rudimentary elements of a planned economy, strictly limited in their scope and always very imperfect in their effectiveness.

If we really wish to escape from this chaos, there are only two ways of doing so: we must either apply rigorous planning to the entire economy or we must return to a free market by eliminating all price controls.

But though all of you look with favor, at least in principle, on the first alternative, very few of you indeed are ready to accept— and even then generally only on behalf of others—the stringent restrictions on liberty that it requires. Be candid. Is it conceivable that you, as men of good will and the champions of the rights of the individual, would establish a system that requires the suppression of every liberty?

You have no choice, then: you must be in favor of economic freedom.

And yet you do not want it. You reject it because it is associated in your mind with the memory of a system you detest, which left the lowly to their fate and which did nothing to establish in human society even a minimum of equality and justice.

But in holding the mechanism of the pricing process responsible for your legitimate grievances, you commit an error fraught with serious consequences. That mechanism is nothing but an instrument for guiding the economy, and as such it is as indifferent to the equilibrium that it establishes as the rudder is to the port to which it steers the ship. If the regimes of the past that you find so hateful did not pursue a very enlightened policy of social legislation, it was because those who, through the mechanism of the pricing process, determined the structure of the social order —those in command of purchasing power, in the first instance, and later the governments that they put into office—did not want any further steps to be taken in that direction.

Whether that mechanism works for good or for ill depends entirely on the will of those who direct it. Instead of destroying it, take command of it, if you want a better world, and you will find it capable of producing all that you most ardently desire.

You syndicalists want to give the workers their fair share of production and to assure them not only material security, but political power, so that they may become the most influential members of society. Does anything in your recent experience justify the belief that price control and its inseparable concomitant, rationing, constitute an effective method of satisfying such hopes? Can you doubt that the "true social policy" I have outlined for you here, which will first create the abundance whose distribution is later to be adjusted, better serves the interests of those on whose behalf you are working than a regime of lies that offers, at low prices, a wealth of goods that are scarcely to be obtained at all?

Like the syndicalists, you socialists also want social justice. But, in addition, you want to mould society to your will and to subject it to your power. As Engels said, you want to liberate man by freeing him from the necessity of obeying all laws not of his own making. But the mechanism of the pricing process is precisely a means of freely directing the will of men and of fixing the structure of the society that they constitute. The more purchasing power you have at your disposal, the more will this means become available to you. Take advantage of it. You will find that in making men freely want what you want them to want, you will obtain results that no amount of compulsion, no matter how rigorous, would ever have produced.

You Christians, like all men of good will, feel an instinctive sympathy for policies that entrust to the state the performance of those tasks which your conscience and your faith require that you yourselves perform as a matter of duty. But if you obey the dictates of your conscience and your religion, not only in your thoughts but in your deeds, the free employment of your purchasing power will permit you to create, by virtue of the mechanism of the pricing process, better than any system of compulsion, the fraternal society that you so ardently desire. If you do not want a liberal regime to be selfish, you have only to be altruistic yourselves. And when the spirit of charity that fills your hearts has exhausted every influence that it is capable of exerting on your personal behavior, the procedures of liberal intervention enumerated in the preceding chapter will furnish you with the means of completing the work of individual and private philanthropy by collective and public generosity.

You conservatives wish to maintain and preserve public order in the interests of social peace. Do you really believe that a system of distribution based on prices arbitrarily fixed by the authorities and adjustable by them alone will ever be accepted by the whole nation as the expression of social justice? You know well enough that the edifice you seek to erect will be constantly battered by a flood of claims and counterclaims.

To be sure, in an unhampered market, strikes will occur. But a strike, by accelerating the process of adjustment, is an instrument of equitable distribution. Suitably regulated, a strike is infinitely less dangerous for society than the great waves of claims and counterclaims and the abrupt fluctuations in total purchasing power that are the necessary consequences of any system of wage controls.

You internationalists want to create large regional communities. Do you think that such international communities can ever be established as long as the disparities maintained by price and foreign-exchange controls make autarky the condition of national existence? The unification of Europe will remain a meaningless program until monetary convertibility and a free market have once again pieced together the broken threads of international solidarity.

Thus, by working together in the framework of a free economy, you can secure all those benefits that your system of economic controls was supposed to confer on the world.

Advocates of a controlled economy, whatever your political party, pay heed to what I say.

I tell you that the only way to attain the noble ends that you seek to realize is to resort to a policy of liberal intervention. Some may call it social liberalism; others, liberal socialism; but for all it will be the means of establishing a society of free men and of realizing that humane and just order which all your efforts have as their goal.

You are so eager to improve the lot of mankind, you have experienced so much disillusionment, that you surely will not let my words go unheeded.

If I am wrong, say so. But if I am right, then agree to unite your efforts, your wills, your capacities for action and the direction of affairs, and the influence you have over your followers, to put into effect a policy that will once again make the world a fit place to live in.

Then the day will not be far distant when mankind will finally be able to reap the fruit of its triumphant technology and witness the dawn of a truly bountiful society, established by the people and for the people, which will inspire their confidence and their devotion because it will once again have found a meaning and a mission.

I call upon you, the men of good will in all political parties, who advocate a controlled economy because you want to direct your fellow men toward the richer, purer, and more fraternal society whose image you hold in your hearts, to unite to bring such a society into existence and save, while there is still time, what yet remains of civilization.

7

The Doctrine of Original Sin and the Theory of the Elite in the Writings of Frédéric Le Play*

LUIGI EINAUDI

1. As a man of science, Frédéric Le Play has had the misfortune of falling into the hands of two kinds of specialists: the statisticians and the social reformers. He is himself to blame for this, because his insistence on his "method" has given rise to the belief that the latter constitutes the substance of his thought, and his constant preachments against Articles 826 and 832 of the Civil Code of Napoleon have made him the recognized leader of all the good people who believe that the securing of the freedom of a testator to bequeath his property as he thinks best is one of the reforms, or even "the" reform, absolutely essential for the solution of the gravest social problems. It is unfortunate, I think, that such a fate should have befallen Le Play's reputation. Yet I say this as one who has a high regard indeed for the method of drawing up a family budget that goes under his name, and I am by no means

* "Il peccato originale e la teoria della classe eletta in Federico Le Play," *Rivista di storia economica*, Volume I, No. 2 (Turin, 1936), pp. 85-118; reprinted in *Saggi bibliografici e storici intorno alle dottrine economiche* (Rome, 1953), edizioni di storia e letteratura, pp. 307-343.

in favor of those provisions of the Napoleonic Code which leave a testator the right to dispose freely of scarcely a quarter of his estate and compel him to divide his real property among the coheirs.

2. On both of these points I fully agree with Le Play's teachings. To deprive parents of the right to dispose of their private fortune as they think best—rewarding the good and industrious children and punishing the lazy and ungrateful ones, or at least deferring until the following generation of grandchildren the enjoyment of the share that would have belonged to the rejected child—or still worse, to deny parents the right to bequeath their property in kind, especially the house and the family possessions, only results in the splitting up of the family. Parents rarely have good reason for showing partiality as between one child and another, and generally do not do so. They prefer to let the children divide up the inheritance amicably among themselves. However, in those exceedingly rare cases in which parents do feel it their duty to favor one of their children over the others, or to bequeath their property in kind, they should be free to do as they think right.

Napoleon and his advisers were opposed to allowing a testator this much freedom because they were bent on destroying the old ruling classes and therefore on breaking up the landed estates. But Le Play reminds us that Napoleon, in order to reconstitute a new ruling class, re-created the *majorats*. In Italy, where a testator has the right to dispose freely of half of his estate,[1] this is not a live question. Here a testator is permitted sufficient freedom of action, while at the same time children may defend themselves against unjust discrimination on the part of their parents; nor are the latter prohibited—provided the rule of the rightful share * is observed—from specifying in their bequests the particular possessions that they wish to hand down to this or that child as a part of his legacy.

Le Play praised the inheritance law existing in Savoy, which

* The rightful share, or lawful portion, is the part of a deceased person's estate assured by law to his heirs regardless of his will. [Translator's note.]

was that of Piedmont and later became that of Italy, and he probably would not have asked the Italian legislator for anything
better. But he would have been the first to protest against the
recent summaries of his doctrine contained in the manuals of the
history of economics, which, reducing it to its minimum, would
have the reader believe that the name of Le Play is to be identified only with the well-known attacks on the morcellation of
estates and with proposals in favor of family-owned property, the
rights of the testator, the conservation, by law, of the *famille-
souche*,* etc., etc. Le Play appreciated good laws, to be sure; but
what he exalted above all was good traditions, sound practices, and
stable customs, and if the laws but left these intact, he would ask
for nothing more in the way of legislation. The real problem that
he studied was the origin of good and stable traditions, practices,
and customs, and the reasons for the prevalence of their opposites;
and it is in the study of these questions that his real contribution
to the social sciences consists.

* Le Play uses the word *famille-souche* to designate a type of family organization similar to what A. E. Schaeffle had previously called the *Stammfamilie*. American sociologists (see No. 64 below) have used the term "stem-family" with this
denotation; but, in view of the metaphor implicit in the etymology of the French
word, it would probably be more appropriate to render it as the "trunk-and-
branch" type of family. Situated midway between the patriarchal and the unstable
forms of family organization, it combines, in Le Play's view, the best features of
both. It consists of a parental household, (the trunk), which represents the continuing element of stability, and a number of individuals (the branches) attached
to the parental home by ties of consanguinity and moral obligation. It may include
aged grandparents, unmarried uncles and aunts, sisters, brothers, domestic servants,
orphaned children, etc. The head of the family—usually, but not always, the oldest
male—has final authority, which he may delegate to his heir when the latter
reaches maturity. Though daughters usually go to the families of their husbands,
nobody is required to leave, and anyone may return. There is always room for the
unmarried or the unmarriageable, and the family is always in touch with its off-
shoots. One married child is kept in the parental household as the "associate heir."
The head of the family sets up the other sons in a trade or provides them with
capital from the savings set aside by the family, which also provides dowries for
the daughters who leave. In case of the death of the heir or the "associate heir,"
one of the other children "makes it a point of honor to return and fill the position
of head of the family." Thus the family is assured of both leadership and continuity. (See Le Play, *Les ouvriers européens*, Vol. I, 2nd ed. [1879], chap. XIV,
pp. 441 ff., especially p. 457.) [Translator's note.]

3. I am also an admirer of the "method" that Le Play invented for drawing up a family budget—so much so, in fact, that for more than a quarter of a century, in figuring up our own accounts, my wife and I (or, I should say, my wife compiles a list of our annual expenditures, while I may perhaps succeed, with the help of scattered notebooks, in reconstructing the account of our income) have been following [2] his plan precisely, although with some modification in the fourth section, which refers to expenditures for religion and charity, recreation, and medical care. (The first is devoted to food; the second, to shelter; and the third, to clothing.) Le Play's budgets are very detailed, and each item acquired has to be indicated not merely under its appropriate category, but according to its species, with the quantity shown in weight or volume or number, as well as the price per unit and the total amounts. So, if we should ever decide to make use of this material, it is quite possible that our findings would make a valuable contribution to the history of the way of life of an Italian middle-class family over a period of time extending from the first decade of the century up to the year in which the cycle will be closed. This possibility of recalling, by means of the entries made in our family accounts, our little personal vicissitudes, I owe to Le Play; and since I do not keep a diary, this collection of notebooks is virtually the only souvenir of our daily domestic life that we shall be able to pass on to our children. For this heritage, therefore, they will be obliged to Le Play.

4. I say this in order to attest my gratitude to Le Play and to inform the reader that in my opinion his model of a family budget is superior to those proposed later. But I must add that the statisticians, in including the family budgets of Le Play in the scheme of statistical methods, have rendered him a very poor service. His disciple Cheysson extracted, in 1890, from Le Play's basic works (*Les budgets comparés de cent monographies de familles publiés d'après un cadre uniforme dans "Les ouvriers européens" et "Les ouvriers des deux mondes,"* prepared in collaboration with Alfred Toqué, with an introduction by E. Cheys-

son, published in the "Bulletin de l'institut international de statistique," Vol. V, Book 1, pp. 1-157) a hundred of the budgets of Le Play and his school and placed them side by side. In doing so, Cheysson very wisely contented himself with publishing the absolute as well as the percentage values of each budget considered *per se,* without attempting to introduce totals or averages. The statisticians, of course, began to complain that this material was unreliable, that the number of cases dealt with was too small, that they exhibited no homogeneity in time and space, and that the data themselves are subject to doubt in regard to the exactness of the weights and even of the amounts paid, which are indicated down to the last cent. Confronted by peasants, who are diffident by nature, how could Le Play pretend to appraise accurately and specifically facts that, as a rule, are even beyond the understanding of the parties concerned? These are, then, not observations of actual facts, however few, but the arbitrary reconstructions of an observer, albeit a most acute and ingenious one. Hence, they are not material that can be utilized by the method of statistics, which presupposes mass phenomena observed in great numbers with a uniform procedure and the certainty of objective relevance.

I too believe that Le Play's method is impracticable for statistical purposes. I must add, however, that in no way does it lessen the value of the family budgets that are today compiled by bureaus of statistics on the basis of distributed questionnaires or of inquiries made among thousands of families to assert that the budgets of Le Play (his own and those whose preparation he supervised) are and should remain something different. They are historical documents, and, as such, not amenable to statistical treatment. The observations they contain refer not to masses, but to particular individuals. Even if we were to go to the extreme of adopting the quite obviously most exaggerated hypothesis that not a single one of Le Play's budgets is an exact reproduction of the actual budget of the particular family in the place and period of time under consideration and that the data thus provided must therefore be declared as of no use for statistical purposes, this would in no way diminish their historical value. History is a reconstruction of individual facts performed by a person who sees the events with his "own" eyes, selects for narration from the vast array of innumerable facts only those of interest to him, disregarding all the others, and colors his findings according to his own personal vision of human affairs.

The statistician has no right to make a choice among the hundred or the thousand family budgets available to him within the limits of the group he has to study. Limitations of time and resources may constrain him to study only ten out of a hundred or a thousand budgets, but the selection ought to be made as much as possible a random one, without the intervention of a deliberate act of judgment or of will on his part. He can be guided in his choice by the appropriateness of taking into account those budgets which throw light upon certain characteristics, for instance, the practice of a given vocation, the number of children, the ownership of the house, etc., etc. But within the limits in which the inquiry is technically and financially feasible, the cases in which these characteristics are exhibited cannot be the object of an arbitrary choice on his part.

The historian, on the other hand, makes his choice according to his own free will. From among many families he selects for observation the one that seems to him the most representative or typical. Why just it and no other should seem so to him even he is perhaps not in a position to say. An impression, a sentence, a way of living, the opinion of persons of repute in the neighborhood—all may have contributed to the choice. The historian may also find it convenient to combine observations relating to two or three families in a composite picture that seems to him really typical. Are not some of the most famous paintings of the great masters abstractions? And yet they succeed better than the most faithful photographs in bringing a whole epoch to life.

Le Play imagined he was performing the work of a statistician, but he wrote history instead. His monographs on Russia depict the social relations between great landowners and peasants, charcoal sellers and shepherds, in the period of serfdom (1844-1853) better than a great many learned academic volumes and famous novels. The figure of the sharecropper in old Castile (1840-1847) comes alive against the background of a society in which the grandee of Spain is much nearer to the worker than one would gather from the stories that depict their relations as a form of guerilla warfare. We have a faithful picture of prerevolutionary France in his monograph of 1856 on the peasant *famille-souche* in the Lavedan valley in Bearn. Sainte-Beuve and Taine, who had a certain familiarity with historical sources, owe very much indeed to Le Play. He had the historian's eye.

5. The difference between those historians—let us say, historians of economics, since we are discussing economic problems, though the statement applies to historians of all kinds—who write books that give the reader the impression of being false from the first line to the last, even though all the facts narrated or reported are true, and those who give us a true picture of the period under investigation even though they gather together only a few arbitrarily selected facts, is entirely a matter of personal vision, of what we have called the historian's eye. Such being the case, the question arises: What kind of historian's eye did Le Play have?

Many years ago, while I was pursuing certain of my studies in the economics of mining (1900), it occurred to me to browse through the collection of *Annales des mines* of the past century; and there I saw for the first time the signature of Frédéric Le Play at the end of some highly informative studies on the art and economics of mining. I do not suppose that anybody still reads these studies, since they probably could provide the modern engineer with nothing that would be of practical value today. To me, however, who have sought and still continue to seek for connections between price and costs of production, between wages, interest rates, and entrepreneurial profits, and for temporal variations in these relationships, these studies of Le Play will always remain masterpieces.

Le Play was a master of the art of engineering—an accomplished master, and therefore, without his being conscious of the fact, also a master of the art of economics. As a theorist in economics he was —and, what is more, he considered himself to be—a heretic. He had no liking for economists, and whenever he could he spoke unfavorably of Adam Smith and the liberal economists, whom he blamed, along with the encyclopaedists and the utilitarians of the eighteenth century, for the evils of modern society. This attitude on his part can be explained by the fact that he had not fully penetrated into the spirit of economics, which is neither liberal nor socialist, nor anything else for that matter, but the science of costs and prices, of choices made from among limited means for attaining the ends aimed at by men. However, under the discipline of his own art of engineering, a field in which he was pre-eminent, he arrived, in the study of concrete problems, at the same conclusions as the economists, by way of the same method and the same forms of reasoning. Whoever reads his monograph on the official price list for bread (see below No. 13) and that on the competition between wood and coal (No. 11) cannot but place him, in spite of his protests, in the ranks of the classical economists.

The mental habit of the engineer, who is accustomed to approach his technical problem, in so far as he aims at attaining his end with a minimum of cost, from the point of view of achieving maximum economy, helped Le Play to keep his eye on reality. He wished to view reality by way of theoretical meditation, but he never divorced the latter from observation. Repeatedly he insists upon the advantage to be derived, even in technical investigations, from observation of the working techniques of craftsmen, miners, and foundry workers. He ascribed to the study of the applied arts as traditionally practised at least as much importance as to the study of books; he therefore remained, to the last, sceptical of the value of professional schools and preferred to them early apprenticeship in the workshop of the master.

6. So far we have treated Le Play only as an eminent writer of industrial monographs—a rival of, though probably greater than, our Giulio, whose picture I tried to draw on a previous occasion (see *La riforma sociale,* January-February, 1935, and, in this volume, pp. 203-212). It was by a combination of accidental circumstances that Le Play, the student of technology and economics, came to construct a theory of the social world. In his books (*Ouvriers européens,* I, 17-34) we read his account of the first observations that he made as a youth in the course of carefree

jaunts along the banks of the Seine near Honfleur in the company of fishermen and peasants and of the influence upon him of friends of the family who brought back to life for him the men of the *ancien régime,* from the rationalist sceptics who inspired the revolution to the traditionalists, who constituted the strength of old France. A very serious accident in the laboratory in the winter of 1829-1830, which forced him to remain inactive for eighteen months, turned his thoughts to the problem of the meaning and purpose of life (*Ouvriers européens,* I, 40). From this time on a new phase in his intellectual activity began. At first by receiving study grants, and later through the generosity of his own and foreign governments, he was enabled to travel, often on foot, over almost all of Europe as far as the Urals, Scandinavia, and the Spanish sierras. The task of studying and reorganizing great mining enterprises afforded him an opportunity to study at the same time the men who worked in them. He asked himself: Why is a man—and he means the man of the people, the peasant, the laborer, the miner, the foundry worker—satisfied or dissatisfied? Why does he wish either to change his position or to remain where he is? Why is one society prosperous and stable and another unstable or disorganized or corrupt?

7. The problem of Le Play would appear to be that of the preacher, the evangelist, the prophet, whose purpose is to combat evil and to champion good; and indeed, to further these ends, he did found societies and associations for the promotion of peaceful social cooperation and grouped around himself men anxious to improve social conditions. But his aim was, at bottom, substantially different. His problem was a purely scientific one: to search for the laws of social uniformity. He proposed to solve the problem by means of rigorously scientific instruments. If we look beneath the outer trappings, which are a source of so much amusement to the scholar accustomed to the language of professional economists,[3] Le Play (April 11, 1806—April 5, 1882) will be seen to belong to the ranks of the great writers of the nineteenth century who turned their attention to the fundamental bases of political life, such as—if we may include among the theorists the

names of some great journalists—Burke, Mallet du Pan, De Maistre, Gentz, Tocqueville, Taine, Mosca, and Pareto.

The last named might no doubt find it somewhat disquieting to see himself grouped with prophets, evangelists, and militants, but truth demands that we look beneath the surface of religious and political formulas to their inner core of scientific substance. With more or less vehemence and awareness of what they were doing, the writers I have mentioned all reacted against the idea that men are guided in their actions by pure reasoning and that a living society could be created by ratiocination. There are powerful, sometimes mysterious forces—whether we call them instinct, or chance, or tradition, or ruling class and political formula, or elite and residues—that ultimately determine the grandeur and the decadence, the permanence and the dissolution, of societies. That Le Play divides peoples (societies) into types, distinguishing between "model" societies, those "dominated by tradition," the "stable," the "unsettled," and the "disorganized," and makes use of the family budget as an instrument for understanding and analyzing them, is not of fundamental importance in determining the character of his vision of the world or in defining the interpretation that this extraordinary engineer—economist by spontaneous intuition and self-taught writer on politics—has given of the reasons underlying the variation in human societies.

His "school" is virtually dead, and only the devotion of a few disciples keeps the spark alive. During and after the war, family budgets were no longer published in the great collection initiated by him. The principle that a testator should be free to bequeath his possessions as he thinks best has inspired such reforms as the increase in the share of the estate that can be freely disposed of by the testator, the right to bequeath property in kind to legatees specified by the testator, more stringent criteria for the determination of what constitutes "enormous damage," * the right to

---

* According to the Code Napoléon, the principal heir had to administer the estate in such a way as to protect the interests of the coheirs until the division of the patrimony had been completed. Any "damage" resulting to the coheirs from a purchase or a sale of real estate by the executor of the will was considered as "enormous" when it was in excess of half of the "just price" and as "most enormous" when in excess of two-thirds. [Translator's note.]

settle accounts in cash in the division of the estate among the coheirs, and the reduction of inheritance taxes when the legatees are members of the testator's immediate family. Still other reforms have been inspired by Le Play's ideas concerning the duty that the employer owes to his workers in his capacity as their patron and protector, the joint ownership of the house by the several members of the family, and the provision of a day of rest on the Sabbath, as well as by his defense of regional and local autonomy. The half century that has passed since Le Play's death has eliminated from these programs for reform all that was merely transitory and has seen the remainder become the common heritage of public opinion or the object of legislative and administrative action.

His doctrine continues to live on by virtue of the contribution it has made to the ever incomplete system of what he called social science, but what in the Italian language is more aptly described as political science. In the illustrious ranks of those mentioned above it would be unjust not to include the name of Le Play.

8. One of his most remarkable efforts was devoted to what he called the "social vocabulary," by which he hoped to define with precision the three hundred words that constitute the language proper to social science (see below No. 2, *Ouvriers européens*, I, 441-449). The prophet or the apostle uses a mystical language calculated to appeal to sentiment and imagination. Since Le Play wished to establish a science, he began by defining words that were in current use. The essence of his doctrine is to be found in the words with which he characterized the ruling classes in society. What others later called a "political class," or an "elite," he called *autorités naturelles*. They are "those whose power in private life derives from the nature of men and things: the father of the family; the director of the factory; the wise man of the community, as indicated by the people's concern and affection." Such men are thus endowed with natural authority and, rising to a position of superiority, by virtue of their ancestry, their social position, and the wisdom of their advice, they direct and command others independently of the legal system of the country.

The highest kind of authority is that derived from the general recognition that one is well fitted to give counsel to others, and this Le Play calls social authority. Those are invested with it

who, by their moral probity, have become the recognized models of private life, who show a strong tendency towards righteousness in their relations with all races, under all conditions, and in all social regimes, and who, by the example of their family and their factory, by their scrupulous observance of the Decalogue and of the customary forms of peaceful social behavior, win the love and the respect of all those around them and thus establish in their community a realm of well-being and peace.

Who of us has not known such a man? Men of this type often hold no official position. They have never been cabinet ministers, senators, or deputies. They did not intrigue for positions as mayors or councillors; they were not offered, or did not accept, the office of *podestà* * or positions of public trust. Sometimes they have acted as conciliators, since their natural office is to sit under the village tree and settle disputes, admonish the ill-bred, and give well-heeded advice to the humble. Such men are superior to those who hold power in this world, for the latter inevitably pass away, while the words of the wise man endure forever.

The scientific investigator arriving in a village in search of sociological information does not know his business if he fails to seek out the man whom public opinion deems the local sage, the chief person of distinction, whether he is rich or of moderate fortune, to whom the inhabitants spontaneously turn for advice. Holders of public office, whose authority is derived from their position in the government, will talk to the inquiring sociologist of the burden of taxes, of demands for governmental aid and intervention, and of projects for the improvement of the local economy. On matters of this kind the village sage will have nothing to say,

---

* A mayor is the head of an Italian community. Now, as in the pre-Fascist era, he is elected by its members. In Fascist times *podestà* was the title given to the office, but the person holding it was appointed by the government, not elected. [Translator's note.]

because nobody there ever thinks of such things; but he will be well informed regarding its customs, its old people, the children, the families, and the perennial reasons for their prosperity or decline.

It pleases Le Play to borrow from Plato ("The Laws," Book XII) the definition of the leader of the people:

For among the great mass of men there are always, in fact, some, though not very many, who are divinely inspired. Such men spring up in ill-governed states quite as much as in those that are well governed, and their society is beyond price. It is always proper for one who dwells in a well-governed state to follow the trail of such men over land and sea, seeking after him who is incorruptible,* so as to confirm thereby those laws of his native land that are sound and to amend any that may be defective. For in the absence of examination and inquiry of this kind, or if it is improperly conducted, a state cannot permanently remain perfect.

9. Those who enjoy this kind of natural authority derive their power from moral probity and custom. In simple societies the father is omnipotent, and, among the heads of families, one acquires particular authority and becomes the founder of a line of noblemen. Real noblemen are those "who, whether by their virtue, their outstanding services, or their observance of the great traditions of their ancestors, have become the models of public life." The nobility is "the flower of the upper and ruling classes in a model society. True nobility does not consist in the transmission of blood, of name, and of titles, but in the practice of the moral law and in devotion to the public interest." The real meaning of nobility was expressed in an unforgettable way by the Marquis Henri Costa de Beauregard when, in 1793, on being in-

---

* The rendering in the text is in accord with the sense given to this passage by Einaudi in his Italian translation. Jowett understands the Greek text to the same effect. However, the passage is susceptible of a quite different interpretation. Taylor, for example, (*The Laws*, London, J. M. Dent & Sons, 1934) construes it as "an inhabitant of a well-governed state whose own character is proof against corruption," and a similar reading ("if so be that he himself is incorruptible") is to be found in the translation of R G. Bury (*The Laws*, London, William Heinemann, Vol. II, 1926). [Translator's note.]

formed that his coat of arms, carved on the stone wall of the castle of Beauregard, had been smashed, and the family records burned at Villard, he said to his wife:

Are they not foolish to imagine that they have made an end of us just because they have destroyed our escutcheon or scattered our archives? Until they tear the hearts from our bodies they cannot prevent them from beating for all that is noble and good, from preferring truth to lies and honor above everything else. Until they tear the hearts from our bodies they cannot forbid them to be warmed by a strain of blood that has never lost its old vigor. Until they tear the tongues from our heads they cannot prevent us from telling our children over and over again that nobility consists exclusively in a refined feeling for duty, in the courage needed to perform it, and in the utmost fidelity to family traditions.[4]

Thus, Le Play's "elite" is not to be confused with the ruling class in the sense in which the latter term is today generally understood. Pareto gives the name "elite" to those who have the highest index numbers * in their respective branch of activity and asserts, therefore, that all who have succeeded in entering the governing class should constitute a part of the "governing elite": the senator who has been nominated in virtue of an inherited patrimony, the deputy who "in certain countries gets himself elected by buying votes and flattering the electorate, if necessary by showing himself now a democrat of democrats, now a socialist, and now an anarchist"; Pericles' Aspasia; Louis XIV's Mme. de Maintenon; Louis XV's Mme. de Pompadour, "who well understood how to infatuate a man of power and took part in his conduct of the government and public affairs." (*Trattato,* §§2027-2036.) Nothing

---

* See §2027 of his *Trattato di sociologia generale,* where he assigns to each individual an index number denoting the degree of his specific capacity "very much the way grades are given in the various examinations in school. The highest type of lawyer, for example, will be given 10. The man who does not get any clients at all will be given 1. Zero will be reserved for the man who is an out-and-out idiot." To those having the highest index numbers in their respective branch of activity Pareto suggests giving the name "elite," subdividing this class into a *governing elite,* "comprising individuals who directly or indirectly play some considerable part in government," and a *nongoverning elite,* comprising the rest. [Translator's note.]

is more repugnant to the spirit of Le Play than this confusion. For him the elite is the very best (therefore he uses the flower as its symbol) of the ruling and upper classes in a prosperous society —that small and very choice part which aims at and accomplishes certain results that he qualifies as "prosperity" for the nation or the state or the group. A class that brings about social ruination, disorder, and decadence can be a ruling class, but it is not an elite.

From the point of view of linguistic propriety, the terminology of Le Play is preferable to that of Pareto. It was repugnant to Le Play to include a notorious paramour like Mme. de Pompadour among the elite, although it seems obvious that she must be considered as having played an important part in the ruling class. Ruling is the function proper even to the leader of a band of liquor smugglers, who, during the era of Prohibition, came to enjoy a very influential position in American political life. For one to belong to the "elite," moral qualities are required that are lacking in smugglers' leaders and in women of ill fame.

10. But the reasons that prompted Le Play to regard only a part of the ruling class as the elite went deeper than considerations of terminology. From 1661 on, France was certainly governed by a ruling class; but from 1661 to 1762, king and courtiers set an example of corruption; from 1762 to 1789, philosophers and literati propagated "fundamental error"; after 1789, literati, hotheads, and plunderers banded together for the purpose of destroying all the good old customs. Le Play does not include among the "elite" those who actually held positions of political and spiritual leadership in France throughout this whole period. The flower of the ruling class might be neglected, persecuted, expelled from France after the revocation of the Edict of Nantes, and decimated by the guillotine, but it remained "the" elite, and, by safeguarding fundamental truth and the tradition of virtue, it preserved France.

Only rarely does it happen, according to Le Play, that the ruling class is also the elite; but on those exceptional occasions when the two classes do coincide, the foundations of a country's enduring greatness are established for centuries. One of these rare occasions was the reign of Henry IV; and it was continued by Louis XIII

(1582-1643) when, under the protection of the Edict of Nantes (1598), Catholics and Protestants rivaled one another in serving the state, and saints like St. Francis de Sales and Jane de Chantal, philosophers and theologians like Descartes and Bossuet, Nicole and Pascal, statesmen like Pasquier, De Harlay, and Sully helped to make the name of France justly renowned all over the world. Some of these great Frenchmen, though fully aware of the splendor of their own fame, consented to Louis XIV's claiming for himself the glory of this golden century rather than crediting it to the work of his predecessors, to which, in truth, it was due.

11. The distinction between ruling class and elite is fundamental for an understanding of Le Play's view of history. The criterion of this distinction is not the form of government adopted, but the observation of the results of the work accomplished by the ruling class. It is difficult to make a summary of the observations scattered throughout the thousands of pages written by Le Play, and I must perforce content myself with a few sidelights illustrative of his thought. A criterion sufficient for excluding a given ruling class from the ranks of the elite is its falling into "fundamental error," i.e., the "belief in the original perfection" of man. This, according to the summary account given in Le Play's "Vocabulary," was

an opinion introduced into France in the eighteenth century by English and German writers, later taught by J.-J. Rousseau, propagated by Parisian *salons,* adopted as an essential principle by the reformist innovators of 1789, of 1830, of 1848, and of 1870; and then admitted, more or less openly, by modern theories hostile to the spirit of tradition. . . . According to the proponents of this error, the child is born with an innate tendency towards the good. Therefore evil, which exists everywhere, is the result of a corrupting action that tends to deprave human nature from infancy. From this opinion, whose falsity is universally recognized by mothers, physicians, and teachers, are logically derived the three false dogmas of systematic liberty, providential equality, and the right of revolution. Observation of societies based on such principles demonstrates that they are incompatible with the maintenance of peace and social stability.

12. A hasty reader might conclude that it is from mere defer-
ence to an article of dogmatic faith that Le Play derives his opinions concerning truth and error, and good and evil; and perhaps
Pareto would classify him among the metaphysicians. But one who
counts among the greatest pleasures of his intellectual experience
the reading of all that Le Play has written has easily convinced
himself that such is not the case. Every one of Le Play's statements
has its origin in factual observation made by himself or by others.
But unlike those who cite indiscriminately the testimony of thinkers and of scribblers, of saints and of yellow-journal romancers, Le
Play accepts evidence only from those whom he knows to be
properly qualified observers. Who is to judge of the qualities
proper to man? Not Rousseau, whose thinking was influenced by
the theory he wished to construct; but the mother, the physician,
the teacher, and the priest, who see the new-born babe, watch over
it during its first years with the anxiety of the parent and the edu-
cator, and have no reason to err or to lie.

Is Rousseau correct in writing in his "Letter to Christophe de
Beaumont, Archbishop of Paris," that the "fundamental principle
of all ethics, on which I have based all my reasoning . . . is that
man is a being good by nature, who loves justice and order; that
there does not exist in the human heart any original perversity;
and that the spontaneous movements of nature are always right"?
Or is Le Play correct in opposing him with a passage from St.
Augustine's "Confessions" (I, vii, xix)? This passage is repeated
too often in the works of Le Play not to be reproduced in its
entirety:

In the weakness of the infant's limbs, and not in its will, lies its
innocence. I myself have seen an infant devoured with jealousy. It
could not yet speak, but it became quite pale and cast bitter looks on
its foster-brother . . . Is it innocent of a child to refuse to share with
another as weak as himself a fountain of milk so abundant and even
overflowing? . . . And this, my God, is the innocence of childhood?
No, there is no innocence. The same sins that we commit in dealing
with our schoolmasters and tutors in order to get nuts, balls, and
birds we later commit in our dealings with king and magistrates in
order to obtain gold, land, and slaves. With the years the object of

our desire changes, and more frightful punishments take the place of the schoolmaster's rod. But fundamentally human nature remains ever the same. Therefore, O God, it could only have been humility, as symbolized by the low stature of children, that Thou wast commending to us when Thou didst say of them, "Of such is the Kingdom of Heaven."

This way of thinking could lead Le Play into error, but in a manner typical of men of science. His method, in so far as it was founded on the observation of reality by persons qualified to observe it, was rigorously scientific.

13. From the erroneous belief in the original perfection of man three false dogmas are derived: 1) systematic liberty; for "man, born perfect, would make the good prevail everywhere if he were permitted to follow his natural inclinations. Universal evil can therefore be the result only of coercive institutions, which have hitherto been at the foundation of every society, and which therefore have to be systematically destroyed in order to return to men their original liberty"; 2) providential equality, since "men, having been born equally perfect, ought to exercise the same power and enjoy the same advantages if society were founded upon justice"; 3) the right of revolution: "Men are indeed born perfect, and they would make the good prevail everywhere if they could all collaborate under conditions of full liberty and equality. All governments have hitherto kept men under contrary conditions—hence the universal dominion of evil. It is therefore necessary to overthrow by force all governments which tolerate compulsion and inequality."

14. Once the fundamental error is refuted, the ground is cut from under the three false dogmas based upon it. The elite is the class that best expresses and fulfills man's essential nature, which, for its part, cannot be adequately defined in any set of dogmas, not even one opposed to those derived from belief in "original perfection." The man whose acceptance of the doctrine of "original sin" is the result of his own observation of the nature of man-

kind does not as a consequence deduce from it the dogmas of legal compulsion, inequality, and absolute obedience. In Le Play's eyes, lawyers, who are the typical apologists of compulsion and legal authority, play only a secondary and often even a negative role in the class of the elite. Prosperous societies resort to legal compulsion only when the moral example of natural and social authorities is not sufficient; and the multiplication of legal restraints is a sign that a society is passing through the transition from prosperity and stability to instability and disorder.

15. If falling into fundamental error constitutes the criterion by which one is disqualified from membership in the elite, the positive criterion of the prosperity of a society under the rule of the elite is the extent to which the Decalogue is observed: the worship of one God and the prohibition of idols; the honor accorded to parents, and the observance of the injunctions against taking the name of God in vain, killing, stealing, giving false testimony, committing adultery, and coveting the goods of another. These are the rules whose observance in private and public life leads a people to prosperity, and whose violation leads it to ruin. Le Play made individual studies of hundreds of families under the most diverse conditions—physical, historical, and political; scrupulously analyzed the material and intellectual circumstances of their lives; and, in seeking the basic causes of happiness or of unhappiness, of prosperity or of poverty, he invariably referred to the Decalogue and studied the attitude of men towards its specific commandments. This is the magic key that opens to us the secrets of a people's history.

Just as he distinguished between elite and ruling class—for the former not only rules over the destiny of a people, as all ruling classes do, but leads it to prosperity—so he distinguished in the history of a people different alternating stages or modes of existence, one of which he called "prosperity," and defined thus:

Prosperity is that condition—both physical and moral—of a society which results from the repeated performance of good acts. Prosperity especially manifests itself in peace and stability. It appears, depending upon place, race, and time, in two extreme forms, simple and complex, each determined by the nature of the means of subsistence. In "simple prosperity" subsistence depends almost exclusively upon the regular gathering of the spontaneous products of the soil, the rivers, and the sea. In "complex prosperity" subsistence depends in great measure on the exchange of the products of human labor. When the nature of a place permits, prosperity produces an accumulation of wealth, intellectual culture, and political power. (No. 2, below, *Ouvriers européens,* I, 471.)

The order of events is, therefore, the following: 1) the existence of an elite, constituted as such because it knows and practises the Decalogue; 2) the example of the elite in teaching the people the practice of the Decalogue; 3) the ensuing peace and social stability, in which "prosperity" consists, and from which are derived wealth, culture, and power, in greater or lesser degree, in accordance with the conditions of place, race, and time.

Opulence, culture, and power can also exist where there is no "prosperity," in the sense of the peace and social stability resulting from the practice of the Decalogue on the part of the elite and of the people guided by them. For example, in the age of Louis XIV the foundations of society were being undermined by the vices of the ruling class; but this was not true of the times of Henry IV and of Louis XIII, during which France became a nation. The political theorist cannot avoid distinguishing among different facts, and he cannot be content to regard an event as explained simply because it occurred. There is an event that is marked by peace and social stability; and we shall consider this type of "event" as the consequence of the observance of the moral law, and shall qualify as the "elite" the ruling class that is able to produce such kinds of "events." There are other "events" that are marked by discord, unrest, social distress, and revolution; and these "events" we shall consider as associated with the existence of a ruling class that does not act in conformity with the Decalogue. All these "events" and "ruling" classes are analyzed and explained by the historian. But what a difference between these two types! And what a very small part wealth, race, climate, and the age, and the abstract schemes founded upon these concepts, have in the historian's explanation of events!

16. From "prosperity" nations can pass to a state of "suffering," which may be either fleeting and easily remediable, as when it is caused by atmospheric disturbances, or lasting, if it is the result of discord and instability, in which case it can lead to social destruction. But the latter kind of suffering is never irreparable. Men of peace are capable of guiding a suffering or a ruined society back to prosperity, while lawyers and literati are not. Nor, as Le Play repeatedly insists, can this be accomplished by young people, because of the predominance in the young of tendencies towards evil. A society that is not ruled by mature and old men cannot be prosperous. Only the mature, provided that they are men of spiritual distinction, are able to acquire that "knowledge of the world" which is learned far more from experience and personal culture than from formal academic instruction. St. Francis Xavier, at Goa, in 1549, gave the following advice to Father Gaspard Barzée as he was about to leave on a mission to Ormuz:

Wherever you are, even if only passing through, try to learn, by talking with the most respectable inhabitants, the inclinations of the people, the customs of the country, the form of the government, the missions, and everything that concerns civil life. You will more easily manage men if you possess such knowledge; you will have a greater authority over them; you will know on which points you have to depend most in your preaching. The counsel of the religious is not always held in high esteem because they do not know the world. . . . But a religious who understands life and has had experience of human affairs is regarded with wonder as an extraordinary man. . . . Knowledge of the world is not gained from manuscripts and printed books, but from living books, from relations with reliable and intelligent men. Thanks to this kind of knowledge, you will do more good than with all the reasoning of the doctors and all the subtleties of the School. (*Ouvriers européens*, I, 474.)

The true master of men, the leader of a people, is not one who writes, but one who speaks. Le Play quotes Plato's *Phaedrus:*

He would be a simple person indeed who should hope to teach others an art by recording his instruction in writing, or to learn it by reading . . . if he thinks written words can do anything more than awaken his memories of what he already knows about the subject. (*Ouvriers européens,* I, 108.)

And he recalls Christ's commandment to the disciples:

Behold, I send you forth as sheep in the midst of wolves. Be ye therefore wise as serpents and harmless as doves. . . . And ye shall be brought before governors and kings, for my sake, for a testimony against them and the Gentiles. . . . But when they shall deliver you up, take no thought how or what ye shall speak, for it shall be given you in that same hour what ye shall speak; for it is not ye that speak, but the Spirit of your Father which speaketh in you. (St. Matthew, X, 16-20, cited in *Ouvriers européens,* I, 573.)

That is, a people is set on the path of righteousness not by those who write its laws or by those who are steeped in the lore of books, but by the man who utters the word of truth in response to the command of his conscience.

17. As a man of limited but carefully selected reading, Le Play quotes principally the Bible (Old and New Testaments), Confucius, the Koran, St. Augustine, St. Bernard, St. Thomas, Aristotle, Plato, Herodotus, Xenophon, Cicero, Tacitus, Seneca, Marcus Aurelius, Bacon, Bossuet, Locke, Vico, Burke, Montesquieu, De Maistre, Montalembert, Tocqueville, De Bonald, and Abbé Huc. He attacked the ideas of Voltaire, Rousseau, Adam Smith, Napoleon I, and Büchner. The essays of Montaigne he kept near his bedside and meditated upon them.

But the book of books for him was man. All his life he followed the method he first adopted when, in the summer of 1829, during the two hundred days of his first journey, traveling 4,250 miles on foot, he visited the regions located between the Moselle, the Meuse, the Rhine, the North Sea, the Baltic, and the mountains of the Erzgebirge range, of Thuringia, and of Hunsdruck:

to familiarize oneself intimately with the peoples and places visited, with the object of establishing a clear distinction between facts of an essentially local character and those of general interest; to be zealous in seeking contact with the social authorities of each locality; to observe their customs; to listen with respect to the judgments they render on men and affairs.

From these preparatory excursions resulted the hundreds of essays which he himself as well as others called "family monographs," but whose pages in fact reflect their author's profound insight into the reasons why nations are contented or suffer, why they prosper and advance or retrogress and decay and then recover and regain social stability and peace.

18. On observing that Le Play begins with a description of each place he visited and that he insists on the influence that the steppe, the forest, the sea, the mine, the farm, the workshop have on those whose lives are bound up with them, readers who feel the need of placing an author in some one of the categories that they have established for their own intellectual or didactic convenience are prone to classify him among the many writers who undertake to explain the history of the world in terms of the geographical, meteorological, mineralogical, and technical characteristics of the inhabited areas and of the work there carried on. Others—who see him as a painstaking describer of customs; as an investigator of the reasons why slavery, serfdom, and various other kinds of labor conditions prevailed during given periods; as an admirer of family traditions and the bonds of customary usage existing between masters and workmen; and as a proponent of legislative reforms designed to conserve the *famille-souche* and family property—if they refrain, out of respect for linguistic propriety, from pronouncing him a reactionary, consider him at least as a conservative of the same stripe as De Bonald or De

Maistre. Still others, recalling his constant insistence upon the importance of religion and his detestation of the economists and the encyclopaedists, call him a forerunner of Christian socialism and of Catholic corporativism. Those who place the emphasis on the passionate preachments contained in his minor writings, his moving appeals to men of good will, and his exhortations on behalf of unity and cooperation for the sake of social peace, place him among the many fanatics obsessed with the idea that they have found the solution of all social problems.

All these classifications and groupings, though perhaps useful for mnemonic purposes, are basically quite false. In spite of the fact that his description of the Russian steppe and of the influence it has had upon the life of the people who inhabit or traverse it is one of the most impressive artistic representations of primitive pastoral life that I know of, Le Play is not a believer in geographical determinism.[5] In spite of the fact that he has, as it were, cast in bronze the essential lineaments of the rural family of the old prerevolutionary regime and described better than anyone else the relations of patronage characteristic of the guild system and the bonds of mutuality thereby established, Le Play is not a reactionary traditionalist. In spite of the fact that he spent the second half of his life in preaching "social reform," he was not an agitator or reformer. Or at least, what is essential to bear in mind in connection with Le Play is not his remarkable gift for accurate observation of the physical world and for re-evoking the societies of the past. It is time that he were recognized as one of the founders of modern political science.

Of course, he did not set to work with the deliberate intention of writing a scientific treatise. Nor did he, like others, lay himself open to the scorn that we generally feel for all those who, in studying man, affect to divest themselves of every human quality and of all interest in the subject and who apply the same standard to every human sentiment and opinion, as if they were dissecting a cadaver or analyzing a mineral. It is easy enough to indulge in little verbal games of this kind, but they add nothing whatever to the understanding of truth. Of what use is it to scoff at those who professed to proclaim the means by which men can attain to the eternal blessedness of Paradise, when the scoffer himself repeats the very same ideas, only translating them into the so-called scientific jargon of research into the laws by which men live in definite societies having the characteristics alpha, beta, and gamma? This sort of thing is just a ridiculous game of *trucco*.*

Le Play never imagined that scientists would waste their time with such linguistic subtleties, and so he spoke of ruling classes and of the elite, of prosperous or decadent societies, of principles likely to keep societies sound or to disintegrate them, and he expressed himself in the eternal language of Moses and of Christ. He listened to the shepherds of the Ural Mountains, the peasants of the Russian steppes, the nomads of Syria, the fishermen of Norway, the miners of Germany, the peasants of the Spanish sierra and the Basque Pyrenees, and found that the same ideals and principles everywhere make for prosperity, and that the causes of social decline are the same the world over. He did not confuse prosperity with opulence, nor decadence with poverty. He analyzed all these concepts and found at the basis of prosperity and opulence, of decadence and poverty, the presence or absence of respect for the moral law.

19. Though all of Le Play's work is a struggle against the fundamental error of believing in the original perfection of man, it is not a struggle against reason. One who flatters man by declaring that he is born in innocence and that he is prompt to recognize truth and to do what is right, may be a demagogue, a tyrant, or a sophist, but he is certainly not a man of science. The scientific investigator starts from the opposite concept, that of original sin, which is based on common observation, and seeks to determine the forces that sometimes succeed in transforming a primitive wild beast into the image of God. Such forces are not riches and power, nor the technical and economic knowledge necessary for acquiring them; neither are they written laws or the commands of the generals who found or destroy great empires. These forces come into being as the slow accumulation of the fruits of experi-

* A game of billiards in which a player, with his own ball, dislodges that of his adversary. [Translator's note.]

ence of good and evil and by virtue of the authority acquired by men of wisdom who have observed how men, all born sinners, can improve their moral condition or drink the bitter dregs of the cup of abomination. Those who believe in the original perfection of man are deluded by pride. It takes humility to face the truth.

20. Saint-Beuve and Montalembert ascribed to Le Play the glory of having made the "great discovery" of the first principle of social science: "in this subject nothing remains to be discovered" (see below No. 2, *Ouvriers européens*, I, chap. XII). Never, perhaps, has a more profound statement been made. In one of his less well-known works (see below No. 13, p. 94), Le Play states that "the most fruitful reforms are those that are accomplished spontaneously, through the tacit agreement of government and people." Gaetano Mosca has developed to a high degree of perfection the theory that political ideals and principles are formulated by the ruling class as an instrument of government. The specific contribution of Le Play consists in having pointed out the criterion for choosing from among the many different political ideals and principles that have governed the world. The elite rules by applying the ideals that the sages have elaborated, in obedience to the moral law, during the course of the centuries. Among the many different ruling classes, with their diverse political formulas, one can consider as the elite only that class which, by applying the eternal principles of the Decalogue, assures a people's continuity and resurgence.

The six volumes of the *Ouvriers européens* are above all else a stupendous history of the vicissitudes of different societies, starting from the moment when the elite, as the exemplar of the eternal ideal, was superseded by other types of ruling classes. We must not allow appearances to deceive us into thinking that only a book written in accordance with the traditional rules is a historical work. Whoever reads the great historical accounts of the grandeur and the decadence of Rome or of the gradual spread of corruption and rebellion during the period of the French Revolution, cannot help being deeply stirred by the narrative, as he passes from enthusiasm to solicitude, from exaltation to anxiety, just as if he were following the account of the life of someone dear to him. Now this miracle, which a few great historians have accomplished in describing the events that took place in these two epochs of human history, whose story never fails to bring new vistas before our imagination and fills us with anxiety or hope for the future of contemporary society, Le Play has performed in dealing with the whole of humanity.

The method he chose was unusual, and he adopted it without the intention of writing history. In the Europe of 1829-1879 he studied certain living fossils, which he called "families," as typical representatives of different stages of human history. The criterion he used in classifying these fossils was the extent of their observance of the eternal Decalogue. He discovered that social groups move toward or away from prosperity, that is, contentment and social stability, to the extent that they heed or disregard the words of the truly elect, i.e., the sages who, without needing to read any books, or at most by reading only one, teach the moral law. These fossils, as we have called them, do not all belong to the same country; yet they represent—thanks to the penetrating vision of the man who selected and described them—the succession of different historical epochs in the same country. Ranging from the happiest type to the most discontented and disorganized, they tell the tragic story of a progressing decadence no less moving than the stirring pages of Gibbon and Rostovzev on the decline of Rome. From page to page, with growing anxiety, we ask ourselves: Where is mankind going?

But the order of the living fossils can be reversed. It was a day of great joy for Le Play when a young friend of his (see below No. 23, p. 209) placed before him a passage of Vico translated into French by Michelet.

Here, at the very birth of domestic economy, they fulfilled it in its best idea, which is that fathers, by their labor and industry, should leave a patrimony to their sons, so that they may have an easy, comfortable, and secure subsistence; then, even if the worst should happen and they should find themselves without a city, in such extremities at least their families may be preserved and, with them, the hope that the nation may some day rise again. (*Oeuvres choisies* [Paris, 1835],

Vol. II, pp. 107-108, but here quoted from the edition of Nicolini [Bari: Laterza, 1913], Part II, p. 407.)

Thus, one of the greatest philosophers of history of all time confirmed the conclusion of Le Play's own constant observations, that the family is the nucleus of society. Le Play translated this into his own language. Vico was thinking of the devastations of war, whereas what Le Play had in mind was internal moral dissolution. As long as some families survive intact, society is not necessarily doomed to destruction. The political techniques employed by ruling classes not inspired by the moral law are not fatally destined to prevail. Their formulas for gaining and holding political power do not take account of the elite, the only class throughout the ages that has given mankind real guidance and direction. Even if only a few sages survive to continue working and teaching and only a few families and social groups still imbue their actions with the precepts of these sages, the great days of prosperity can return. Just as Henry IV in a single decade raised France once again from the material ruin and moral corruption into which she had sunk during the period of the civil wars and the reign of the Valois and laid the foundation of France's greatness in the seventeenth century, so some other wise and strong man may be able to raise France from the ruins of the war of 1870 and rescue her from the intoxication of the great war of 1914-1918.

Those who affect to speak only in scientific terms do not find the moral law among the elements of their sociological laws. Let us pardon them and take the liberty of affirming that Le Play had a much deeper insight into the real reasons underlying the alternating vicissitudes of societies and civilizations.

The preceding essay on the scientific content of Le Play's doctrine is somewhat in the nature of an introduction to the bibliographical description of his own works and some of their sources as well as the works of certain of his students. This description continues the tour of my library which I began elsewhere (*La riforma sociale,* March-April, 1935, and in this volume, pp. 3-26), and on the first stage of which I discussed Francesco Ferrara. The present bibliography too will include only books that are actually in my possession. My reasons for following this procedure are the same as those I have already mentioned. In the first place, only books that the bibliographer himself has actually seen should be included in his list. Moreover, following the same procedure as Morellet, McCulloch, and Papadopoli adopted for the cataloguing of their own books, Bonar for the books of Adam Smith, and Alfred Marshall's widow for those of her late husband, I wish to compile a catalogue of all the books that, by accident or by design, I have accumulated over the years about certain economists or certain economic problems. It is a catalogue that is in many respects deficient when compared with that of a public library, yet in some way instructive. I have also hoped to be of some modest assistance to students wishing to make a judicious selection of books for their own library of economics at not too great a cost.

1. LES OUVRIERS EUROPÉENS. *Études sur les travaux, la vie domestique et la conduite morale des populations ouvrières de l'Europe précédées d'un exposé de la méthode d'observation,** Paris: Imperial Press, 1855. One folio volume, pp. 301. My copy carries the author's dedication to Michel Chevalier and the bookplates of both. Chevalier had given his daughter in marriage to Le Play's son. From Chevalier's library this volume was transferred to that of his son-in-law, Paul Leroy-Beaulieu.

The book's inconvenient format is due to the reproduction in their entirety, in the space of only two pages, of all the thirty-six budgets of the workers' families that were studied: the left sheet for the income, the right for the expenditures. A general introduction precedes and an appendix follows, both dealing with the method and scope of the study, which he calls a "direct inquiry." Such investigations, he says, are preferable to statistical inquiries, which he holds in rather low esteem because: 1) "they abstract from all considerations whose connection is only accessory to facts of interest to the

---

* The Workers of Europe. Studies of the work, domestic life, and moral conduct of the laboring classes of Europe, with an introductory account of the method of observation.

public authorities"; 2) "they do not take into account either the particular nature of individuals or the specific character of the environment in which they live"; 3) they are not concerned with the "direct observation of facts," but confine themselves to the "compilation and more or less plausible interpretation of facts collected from very different points of view, for the most part alien to scientific interest." Therefore, "in spite of their apparent generality and their seductive regularity, statistical reports have rarely contributed to the progress of social science. Statesmen have sometimes made use of them in order to support a given thesis, but experienced men of affairs rarely rely on them in the formulation of policy or in the conduct of their business."

The following quotation from Fontenelle's eulogy on Vauban serves as an epigraph: "He carefully informed himself concerning the value of the lands, their yield, the method of their cultivation, the household possessions of the peasants, their customary food, and the daily produce of their labor—all apparently mundane and insignificant particulars, but nevertheless pertinent to the great art of governing."

These words make clear the purpose and scope of the work. Perhaps, if he had been familiar with it, he might have added the following report by Mirabeau on the method by which Cantillon gathered his information: "In his travels he wished to investigate everything at first hand. He would descend from his carriage to question the peasant in the field and test the quality of the soil by putting a small amount on his tongue. He would take notes and in the evening, after he returned to his inn, an accountant, whom he always brought along with him, would make a fair copy of everything he had noted down."

The edition published in 1855 had not entirely satisfied Le Play, for, yielding to the advice of his friends, he had consented to eliminate from it his theoretical conclusions and his ideas on social reform—"half a volume of truth that my fellow citizens could not tolerate"—confining himself to a few concluding remarks: "The position occupied by a society certainly depends upon its material conditions and political institutions; but the essential factors which determine its superiority are of a moral order."

And so he did not rest until he could bring out a second
edition of his *magnum opus.*

2. LES OUVRIERS EUROPÉENS. *Études sur les travaux, la vie domestique et la condition morale des populations ouvrières de l'Europe d'après les faits observés de 1829 à 1855, avec des épilogues
indiquant les changements survenus depuis 1855.** Second edition,
in six volumes. Tours: Alfred Mame and Sons, 8°.

Vol. I: *La méthode d'observation appliquée, de 1829 à 1879, à
l'étude des familles ouvrières en trois livres ou précis sommaire
touchant les origines, la description et l'histoire de la méthode avec
une carte géographique des 57 familles décrites.*** 1879, pp. xii +
648, 1 c.n.p.***

Vol. II: *Les ouvriers de l'orient et leurs essaims de la Mediter-
ranée; populations, soumises à la tradition, dont le bien-être se
conserve sous trois influences dominantes: le décalogue éternal, la
famille patriarcale et les productions spontanées du sol.**** 1877,
pp. xxxiv + 560, 1 c.n.p.

Vol. III: *Les ouvriers du nord et leur essaims de la Baltique et
de la Manche; populations guidées par un juste mélange de tradition et de nouveauté, dont le bien-être provient de trois influences
principales: le décalogue éternel, la famille-souche et les productions spontanées du sol ou des eaux.***** 1877, pp. xlii + 513, 1
c.n.p.

---

* The Workers of Europe. Studies of the work, domestic life, and moral condition of the laboring classes of Europe, on the basis of facts observed from 1829 to
1855, with appendices indicating the changes that have occurred since 1855.

** The method of observation employed from 1829 to 1879 in the study of
workers' families presented in three volumes, or a synoptic view of the origin, description, and history of the method, with a map showing the location of the fifty-
seven families described.

*** Cover not paginated. In this sense the abbreviation *c.n.p.* will be used here-
after in the text. [Translator's note.]

**** The workers of the East and the Mediterranean: Societies dominated by tradition, which owe their well-being to the influence of the eternal Decalogue, the
patriarchal family, and the spontaneous products of the soil.

***** The workers of the North, the Baltic Sea, and the English Channel: Societies in which tradition and innovation are aptly combined and which owe their
well-being to three principal sources: the eternal Decalogue, the *famille-souche,* and
the spontaneous products of the soil or the sea.

Vol. IV: *Les ouvriers de l'occident. Ire série: Populations stables, fidèles à la tradition, devant les envahissements de la nouveauté, soumises au décalogue et à l'autorité paternelle, suppléant à la rareté croissante des productions spontanées par la communauté, la propriété individuelle et le patronage.** 1877, pp. xlii + 575, 1 c.n.p.

Vol. V: *Id., IIme série: Populations ébranlées, envahies par la nouveauté, oublieuses de la tradition, peu fidèles au décalogue et à l'autorité paternelle, suppléant mal à la rareté croissante des productions spontanées par la communauté, la propriété individuelle et le patronage.*** 1878, pp. 1 + 535, 1 c.n.p.

Vol. VI: *Id., IIIme série: Populations désorganisées, égarées par la nouveauté, méprisant la tradition, revoltées contre le décalogue et l'autorité paternelle, empêchées par la désorganisation du travail et de la propriété de suppléer à la suppression des productions spontanées.**** 1878, pp. 1 + 568, 1 c.n.p.

In this edition, whose format is more convenient, the number of typical families observed increases from thirty-six to fifty-seven, and the second to the sixth volumes are systematically divided into four parts: an introduction, dealing with the social structure of the countries inhabited by the families investigated; the monographs themselves, all composed on the same pattern (place, industrial organization, family composition, means and modes of existence, history, customs and institutions—with appended budgets and accounts of income and expenditures—and diverse elements in the social struc-

---

* The workers of the West: first series: Stable societies standing faithful to tradition in the face of a flood of innovations and subject to the Decalogue and paternal authority, in which the community, individual property, and patronage compensate for the increasing scarcity of spontaneous production.

** *Id.*, second series: Societies shaken by a flood of innovations, forgetful of tradition, and showing little respect for the Decalogue and paternal authority, in which the community, individual property, and patronage poorly compensate for the increasing scarcity of spontaneous production.

*** *Id.*, third series: Disorganized societies, confused by innovation, despising tradition, revolting against the Decalogue and paternal authority, prevented by the disorganization of labor and property from compensating for the suppression of spontaneous production.

ture of the place) *; an alphabetical and methodical glossary of essential words, ideas, and particularities, and an appendix on the changes in social conditions that occurred after 1855. The first volume provides a synoptic view of the whole inquiry: the origin, description, and history of the "method" employed. Le Play does not speak of his "doctrine," but of his "method," which consisted in the search for the essential truths about society.

In the compilation of the family monographs, Le Play often made use of the works of others. "According to information collected at the place of inquiry" is the expression he usually adopts to indicate the collaboration of A. de Saint-Léger, A. Daux, Ad. Focillon, A. Saglio, A. Cochin and E. Landsberg, Courteille and J. Gautier, or exclusive reliance on the work of E. Delbet, A. de Saint-Léger and E. Delbet, Ad. Focillon, E. Landsberg, Narcisse Cotte, Ubaldino Peruzzi (a monograph on the Tuscan sharecropper in the fourth volume), S. Coronel and F. Allan, T. Smith, Ratier, A. Paillette and Sergio Suarez, A. Duchatellier, A. Dauby, De Barive, T. A. Toussaint and T. Châle. Collaboration or single authorship here refer to the collection and first elaboration of the material and to the discussion of the results. The definitive redaction and the conclusions bear the uniform imprint of Le Play himself.

The subtitle of each volume sums up the characteristic features of each family's position in the scale of social values.

3. LES OUVRIERS DES DEUX MONDES. *Études sur les travaux, la vie domestique et la condition morale des populations ouvrières des diverses contrées et sur les rapports qui les unissent aux autres classes, publiées sous forme de monographies par la Société internationale des études pratiques d'économie sociale.***

---

* *Élément diverses de la constitution sociale* refer to social phenomena before which the worker is merely passive and the good or bad consequences of which cannot be attributed to him, e.g., the Napoleonic Code's provisions concerning the division of the family property among the children of the testator. [Translator's note.]

** The workers of the Old World and the New. Studies of the work, domestic life, and moral condition of the laboring classes in different countries and their bonds of unity with other classes. Published in the form of monographs by the Société internationale des études pratiques d'économie sociale.

In 1856 Le Play founded the Société internationale des études pratiques d'économie sociale. One of its functions was to promote the writing and publication of family monographs modeled after those contained in the *Ouvriers européens* and issued by the same publisher.

A first series of five volumes bears the following dates: I, 1857, pp. 464; II, 1858, pp. 504; III, 1861, pp. 470; IV, 1862, pp. 500; V, 1885, pp. iii + 536. Publication proceeded rapidly in the first five years, with thirty-seven monographs contained in the first four volumes. The first chapters of the fifth volume, with three monographs, appeared in 1875; the last, between 1883 and 1885. The complete volume is dated April 15, 1885. It was from the monographs contained in the first four volumes of this work that were drawn, in great part, the twenty-one monographs that were to increase the second edition of the *Ouvriers européens* (1877-1879). Thus, the two publications overlap to a certain extent; up to the first third of the fifth volume, both were published under the personal supervision of the founder of the society.

Le Play died in 1882. After the appearance of the fifth volume the society initiated a second series in 1887 published by Firmin-Didot and Co.: I, 1887, pp. viii + 532; II, 1890, pp. x + 560; III, 1892, pp. xvi + 483; IV, 1895, pp. viii + 535; V, 1899, pp. xii + 590.

A third series is composed of two complete volumes: I, 1904, pp. viii + 578, together with a supplement of forty-eight pages and a map; II, 1908, pp. viii + 519, with a supplement of thirty-two pages. Both supplements were devoted to monographs on factories.

Among the names of Le Play's collaborators in the three series of the *Ouvriers des deux mondes* we find, besides those already mentioned (A. Focillon, E. Delbet, A. de Saint-Léger, U. Peruzzi, Narcisse Cotte, A. Dauby, T. Châle, T. A. Toussaint, Courteille and J. Gautier, S. Coronel and F. Allan) the names of industrialists, workers, agriculturists, and priests, in appreciation of their specialized knowledge of the facts under investigation. And side by side with these we find the names of scholars who later acquired fine reputations: Pierre du Maroussem, who contributed nine family monographs, in addition to the two already mentioned dealing with factories; Urbain Guerin, who contributed nine more; Armand Julin, two; Claudio Jannet, one; Victor Brants, two; A. Delaire, three; Augustin Cochin, one; Ippolito Santangelo Spoto, three (among them a remarkable paper on a recent chapter in the vicissitudes attendant upon the curious social experiment initiated by the Bourbon monarch Ferdinand IV in the colony of St. Leucio near Caserta) ; and the Countess Maria Pasolini, who contributed a monograph on the sharecroppers in Romagna.

4. LA RÉFORME SOCIALE EN FRANCE, *deduite de l'observation comparée des peuples européens,** Paris: Plon, 1864, 8°. Vol. I, pp. xii + 440; Vol. II, pp. 4 n.p. + 480.

This book went through several editions, of which the sixth, "corrected and revised," was the last published during the lifetime of the author. It was issued by Alfred Mame and Sons, 1878, in four volumes, 16°: I, pp. xc + 2 n.p. + 371; II, pp. 4 n.p. + 460; III, pp. 4 n.p. + 529; IV, pp. 4 n.p. + 468. In 1901 an eighth edition appeared, which the publisher, in a "prefatory note to the reader" declared to be a simple reprint of the sixth edition, the only variation being a return to the division into three volumes used in the preceding third, fourth, and fifth editions.

The rearrangements and other changes between the first and the sixth edition are manifold and testify to the care with which Le Play each time revised this book, which, despite its rather bulky size, had the largest sale of all his works. Prefatory remarks, introductions, appendices, and addenda methodically make clear the scope and content of the work. The chapters become books and the paragraphs chapters. The first edition, which has an introduction dealing with "Les idées préconçues et les faits" (preconceptions and the facts) and a conclusion on "Les conditions de la réforme" (the conditions of reform), is made up of seven chapters, dealing with religion, prosperity, the family, labor conditions, nonfamily associations, private relations, and government. In the sixth edition the material in each book is identical with that in each of the old chapters; but the fifth book, on asso-

* Social reform in France, based on a comparative study of the peoples of Europe.

ciations, is divided into two parts: "communautés" (community of property, cooperatives, and joint stock companies) and "corporations"; and the seventh, on government, is also divided into two parts: one on the selection of models, and the other on corruption and reforms in France. In 1878 Le Play added an epilogue to the text of the 1864 edition. The appendices increase from five to eleven. The copious alphabetical and analytical index of the first edition is transformed in 1878 into two indices, one of words used in a particular sense, and the other of the authors quoted.

5. L'ORGANISATION DU TRAVAIL, *selon la coutume des ateliers et la loi du décalogue, avec un précis d'observations comparées sur la distribution du bien et du mal dans le régime du travail, les causes du mal actuel et les moyens de réforme, les objections et les réponses, les difficultés et les solutions.**

The second edition, which I have at hand, was published by Mame at Tours, 1870, pp. xii + 564. In it appears the following epigraph, taken from the "Testament politique" of Richelieu (I, II, 10) : "Les politiques veulent, en un État bien réglé, plus de maîtres ès arts mécaniques que de maîtres ès arts libéraux" ("In a well-constituted state, the true policy is to have more masters of mechanical arts than masters of the liberal arts.") Included also is important documentation on the right of testamentary bequest in France, the brutal behavior of peasants toward their aged parents, and the erroneous opinion regarding the superiority of youth to old age.

6. L'ORGANISATION DE LA FAMILLE *selon le vrai modèle signalé par l'histoire de toutes les races et de tous les temps, avec trois appendices par MM. E. Cheysson, F. Le Play et C. Jannet.*** Paris: Téqui, 1871, pp. xxvii + 318.

---

* The second edition of this work was translated into English by Gouverneur Emerson, under the title *The Organization of Labor*, Philadelphia: Claxton, Remsen and Haffelfinger, 1872, pp. xxii + 3 n. p. + 392, 12°. [Translator's note.]

** The true model of family organization, as demonstrated by the history of all races and all times, with three appendices by MM. E. Cheysson, F. Le Play, and C. Jannet.

The first appendix, the work of E. Cheysson, an engineer, is a historical document of exceptional importance: the story of the impending ruination of the Melouga family brought on by the Civil Code in 1869. This was the same family that Le Play, in 1856, had considered as an ideal model of social organization. The second appendix is a report prepared by Le Play on the way in which small patrimonies are eaten up by rapacious lawyers. The third is an exposition by Jannet of the juridical system characteristic of the countries in which the institution of the *famille-souche* has taken root.

7. LA PAIX SOCIALE APRÈS LE DESASTRE, *selon la pratique des peuples prospères.** Reply of June 1, 1871, to questions received by the author between September 4, 1870, and May 31, 1871. Second edition, with an epilogue added in 1875, Tours: Mame, 1876, pp. 167.

A booklet consisting of questions and answers, written for the purpose of popularizing those of his ideas which he sees confirmed by the disaster of the war of 1870.

8. LA CONSTITUTION DE L'ANGLETERRE, *considérée dans ses rapports avec la lois de Dieu et les coutumes de la paix sociale, précédée d'aperçus sommaires sur la nature du sol et l'histoire de la race, avec la collaboration de M. A. Delaire.*** Tours: Mame, 1875, Vol. I, pp. lxiii + 340; Vol. II, pp. 4 n.p. + 437.

A picture of England's prosperity during the first two-thirds of the nineteenth century. (Le Play uses the term "prosperity" rather than "grandeur" because the latter is alien to his conception of really great peoples and is often incompatible with prosperity in the moral rather than the material sense.) The four foundations of prosperity are, in his opin-

---

* The return to peaceful social cooperation after the debacle, as shown by the example of prosperous societies.

** The constitution of England, considered in its relations to the law of God and the customs of peaceful society, preceded by a few brief observations on the nature of the soil and the history of the race, in collaboration with A. Delaire.

ion, the authority of parents, enjoined by God's Testament and fortified by the law; the hierarchy derived from the *familles-souche* and identified with the soil; the national monarchy; and the subordination of public life to the laws of God.

9. LA RÉFORME EN EUROPE ET LE SALUT EN FRANCE. *Le programme des unions de la paix sociale, avec une introduction de M. H.-A. Munro Butler Johnstone.** Tours: Mame, 1876, pp. 300.

Together with Nos. 7 and 8, this book represents Le Play's contribution to the movement of social reconstruction that developed out of the ruins of 1870. While Bonapartists, Legitimists, and Orleanists were losing in vain disputes the battle for the return of the hereditary monarchy, Le Play kept insisting that the true problem did not consist in the restoration of any particular form of government, but in the development of the ideas, customs, and institutions of peace and social stability. Among the institutions likely to prevent social convulsions he lists the privy council, the parliament, the cabinet, and the supreme court of justice. The members of the first and the last are to hold office for life, to be held legally accountable for their acts, and invested with the right to veto all legislation that violates the laws of God and the law of nations. However, the elasticity of the powers inherent in sovereignty is not derived from written law, but from custom.

10. LA CONSTITUTION ESSENTIELLE DE L'HUMANITÉ, *exposé des principes et des coutumes qui créent la prosperité ou la souffrance des nations.*** Tours: Mame, 1st ed., 1881; 2nd ed., 1893, pp. xvi + 360.

A note in the second edition informs us that this book contains the definitive expression of Le Play's ideas. He died a

---

* Reform in Europe and the salvation of France. Program of the unions de la paix sociale, with an introduction by H.-A. Munro Butler Johnstone.

** The essential constitution of humanity, an exposition of the principles and customs responsible for the prosperity or the suffering of nations.

few months after completing it. Special attention should be given to the appendix, dealing with the propaganda literature put out by the various associations which Le Play founded and containing an historical account of the publishing house of Alfred Mame of Tours.

11. *De la methode nouvelle employé dans les forêts de la Carinthie pour la fabrications du fer et des principes que doivent suivre les propriétaires de forêts et d'usines au bois pour soutenir la lutte engagée dans l'occident de l'Europe, entre le bois et le charbon de terre.** Paris: Carilian Goeury et V°ʳ Dalmont, 1853. Excerpt from the *Annales des mines,* fifth series, Vol. III, 8°, pp. 205 and six tables.

A typical example of the kind of work that one finds scattered throughout the *Annales des mines.* An exact comparative analysis of the costs of production and the price of iron manufactured according to each of the two methods. A demonstration of the connections existing between the laws relating to the inheritance of landed property, the breaking up of estates, the denuding of forests, and the price of iron.

12. *Enquête sur la boulangerie du département de la Seine, ou recueil de dépositions concernant le commerce du blé, de la farine et du pain, faites en 1859, devant une commission présidée par M. Boinvilliers, président de la section de l'intérieur, recueillies par la sténographie, revues par M. Le Play, conseilleur d'état rapporteur, puis par les déposants, coordonées at complétées par une table alphabétique et analytique des matières.*** Paris: Imprimerie nationale, 4°, pp. 8 n. p., xi + 834.

---

* On a new method employed in the forests of Carinthia for the production of iron, and the principles to be observed by the owners of forests and timber mills in order to withstand the competition of coal in Western Europe.

** An inquiry into the bakery business in the Department of the Seine, being a collection of despositions concerning the commerce in wheat, flour, and bread made in 1859 before a commission presided over by M. Boinvilliers, president of the Section de l'Intérieur, stenographically recorded, and revised first by M. Le Play, member of the Conseil d'Etat, and later by the deponents; coordinated and completed by an alphabetical and analytical index.

13. *Question de la boulangerie du département de la Seine. Deuxième rapport aux sections réunies du commerce et de l'intérieur, du Conseil d'État, sur le commerce du blé, de la farine et du pain, par M. F. Le Play, conseiller d'État, rapporteur.** Paris: Imprimerie impériale, 1860, 4°, pp. 299.

A "first report," which should precede No. 12, was distributed on January 23, 1858, and was also prepared by Le Play. On the basis of this the Conseil d'État resolved on June 22, 1858, to conduct an inquiry, the results of which are contained in No. 12, and to entrust to Le Play the preparation of the second report (No. 13). The methodically prepared and minutely detailed alphabetical indices and notes are characteristic of the scrupulous care that Le Play gave to all his work, including the volume of depositions.

Characteristic too are the conclusions—drawn strictly and exclusively, as was the author's wont, from factual observations made in Paris, in the *départements* of France, and, for purposes of comparison, in London and Brussels—in favor of the gradual abolition of the system of government controls on the commerce in grain, flour, and bread. They were characteristic because Le Play, engineer, observer, and traditionalist, reasoned in the same way and came to the same conclusions as Adam Smith, the very man whom he held responsible in great part for the social evils of his day. The truth is that economic schools do not exist; the only distinction one can make is, as Pantaleoni used to say, between those who know economics and those who do not, or, as I prefer to say, between those who know how to reason within the limits of their knowledge and those who do not.

Le Play, who knew how to reason and had a deep insight into many things, reasoned like a perfect economist in purely economic matters and possessed the additional gift of being able, with the same soundness of judgment, to connect economic facts with the other aspects of life. Just as No. 11

---

* The problem of the bakery business in the Department of the Seine. Second report made jointly to the Section du Commerce and the Section de l'Intérieur of the Conseil d'Etat, on the commerce in wheat, flour, and bread, by M. F. Le Play, member of the Conseil d'Etat and reporter.

demonstrates the connection between the inheritance laws and the management of forests, so No. 13 shows the connection between the official regulation of bakeries and the difficulty that shopkeepers' assistants encounter in raising their social status. Like that of Giulio recorded elsewhere (*La riforma sociale*, January-February, 1935, pp. 100 ff. and in this volume, pp. 203-212), the procedure followed by Le Play in establishing these relationships constitutes a model, hitherto unsurpassed, and always worthy of study, of the way in which concrete economic investigations should be conducted.

14. *Voyages en Europe, 1829-1854, extraits de sa correspondance, publiés par M. Albert Le Play, sénateur.** Paris: Plon Nourrit and Co., 1899, 16°, pp. 4 n. p. + 345.

The letters are preceded by a brief preface written by Le Play's son; a biographical note by Lefébure de Fourcy, Inspector General of Mines; and a bibliography which is interesting because of its references to publications outside the field of economics.

On Le Play and His Doctrine

15. AUBURTIN, FERNAND. *Frédéric Le Play d'après lui-même. Vie, méthode, doctrine. Notice et morceaux choisies.*** Paris, Giard and Brière, 1906, 16°, pp. 6 n. p. + vi + 608, with a reproduction of Le Play's statue in the gardens of the Luxembourg.

16. DE BESSE, P. LUDOVIC. *Le clergé de France et Frédéric Le Play,**** Paris: Libraire S. François (but printed in S. Remo, 1909, with the imprimatur of the Bishop of Ventimiglia), 1909, 16°, pp. 8 n. p. + iv + 522.

No. 15 contains ample quotations from Le Play's works. No. 16 considers his doctrine of the "providential man" from the Catholic point of view.

---

* Travels in Europe, 1829-1854. Extracts from his correspondence published by Senator Albert Le Play.
** Frédéric Le Play: a self-portrait. His life, method, and doctrine. A general sketch and selected excerpts from his works.
*** The clergy of France and Frédéric Le Play.

17. *Programme de gouvernement et d'organisation sociale d'après l'observation comparée des divers peuples, par un groupe d'économistes avec une lettre-préface de M. F. Le Play.** Paris: Tardieu, 1881, 8°, pp. 4 n. p. + viii + 312.

The compilers' identity is not given, but they belonged to a group of Le Play's friends, and the program seems to have been inspired by him.

18. CATINEAU, P.-H. *Réforme sociale. Deux lettres à M. F. Le Play.*** Paris: Librairie des sciences sociales, 1873, 16°, pp. xi + 79.

19. *Id., Paix ou guerre. Troisième lettre à . . . id.**** Paris, 1873, 16°, pp. 8 n. p. + 94.

Three letters from a former student of the Polytechnical Institute, a follower of Fourier, in which the writer criticizes Le Play's position regarding "original sin," alleging it to be a myth and not a datum of observation, and professes himself, like Rousseau, a believer in the original goodness of man.

20. VIGNES, J.-B. MAURICE. *La science social d'après les principes de La Play et de ses continuateurs.***** 2 volumes, 8°, Paris: Giard and Brière, 1897 (Vols. IX and X of the Bibliothèque sociologique internationale); I, pp. 4 n. p. + 460; II, pp. 4 n. p + 455.

Le Play had followers, of whom some carried on their work in accordance with his principles, while others, under the influence of Demolins and De Tourville, broke away. The review that served as the organ of the former group was *La réforme sociale;* that of the others was for many years *La*

---

* A program of government and social organization based on a comparative study of different peoples, by a group of economists, with a prefatory letter from Le Play.

** Social reform: two letters addressed to M. F. Le Play.

*** Peace or war: third letter addressed to M. F. Le Play.

**** Social science according to the principles of Le Play and his followers.

science sociale. The work of Vignes synthesizes the doctrines not only of Le Play, but of the various groups of his disciples.

21. SOROKIN, PITIRIM. *Contemporary Sociological Theories.* New York and London: Harper and Brothers, 1928, 8°, pp. xxiii + 785.

The second chapter (pp. 63-98) is dedicated to the "School of Le Play." His "deserves to be put among the few names of the most prominent masters of social science." This chapter should be especially consulted for its bibliography of the works of those of Le Play's disciples who later broke away from his school and for its critical summary of the scientific generalizations of the entire school. However, in this work, as well as in that of Vignes, attention is directed to the secondary aspects of the doctrine: nomenclature; the method of drawing up family budgets; geographical environment; types of families (patriarchal, unstable, disintegrating) ; relations among labor, property, family, state, etc.

Collaborators and Disciples

Since the present bibliography is intended for those desirous of becoming acquainted with Le Play's ideas, I shall not include here the few books I have collected that were written by those who later broke away from his school (see Nos. 18, 19, and 21), but only works that seem to me to be derived directly from his principles. The collected volumes of *La réforme sociale* and the various bulletins published by the unions pour la paix sociale are indispensable to the scholar and can be consulted in public libraries. Among the separate works that are worth mentioning are the reports of certain congresses and the books of Jannet, Du Maroussem, and De Ribbe.

22. LA RÉFORME SOCIALE ET LA CENTENAIRE DE LA RÉVOLUTION. *Travaux du congrès tenu en 1889 par la Société d'économie sociale et les unions de la paix sociale fondées par F. Le Play, précédés d'une lettre de M. H. Taine et d'une introduction sur les prin-*

cipes de 1789, l'ancien régime et la révolution.* Paris, 1890, 8°, pp. 4 n. p. + xiii +645 + cxxiv.

In an illuminating letter Hippolyte Taine recalls that in conversation with Le Play he ventured to suggest as his collaborators Balzac, George Eliot, Turghenieff, and Flaubert. This is perhaps the most profound observation I have ever read on Le Play and the one that most accurately measures his intellectual stature, for he was indeed a co-worker with the great novelists who have plumbed the inmost depths of human nature. "Political Economy in Balzac" could very well be the subject of a rather worthwhile doctoral dissertation; but far more significant is the question as to what contribution Alessandro Manzoni, Balzac, and Le Play may have made to the development of political science, for the answer would help to make clear what was common to the genius of these men, all of whom lived at the same time. In addition, this volume contains reports and speeches that are helpful in illuminating the critical attitude taken by Le Play and his school toward the principles of 1789.

23. *Fêtes du centenaire de La Play et XXVe congrès de la Société internationale d'économie sociale,* Paris, 1907, 8°, pp. 4 n. p. + 220, with a reproduction of the statue unveiled at this time ** in the gardens of the Luxembourg.

Interesting because of the many articles on Le Play's work and the societies he founded. Two essays, one by Albert Sorel on his reading of *La réforme sociale,* and the other, by François Escard, entitled "Le Play at Work" (see above) and consisting of personal reminiscences, are essential for an understanding of the man and the charm that he exercised over others.

---

* Social reform and the centenary of the Revolution. Proceedings of the congress held in 1889 by the Société d'économie sociale and the unions pour la paix sociale founded by F. Le Play, preceded by a letter from H. Taine and by an introductory essay on the principles of 1789, the *ancien régime,* and the Revolution.

** On the occasion of the hundredth anniversary of Le Play's birth and the twenty-fifth congress of the Société internationale d'économie sociale.

24. *La désertion des campagnes. XXIXe congrès etc.** Vol. II, Paris, 1910, 8°, pp. viii + 366 + 123.

The twenty-ninth congress of the Société internationale d'économie sociale and the unions de la paix sociale was devoted to the study of the problem of the flight from the farm. The first volume contains reports of the sessions; the second, mentioned above, the records submitted.

25. *Les classes moyennes dans le commerce et l'industrie. XXXe congrès etc.*** Paris, 1910, 8°, pp. 4 n. p. + 455.

The concept of the middle class and the different types of associations—for granting credit, furnishing supplies and provisions, and promoting sales and consumption—that it sets up for the purpose of defending and advancing its welfare.

26. *L'oeuvre essentielle de demain. 34e congrès etc.**** Paris, 1916, 8°, pp. 6 n. p. + vi + 185.

During the war the surviving followers of Le Play, although becoming ever less numerous, assembled for the purpose of discussing the necessity of an increase in the birth rate; ways and means of defending the race against all the factors making for its degeneration; and the promotion of a "back-to-the-land" movement. The revival of family feeling and of respect for tradition and the dignity of labor, which had filled Taine, Renan, and Le Play with so much hope after the disaster of 1870 and 1871, does not appear to have found any echo after the victory of 1918.

27. DE TOURVILLE, HENRI. *Histoire de la formation particulariste. L'origine des grands peuples actuels.* Paris: Firmin Didot, 1904, 8°, pp. viii + 547, 1 c. n. p.

* The flight from the farm.
** The middle classes in commerce and industry.
*** The essential task of tomorrow.

28. *Id., D'après ses lettres (1842 à 1903)*, with an introduction and notes by Dieux Marie André (pp. 7-17), Paris: Blond, 1928, 16°, pp. 268, c.n.p.

29. JANNET, CLAUDIO. *Les institutions sociales et le droit civil à Sparte.* Paris: Durand and Pedone-Lauriel, 1873, 16°, pp. 158.

30. *Id., Les institutions sociales et le droit civil à Sparte.* Second edition, revised and enlarged, Paris: Durand and Pedone-Lauriel, 1880, 16°, pp. 156, 1 c. n. p.

31. *Id., Les États-Unis contemporains ou les moeurs, les institutions et les idées depuis la guerre de la sécession. Ouvrage précédé d'une lettre de M. Le Play.** Fourth edition, Paris: Plon, 1889, 16°, Vol. I, pp. 4 n. p. + xliii + 350; Vol. II, pp. 4 n. p. + 383.

In a letter to the author, Le Play recalls the conclusion arrived at by Tocqueville in *La démocratie en Amérique:* "The gradual development of equality is a providential event. Among its principal characteristics are the following: it is universal; it is durable; it every day withdraws itself further from control by any human power. All events and all men have contributed to its development. Would it be reasonable to believe that a social movement that has gone so far could be brought to a halt for a single generation? Does anyone suppose that, after having destroyed the feudal system and vanquished kings, democracy will ever retreat before the bourgeoisie and the rich? Will it now stop its course after having become so strong and its enemies so weak?"

Jannet's book constitutes a serious and judicious commentary on these observations and demonstrates what, in his opinion, were the dangerous consequences of the error committed by Franklin, LaFayette, and Jefferson in believing that the victory of the thirteen colonies was due to the spirit of democracy, whereas it was in fact due to the respect for the aristocratic traditions exemplified by the first two presidents, Washington and John Adams. The book was written from 1873 to 1877 while the author was in the United States and had the opportunity to observe the dangers resulting from

---

* The United States today: manners, institutions, and ideas following the Civil War, with a prefatory letter written by Le Play.

the disintegration of the ruling classes in the South after the Civil War.

32. *Id., Le socialisme d'état et la réforme sociale.** Second edition, Paris: Plon, 1890, pp. 4 n. p. + xv + 606.

Studies of different schemes for social reform: labor legislation; compulsory insurance; professional and industrial syndicates; cooperative societies; reform of the inheritance laws, etc., which, in imitation of Bismarck, were being proposed or adopted in Europe in order to resist the advance of socialism. In conformity with Le Play's doctrine, "the real remedy for the evil is a new evangelical conquest of the domestic barbarians, whose number the revolution has multiplied concomitantly with the increase in the density of population brought about by modern economic progress."

33. BAUDIN, LOUIS. *Frédéric Le Play (1806-1882, textes choisies et préface)* (pp. 3-54). Paris: Dalloz, 1947, 16°, 3 c. n. p., pp. 316.

34. DEMOLINS, EDMOND. *Le mouvement communal et municipal au moyen âge. Essai sur l'origine, le développement et la chute des libertés publiques en France, précédé d'une lettre de M. F. Le Play* (pp. ix-xiii). Paris: Didier, 1875, 16°, pp. xl + 350, 1 c. n. p.

35. *Id., Les français d'aujourd'hui. Les types sociaux du midi et du centre.* Paris: Firmin Didot, n.d., 16°, 2 c. n. p., pp. xii + 465, 1 c. n. p.

36. *Id., Les grandes routes des peuples. Essai de géographie sociale. Comment la route crée le type social. Les routes de l'antiquité.* Paris: Firmin Didot, n. d., 16°, pp. xii + 456, c. n. p.

37. *Id., Les grandes routes des peuples. Les routes du monde moderne.* Paris: Firmin Didot, n. d., 16°, 1 c. n. p., pp. vii + 540.

On the two outside pages of the cover is printed a map of the main land routes of the modern world.

38. ROUX, PAUL. *Précis de science sociale. Méthode et enquêtes.* Paris: Giard, 1914, 16°, 3 c. n. p., pp. 264 + 24.

---

* State socialism and social reform.

39. BOISSONADE, GUSTAVE. *Histoire de la réserve héréditaire et de son influence morale et économique,* awarded a prize by the Institut de France (Académie des sciences morales et politiques). Paris: De Guillaumin, 1873, 8°, pp. xv. + 746, 1 c. n. p.

40. DU MAROUSSEM, P. *La question ouvrière.* Paris: Rousseau, 8°; I: *Charpentiers de Paris, compagnons et indépendants, avec préface de M. Th. Funck-Brentano,* 1891, pp. 298; II: *Ébénistes du Faubourg Saint-Antoine, Grands magasins, "sweating-system," avec préface de M. Th. F.-B.,* 1892, pp. 4 n. p. + 311; III: *Le Jouet parisien, Grand magasins, "sweating-system," avec introduction de M. Th. F.-B.,* 1894, pp. 307; IV: in collaboration with CAMILLE GUERIE, *Halles centrales de Paris et commerce de l'alimentation,* 1894, pp. 4 n. p. + 304 with a plan of the market.*

After Le Play's death the most faithful interpreter of his method of observing and selecting typical facts, though not of his philosophy of history, was Du Maroussem. In a broader framework, these monographs of Maroussem are real masterpieces of exact inquiry, involving a rigorous sifting of the data and a judicious reconstruction of family life and occupations and of the material, intellectual, and moral environment in which that life unfolds. Why are not the books of economists all well written? Why, even in simple description or narration, do they put the reader to sleep instead of fascinating him, as Du Maroussem knew so well how to do? Nine times out of ten the reluctance of authors to undergo the painful labor of revising and rewriting inflicts agonizing torments on their readers. Distributing the proof sheets of his books generously among his friends, Le Play (see the reminiscences of Escard cited in No. 22) would importune them for criticisms and suggestions and kept patiently enlarging and recasting his works.

* The labor question: I. Carpenters of Paris, associated and independent, with a preface by Th. Funck-Brentano; II. Cabinet makers of the Faubourg Saint-Antoine and the "sweating-system" practised by the large contractors, with a preface by Th. F.-B.; III. The Parisian toy business and the "sweating-system" practised by the large contractors; IV. The central markets of Paris and the commerce in produce.

41. FRANÇOIS-PONCET, ANDRÉ. *La vie et l'oeuvre de Robert Pinot.* Paris: Colin, 1927, 8°, 2 c. n. p., 1 portrait, pp. 356, 1 c. n. p.

42. DE RIBBE, CHARLES. *Pascalis, étude sur la fin de la constitution provençale, 1787-1790.* Paris: Dentu, 1854, 8°, pp. 330, with a portrait of Pascalis.

43. *Id., L'ancien barreau du parlement de Provence ou extraits d'une correspondance inédite échangée pendant la peste de 1720 entre François Decormis et Pierre Saurin, avocats au même parlement.* Paris: Durand, 1861, 8°, pp. 192.

44. *Id., Les familles et la société en France avant la révolution, d'après des documents originaux.* Paris: Albanel, 1873, 16°, pp. 4 n. p., vii + 563; 4th ed., Tours: Mame, 1879, 16°, Vol. I, pp. xx + 339; II, pp. 4 n. p. + 377.

45. *Id., Une famille au XVIe siècle, document original précédé d'une introduction par . . . et d'une lettre du R. P. Félix.* Paris: Albanel, 1867, 16°, pp. 4 n. p., 132; 3rd ed., Tours: Mame, 1879, 16°, pp. 220.

46. *Id., Le livre de famille.* Tours: Mame, 1879, 16°, pp. vi + 283.

47. *Id., Une famille rurale aux XVII siècle d'après un document inédit.* Paris: Tardieu, 1882, 16°, pp. 64.

48. *Id., Une grande dame dans son ménage aux temps de Louis XIV, d'après le journal de la comtesse de Rochefort,* II. Paris: Palmé, 1889, 16°, pp. 4 n. p. + 384. A second edition was issued by the same publisher in 18° in 1890.

49. *Id., La société provençale a la fin du moyen âge, d'après des documents inédits.* Paris: Perrin, 1898, 8°, pp. 4 n. p., xii + 572.

50. *Id., Le Play, d'après sa correspondance.* Paris: Firmin Didot, 1884, 16°, pp. 4 n. p. + 454, with a bust of Le Play.

De Ribbe's books have been cited in order to demonstrate that the essence of Le Play's thought does not consist in this or that technical method, in some particular form of family budgets, or in a special nomenclature. De Ribbe discovered another method, that of *livres de raison.*

"There was at one time among almost all the most estimable, Christian, and well-ordered families—in a word, the backbone of the French nation—a custom that proves with what seriousness and practicality they conducted their lives. Under the name of *livres de raison* they kept books of domestic record and memoranda that came in time to serve as a guarantee of sound, businesslike procedures in the management of their affairs. The *livre de raison* was originally a modest record of accounts . . . but sometimes its scope was broadened: more exalted matters were included, and moral ideas and reflections were spontaneously set down next to, or in connection with, the entry of some item of income or expenditure. The head of the family, whenever he was struck by some fact or circumstance, used to record his observations or recommendations regarding it, and to these he would attach serious importance. In this way the family account book became the guardian of the family tradition. . . . It was the work of the father, as almost the natural prerogative of the head of the house. At his death the book was continued by the mother, until the first-born had reached maturity and married and was in a position to take over the management of domestic affairs."

A great part of De Ribbe's work is founded upon these *livres de raison*. He drew from them the history of the families that had prospered, not by good luck, but by virtue of their own moral probity. Such books are not kept by the man who gets a windfall, because he does not want others to know how he obtained his money, nor by the man who squanders his fortune, because he does not pay attention to matters of this kind. The surviving *livres de raison* thus transmit to us the history of God-fearing families, of those in which the mother, with but scant means, brought up many orphans, and of those in which family possessions were handed down from generation to generation to the first-born, while the younger brothers flocked to different parts of the world, providing the king with soldiers, sailors, and magistrates, and the motherland with colonists.

Since families of this kind are the only ones that really make a nation, while the others either do not count or actually contribute to its destruction, it is possible to learn from these *livres de raison* the reasons why nations have survived in spite of the corruption of those who temporarily constituted their ruling classes, and why these same nations become great as soon as the scions of such families attain positions of influence in the government. In addition to the *livres de raison,* diaries and letters may serve as historical sources of information concerning the facts of everyday life. It is out of ordinary things like these, precious relics that throw light on the past, that De Ribbe weaves the substance of his book.

51. GUIBERT, LOUIS; LEROUX, A.; DE CESSAC, J.; LECLER, A. *Livres de raison registres de famille et journaux individuels, limousins et marchois.* Paris: Picard, 1888, 8° (cover and frontispiece are missing), pp. 484.

52. TAMIZEY DE LARROQUE, PH. *Deux livres de raison de L'Agenais suivis d'extraits d'autres registres domestiques et d'une liste récapitulative des livres de raison publiés ou inédits.* Auch: Cochraux, 1893, 1 c. n. p., pp. xiii + 206, 1 c. n. p.

53. DE PESQUIDOUX, JOSEPH. *Le livre de raison. Première série,* Paris: Plon, 1939, 16°, 4 c. n. p., pp. 242, 1 c. n. p., 29th edition; *Le livre de raison. Deuxième série,* Paris: Plon, 1938, 16°, 4 c. n. p., pp. viii + 278, 1 c. n. p., 18th edition; *Le livre de raison. Troisième série,* Paris: Plon, 1932, 16°, 4 c. n. p., pp. iv + 256, 1 c. n. p., 2nd edition.

54. DE VAISSIÈRE, PIERRE. *Gentilshommes campagnards de l'ancienne France. Étude sur la condition, l'état social et les moeurs de la noblesse de province du XVIe au XVIIIe siècle.* Awarded a prize by the Académie française (second Gobert prize). Paris: Perrin, 1904, 8°, 4 c. n. p., pp. 432 + 1 c. n. p.

55. BAUDRILLART, HENRI. *Gentilshommes ruraux de la France,* published by Andre Baudrillart and preceded by a biographical introduction by C. Benoist (pp. vii-xxiii). Paris: Firmin Didot, 1893, 8°, 1 c. n. p., 1 portrait, pp. lxviii + 358, 2 c. n. p.

Sources

I have mentioned above (see §17 of this text) the authors with whose works Le Play was chiefly familiar. Here I should like to list just two of his sources that are less generally known.

56. DES SERRES, OLIVIER, seigneur de Pradel (1539-1619). *Le théâtre d'agriculture et mesnage des champs.* New edition based on the text of 1600, Paris: Huzard, Year 12 (1804), 4°; I, pp. cxcii + 682, with a portrait; II, pp. xliv + 948. With two illustrations: the portrait and a commemorative stele.

This is the best edition of the famous treatise on agriculture of which Scaliger wrote: "Dedicated to the king [Henry IV] who for three or four months had it brought to him after dinner . . . and, in spite of his usual impatience, used to read it for half an hour."

Le Play looked upon Henry IV as the ideal monarch, and he and his friends felt obliged to the king for having kept at his bedside De Serres' treatise, of which the first book deals with the duties of a country gentleman as cultivator of the soil, builder of houses, and ruler of men. In particular, the sixth chapter of this first book "de l'office du Père-de-famille envers ses domestiques, et voisins" ("On the duty of the father of the family towards his servants and neighbors") is the picture of the era of the prosperous society when it was *"l'honneur de la noblesse française d'habiter aux champs, n'allant aux villes que pour faire service au Roy et pourvoir aux affaires pressées"* ("the honor of the French aristocracy to live in the country and to go into town only to serve the king and to attend to urgent affairs") ; and the head of the family considered as the prime requisite for success in the management of his estate the choice *"d'une sage et vertueuse femme, pour faire leurs communes affaires avec parfaite amitié et bonne intelligence . . . , estant la femme l'un des plus importants ressorts du mesnage, de laquelle la conduite est à préférer á toute autre science de la colture des champs"* ("of a wise and virtuous helpmeet, so that they might carry on their common work together with perfect mutual affection and understanding . . . for a wife is such a pillar of strength in the household that her management of it is worth more than any amount of knowledge of agricultural techniques").

This is a truth not understood by a great many modern investigators into the causes of prosperity or adversity in agriculture. They dwell on prices, taxes, governmental subsidies, markets, consumers' and producers' cooperatives, and other such inanities, whereas the only basis for determining the

causes of the success or the failure of an agricultural family—
or of any family, for that matter—is the character of the
mother of the family—something not at all amenable to statistical treatment.

The edition of 1804 is enriched by a dissertation by François de Neufchateau; an "Essai historique sur l'état de l'agriculture en Europe au seizième siècle" ("Historical essay on
the state of agriculture in Europe in the sixteenth century")
by Grégoire, an ordained bishop and Jansenist; a bibliographical note on the editions of the *Théâtre,* prepared by
J. B. Huzard; copious indices, etc. All this is evidence of the
revival of some studies during the Napoleonic regime, even
if they express, albeit in veiled and guarded fashion, a spirit
profoundly opposed to the principles of an autocrat intent
on attracting all the best men in the country into his service
and on making himself the sole center from which the impulse for every kind of activity was to emanate.

57. VASCHALDE, HENRI. *Olivier de Serres, Seigneur du Pradel.
Sa vie et ses travaux. Documents inédits illustrés de portraits, gra-
vures, et fac-simile.* Paris: Plon, 1886, 8°, 2 c. n. p., 1 ill., 2 c. n. p.,
pp. 232, 1 c. n. p

58 HUC, M. *Souvenirs d'un voyage dans la Tartarie, le Thibet
et la Chine pendant les années 1844, 1845, et 1846.* 2nd edition,
Paris: Le Clare, 1853, 8°, I, pp. 440, with a map; II, pp. 2 n. p.
+ 518.

59. *Id., L'empire chinois, faisant suite à l'ouvrage intitulé
Souvenirs etc.* 2nd edition, Paris: Gaume, 1854, 8°; I, pp. 2 n. p. +
xxiv + 471, with a map; II, pp. 4 n. p. + 487.

60. *Id., Le christianisme en Chine, en Tartarie, et au Thibet.*
Paris: Gaume, 8°; I, 1857, pp. 4 n. p. + xvi + 469, with a map;
II, 1857, pp. 4 n. p. + 455; III, 1857, pp. 4 n. p. + xxii + 462;
IV, 1858, pp. 4 n. p. + 476.

These works of the missionary Huc are cited by Le Play
in nearly all his books. And rightly so, for there are few
writers of travel books who, like Huc, are capable of grasping
the fundamental characteristics of the life of the peoples they
visit, and far too many scientific reports deal with particular
details of no decisive significance.

The following quotation from the *Souvenirs* (see above No. 58, vol. I, pp. 287-288) corrects a customary and widespread misconception about slavery that is based upon the mere sound of the word: "Those Tartars who do not belong to the family of the prince are slaves; they live in absolute dependence upon their masters. Besides paying homage and rents, they are obliged to tend the flocks of their masters, and they are permitted to own cattle on their own account. But it would be erroneous to believe that in Tartary slavery is as harsh and cruel as it was among some peoples. The families of nobles hardly differ in any respect from the families of slaves. In studying their mutual relations it would be difficult to distinguish the one from the other. Both live in tents; both alike spend their lives in pasturing their flocks. Among them one never sees luxury and opulence in insolent contrast to poverty. When the slave enters the tent of his master, the latter always offers him tea with milk; they like to smoke together and exchange pipes with each other. Outside the tent the young slaves and the young lords amuse themselves in wrestling matches—all together and without distinction; the stronger throws the weaker to the ground, and that is all. It often happens that families of slaves become owners of many herds and spend their lives in affluence. We have known many of them who were richer than their masters, but this fact did not in the least diminish the latter's authority."

The missionary considers such observations a basis for concluding that even this form of slavery is nevertheless contrary to the dignity of man, but that it does not need to be abolished by law, since the moral teaching of Christianity is sufficient for the purpose. To this the scholar considers it pertinent to remark that, in the absence of accurate observation of individual cases by a qualified observer, "slavery" is a word of indeterminate signification.*

---

* The following publications, not listed by Einaudi, are available in English. [Translator's note.]

61. ELLWOOD, CHARLES A. "Instruction in the Observation of Social Facts According to the Le Play Method of Monographs of Families," *American Journal of Sociology*, 2 (1897); 662-679.

62. FARMER, PAUL. "The Social Theory of Frédéric Le Play," *Teachers of History, Essays in Honor of Lawrence Bradford Packard*, ed. by H. Stuart Hughes et al., Cornell University Press, Ithaca, New York, 1954, pp. 58-78. (Continued on p. 216.)

Le Play's publisher (Mame of Tours) offers for sale in a recent catalogue five of the six volumes of the *Ouvriers européens* (see above No. 2; the second volume is out of print) at nine francs a volume; *La constitution de l'Angleterre* (see No. 8 above) at five francs; and *La paix sociale après le desastre* (see No. 7 above) for sixty centimes. The Société d'économie sociale (Rue Guyot, 31, Paris, XVIIᵉ) may still have in stock Number 3 and Numbers 22 to 25 at rather low prices. Nearly all the rest is mechandise for the antiquarian. Some years ago one might have bought a few remaining copies of *Les ouvriers européens* for considerably less than a hundred francs. But at present they are going up again in price, and a copy selling at a mere one hundred francs would now seem rather cheap. It is more difficult to find the entire collection of the *Ouvriers des deux mondes.*

Le Play's works, however, taken all in all, have not yet passed into the category of rare books, with the exception of those of the type of Numbers 11 to 13; nor do they seem likely to become rare soon, because Le Play's zeal for propaganda prompted him to have an enormous number of copies printed in each edition of his books and continually to reissue them in new editions. The essential condition for collecting his works is not to offer high prices; for, with the exception of Numbers 1-3, each copy of which naturally costs more than a hundred francs, all the remaining can be collected—even without going book-hunting in the stalls along the Seine, where, in any case, the places whose whole stock one could hope to buy up for a song have long since passed into the realm of legend—by consulting the catalogues of antiquarians, at prices fluctuating from five to fifty francs for each. The one requisite is to have sufficient patience and not to weary of poring over the pages of many catalogues to find very little.

---

63. HERBERTSON, DOROTHY. *The Life of Frédéric Le Play,* ed. by Victor   Branford and Alexander Farquharson. First publication in 1950 as Section 2, Volume XXXVIII (1946) of the *Sociological Review.* Also printed separately with index, 1950, Le Play House Press, Ledbury, Herefordshire, 120 pp.

64. ZIMMERMAN, CARLE CLARK and FRAMTON, MERLE E. *Family and Society, A Study of the Sociology of Reconstruction,* New York: D. Van Nostrand and Company, 1935, pp. xv + 611.

NOTES

1. This provision was in effect in 1936; later the portion of the estate at the free disposition of the testator was unfortunately reduced. (Footnote added in 1952.)
2. Or rather, we used to do so up to twenty years ago, when the vicissitudes of tumultuous times made us forget this useful practice. (Note added in 1952.)
3. G. L. Bousquet, in his suggestive study, "Le douar Aghbal," in the *Revue d'économie politique* of January-February, 1935, p. 99, after having said, "... *c'est un auteur dont les buts n'ont rien de scientific*" ("... he is an author whose aims are in no way scientific"), nevertheless attests his great indebtedness to Le Play and recommends him especially *"aux gens épris d'abstractions comme antidote"* ("as an antidote to those infatuated with abstractions"). The present essay has the purpose of throwing light upon the scientific elements in Le Play's theory. But, since his is an historical theory, it can serve as an antidote only to the abstract theory of those who would like to use a certain abstraction to interpret reality even in cases where another abstraction would serve the purpose.
4. Costa de Beauregard, *Un homme d'autrefois* (Paris, 1900), p. 146.
5. Nor is Taine, for that matter, in spite of the fine, but altogether misleading, introductory chapter to his "History of English Literature," which has little to do essentially with the text that follows. Yet everyone stops here and judges him accordingly. Whenever his name is mentioned, all the parrots repeat in chorus: "race," "milieu," and "age." These are supposed to be the three factors from which, in his introduction, he derives *l'état moral* (the moral condition) of a people; and from this "moral condition" are derived, in their turn, its literature, its philosophy, its society, and its art. This is ridiculous enough, to be sure, but let us read on: *"Tout vient du dedans chez lui, je veux dire de son âme et de son génie; les circonstances et les dehors n'ont contribué que mediocrement à le développer"* ("With him, everything comes from within, that is to say, from his soul and his genius; circumstances and external factors contributed only slightly to his development.") Here, of course, he is speaking of Shakespeare, for whom Taine is quite willing to throw out the window the three factors, which are good only for describing those writers concerning whom one would be at a loss what to say if one did not fit them into the framework of "race," "milieu," and "age." But by now Taine has been tagged with these labels, and we are never allowed to forget them!

Index

Prepared by Vernelia A. Crawford

Note: This index to *European Economic Thought* includes the titles of essays and parts, each listed under the appropriate subject classifications. With the exception of these specific page references, which are hyphenated, the numbers in each instance refer to the *first* page of a discussion. A page number followed by a figure in parentheses indicates the number of a footnote or bibliographic reference.